Multilingual AI

Multilingual AI

Ange Ndong
Elise Okoumba

Kruger Brentt
Publishers
2026

Kruger Brentt Publishers UK. LTD.
Company Number 9728962

Regd. Office: 68 St Margarets Road, Edgware, Middlesex HA8 9UU

ISBN: 978-1-78715-619-7

For information on all our publications visit our website at http://krugerbrentt.com/

Preface

Multilingual AI explores the rapidly evolving field of artificial intelligence that enables machines to understand, generate, and interact in multiple human languages. As global communication becomes increasingly digital and interconnected, the ability of AI systems to process diverse languages is critical for applications in translation, virtual assistants, content creation, and cross-cultural collaboration. This book provides students, researchers, and professionals with a comprehensive understanding of multilingual AI technologies, their challenges, and practical applications.

The book begins with an overview of the principles of natural language processing (NLP) and machine learning as they apply to multiple languages. It then delves into key techniques such as multilingual embeddings, transfer learning, cross-lingual models, and large language models trained on diverse datasets. Challenges unique to multilingual AI—such as linguistic diversity, low-resource languages, and cultural nuances—are explored in detail.

Practical applications across industries are highlighted, including machine translation, conversational AI, sentiment analysis, and multilingual information retrieval. The book also addresses ethical and societal considerations, such as bias, fairness, and accessibility, emphasizing responsible AI deployment across different linguistic and cultural contexts.

Emerging trends, including zero-shot and few-shot learning, AI-driven language preservation, and real-time multilingual interaction systems, are discussed to provide a forward-looking perspective. Case studies and examples illustrate how multilingual AI is transforming global communication and bridging language barriers.

We hope that Multilingual AI will serve as a valuable resource for learners and professionals, equipping them with both the theoretical foundations and practical insights necessary to develop, evaluate, and implement AI systems capable of supporting a truly global and inclusive digital environment.

Ange Ndong
Elise Okoumba

Contents

CHAPTER 1

Introduction to Multilingual AI

1.1 WHAT IS MULTILINGUAL AI?

Multilingual AI refers to artificial intelligence systems that are capable of understanding, processing, and generating human language across multiple linguistic domains. As the world becomes increasingly interconnected, the need for AI systems to function seamlessly across different languages has grown significantly. From virtual assistants to automated translation tools and multilingual chatbots, multilingual AI plays a pivotal role in breaking down communication barriers and ensuring inclusive access to information and services across global populations. This field merges advancements in natural language processing (NLP), machine learning, and computational linguistics to create models that can perform effectively across diverse linguistic landscapes.

Multilingual AI represents a transformative leap in how humans and machines interact across language boundaries. By enabling seamless communication and expanding access to knowledge, it holds the potential to democratize information and foster global understanding. While significant progress has been made, ongoing efforts are needed to address technical, linguistic, and ethical challenges. Through collaborative innovation and a commitment to inclusivity, multilingual AI can continue to evolve into a powerful force that connects people, empowers communities, and enhances human potential across every language and culture.

The ethical development of multilingual AI is crucial to ensuring that its deployment does not inadvertently reinforce biases or exclude marginalized groups. Language carries cultural identity and meaning, and mishandling it can result in misrepresentation, stereotyping, or harm. Developers must address issues such as linguistic bias, discriminatory outputs, and unequal access to AI technologies. Ensuring that datasets are diverse, representative, and ethically sourced is essential. Transparency in model behavior, explainability in decision-making, and mechanisms for user feedback and correction are also vital for responsible deployment. Collaborative efforts with language communities, particularly for indigenous and endangered languages, are key to fostering inclusivity and respecting linguistic heritage.

The future of multilingual AI is poised to benefit from several exciting innovations. Advances in multimodal learning, where AI models integrate text, audio, and visual inputs, are expected to improve language understanding and generation in more natural and context-aware ways.

Federated learning and privacy-preserving AI approaches will enhance data security while enabling decentralized training across diverse language communities. Greater integration of linguistic theory and cognitive science into AI development can help create models that better mimic human language understanding. Additionally, as AI regulation and ethical frameworks evolve, future multilingual AI systems will be held to higher standards of fairness, transparency, and accountability, especially in sensitive applications such as healthcare, law, and education.

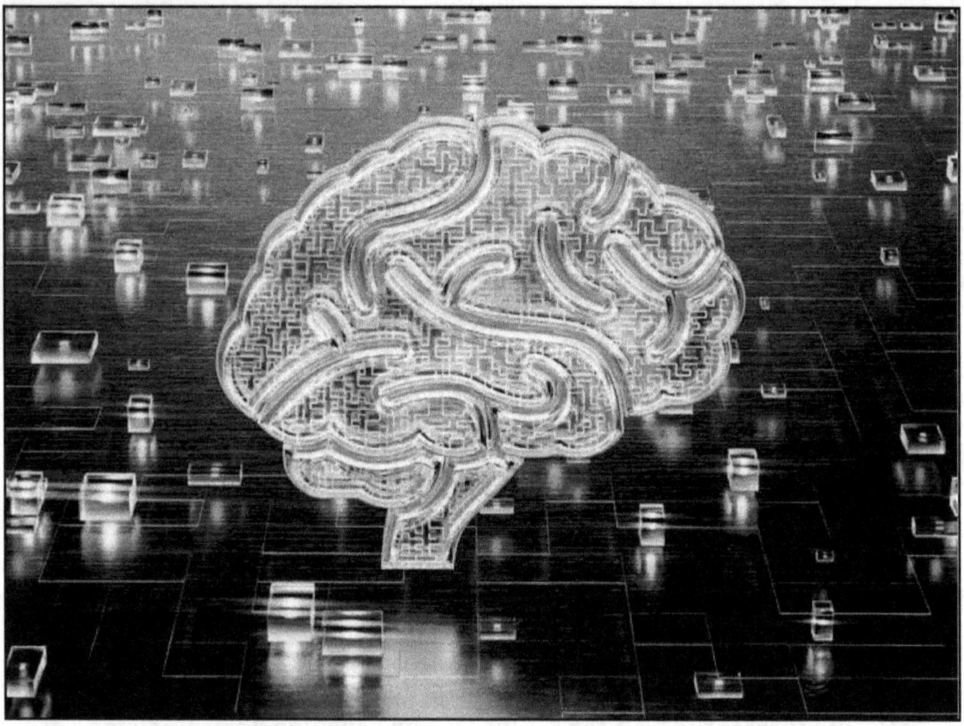

Fig: Multilingual AI—Bridging the Language Gap in Document Processing

1.1.1 Evolution and Growth

The evolution of multilingual AI has been closely tied to advancements in NLP and computational models. In the early stages, machine translation systems such as rule-based and statistical models were limited in their performance and scope, often requiring handcrafted rules and large amounts of aligned bilingual data. The introduction of neural machine translation (NMT) and transformer-based architectures like Google's Transformer model marked a turning point. These models allowed for better contextual understanding and fluency in translation tasks. The development of multilingual language models such as OpenAI's GPT, Google's mT5, Meta's M2M-100, and XLM-R has further expanded capabilities, enabling a single model to work across hundreds of languages simultaneously. These models are trained on massive multilingual corpora and are capable of cross-lingual transfer, allowing them to perform well on low-resource languages even with limited training data.

1.1.2 Core Principles and Techniques

At the heart of multilingual AI lies the concept of shared representation learning, where the model learns to map different languages into a common semantic space. This enables the model to understand and generate text in multiple languages while maintaining contextual coherence. Techniques such as cross-lingual embeddings, multilingual pretraining, and zero-shot learning have become foundational in this field. Cross-lingual embeddings allow the model to capture meaning across languages, while multilingual pretraining leverages large-scale multilingual datasets to train models capable of handling diverse linguistic inputs. Zero-shot and few-shot learning further allow these models to perform tasks in languages they were not explicitly trained on, thereby increasing their versatility and accessibility.

1.1.3 Challenges

Despite its promise, multilingual AI faces several significant challenges. One of the major issues is data imbalance, as high-resource languages like English, Chinese, and Spanish dominate the training datasets, while low-resource languages often lack sufficient digital representation. This imbalance can lead to biased performance and reduced accuracy in underrepresented languages. Another challenge lies in the structural and grammatical diversity of world languages, which vary significantly in syntax, morphology, and semantics. These differences make it difficult to create models that perform uniformly well across all languages. Additionally, cultural context, idiomatic expressions, and dialectal variations pose complexities that current models still struggle to address effectively. Ethical concerns such as algorithmic bias, data privacy, and the potential for misinformation also require careful consideration in multilingual AI applications.

1.1.4 Applications of Multilingual AI in Real-World Scenarios

Multilingual AI has found widespread application in various sectors, transforming the way organizations operate and engage with diverse audiences. In communication and customer service, multilingual chatbots and virtual assistants provide instant support to users in their native languages, enhancing user satisfaction and accessibility. In healthcare, multilingual AI facilitates patient-doctor communication, medical record translation, and health education in multicultural settings. The education sector benefits through AI-powered language learning tools and inclusive educational platforms that support learners from different linguistic backgrounds. In government and legal sectors, multilingual AI enables translation of official documents, public service announcements, and legal texts, promoting transparency and citizen engagement. Additionally, media and content creation industries use multilingual AI to localize content, subtitles, and marketing campaigns, allowing brands to reach global audiences effectively.

1.1.5 Multilingual AI and Low-Resource Languages

Addressing the needs of low-resource languages is a critical focus within multilingual AI. Many communities worldwide speak languages that are underrepresented in digital platforms due to a lack of training data and linguistic resources. Researchers are working to overcome this through transfer learning, where knowledge from high-resource languages is used to improve performance in low-resource ones. Initiatives such as Masakhane and Common Voice are crowdsourcing language data and fostering collaboration among native speakers, linguists, and AI researchers. These efforts aim to create inclusive AI systems that support linguistic diversity and ensure that technological benefits are equitably distributed across all populations, regardless of their native language.

1.2 IMPORTANCE IN A GLOBALIZED WORLD

In a world where language shapes access to opportunities, multilingual AI stands as a transformative force for global equity and progress. By breaking down linguistic barriers, it empowers individuals, businesses, and nations to participate fully in the digital economy. From healthcare and education to cultural preservation and international trade, AI's ability to process and generate multiple languages fosters inclusivity and innovation.

However, realizing this potential demands responsible development, ethical frameworks, and ongoing efforts to bridge the digital divide. As AI continues to evolve, prioritizing multilingual capabilities will be essential in building a truly connected and equitable global society—one where language is no longer a barrier but a bridge to shared understanding and collaboration. The future of multilingual AI holds immense potential, driven by advancements in neural machine translation, zero-shot learning, and adaptive language models.

Emerging technologies like Meta's No Language Left Behind (NLLB) initiative and OpenAI's multilingual GPT models aim to support hundreds of languages with near-human accuracy. In the coming years, AI could enable real-time multilingual communication in augmented reality (AR) and virtual reality (VR) environments, revolutionizing international diplomacy, tourism, and remote work. Governments and corporations investing in multilingual AI infrastructure will gain a competitive edge in global markets, while marginalized communities will benefit from greater digital inclusion. However, achieving this vision requires sustained collaboration between linguists, technologists, and policymakers to ensure that AI serves as a unifying force rather than a tool of exclusion.

Fig: Shaping Inclusive AI for Every Language

1.2.1 Bridging Communication Gaps in a Multicultural Society

One of the most significant contributions of multilingual AI is its ability to bridge communication gaps in an increasingly interconnected world. Traditional AI models, often trained primarily on English-language data, have historically excluded non-English speakers, creating a digital divide. Multilingual AI addresses this imbalance by enabling real-time translation, transcription, and interpretation across languages. Applications such as Google Translate, DeepL, and OpenAI's GPT models now support dozens of languages with increasing accuracy, allowing businesses, travelers, and international organizations to communicate effortlessly. In healthcare, for example, multilingual chatbots can assist patients in their native languages, reducing miscommunication and improving medical outcomes. Similarly, in legal and diplomatic settings, AI-powered translation ensures that documents and negotiations are accurately interpreted, minimizing errors that could have far-reaching consequences.

1.2.2 Enhancing Global Business and Economic Inclusion

The global economy thrives on cross-border trade, investment, and collaboration, all of which rely heavily on effective communication. Multilingual AI empowers businesses to expand into new markets by automating customer service, marketing, and compliance processes in local languages. E-commerce platforms like Amazon and Alibaba leverage AI-driven language models to provide product descriptions, reviews, and customer support in multiple languages, enhancing user experience and driving sales. Financial institutions use multilingual AI to detect fraud, analyze market trends, and provide personalized banking services to diverse populations. Moreover, startups and small enterprises, which previously struggled with language barriers, can now compete globally thanks to affordable AI-powered translation and localization tools. By democratizing access to international markets, multilingual AI fosters economic inclusion and reduces disparities between developed and developing regions.

1.2.3 Revolutionizing Education and Knowledge Dissemination

Education is another sector where multilingual AI is making a profound impact. With millions of students worldwide learning in non-native languages, AI-powered tools such as Duolingo, Khan Academy, and Coursera provide personalized, language-inclusive learning experiences. These platforms use natural language processing (NLP) to adapt content to learners' linguistic proficiencies, ensuring comprehension and retention. Additionally, AI-driven transcription and translation services enable universities to offer multilingual courses, breaking down barriers for non-English-speaking students. Research and academic collaboration also benefit from multilingual AI, as scholars can now access and contribute to global knowledge repositories without language constraints. Open-access journals and digital libraries employ AI to translate and summarize research papers, accelerating scientific progress and innovation across linguistic boundaries.

1.2.4 Supporting Cultural Preservation and Linguistic Diversity

While globalization promotes connectivity, it also risks marginalizing minority languages and cultures. Multilingual AI plays a crucial role in preserving endangered languages by digitizing oral histories, translating ancient texts, and enabling speech recognition for underrepresented dialects. Organizations like UNESCO and the Endangered Languages Project collaborate with AI researchers to develop tools that document and revitalize at-risk languages. Furthermore, AI-generated content in local languages—such as news articles, literature, and media—helps sustain cultural identity in an increasingly homogenized digital landscape. By ensuring that all languages, not just dominant ones, are represented in AI datasets, developers can prevent linguistic extinction and promote cultural heritage in the digital age.

1.2.5 Challenges and Ethical Considerations

Despite its benefits, multilingual AI faces significant challenges, including bias, data scarcity, and ethical dilemmas. Many AI models still exhibit biases favoring widely spoken languages like English, Mandarin, or Spanish, while low-resource languages suffer from inadequate training data. This imbalance can lead to inaccurate translations or reinforce stereotypes, particularly in sensitive contexts like legal or medical AI applications. Additionally, the collection and use of linguistic data raise privacy concerns, especially when dealing with indigenous or minority languages. Ensuring ethical AI development requires inclusive data sourcing, transparent algorithms, and collaboration with native speakers to refine language models. Policymakers and tech companies must also establish guidelines to prevent AI from being weaponized for misinformation or surveillance across linguistic groups.

1.3 EVOLUTION OF LANGUAGE TECHNOLOGIES

The evolution of language technologies represents one of the most transformative journeys in the realm of artificial intelligence. From early rule-based systems to today's advanced neural network models, language technologies have undergone significant change in their ability to process, understand, and generate human language. Multilingual AI stands at the forefront of this evolution, enabling machines to interact in multiple languages and bridge communication gaps across global communities. As the digital world becomes more interconnected, the demand for language technologies that support linguistic diversity and cultural inclusion has intensified.

The evolution of language technologies toward multilingual AI marks a pivotal shift in how humans and machines interact. From simple rule-based systems to powerful neural models capable of understanding and generating text in hundreds of languages, the journey has been both complex and transformative. Multilingual AI has opened new possibilities for communication, inclusion, and innovation across the globe. While challenges remain, particularly in addressing data disparities and ensuring ethical use, the progress achieved so far underscores the potential for technology to transcend linguistic boundaries and enrich human connection. By continuing to invest in equitable development, multilingual AI can play a key role in shaping a more inclusive and linguistically diverse digital future.

As multilingual AI becomes more widespread, ethical considerations must be central to its evolution. Language technologies can amplify existing biases, marginalize communities, or propagate misinformation if not carefully designed and tested. Ensuring fairness, transparency, and accountability in multilingual models is essential. This involves using diverse and representative datasets, auditing model outputs for bias, and developing guidelines for responsible use. User privacy is another critical issue, particularly in applications that process sensitive personal data. Developers must implement robust security measures and obtain informed consent. Collaboration with affected communities is vital to ensure that AI systems reflect local values, linguistic norms, and social contexts.

Looking ahead, the future of multilingual AI promises continued innovation and expansion. Advances in multimodal learning, where models integrate text, speech, and visual information, are likely to enhance understanding and generation capabilities. Personalization will become more prominent, allowing AI systems to adapt to individual users' linguistic preferences and communication styles. Federated learning and decentralized AI approaches will allow for more secure and inclusive model training, particularly in resource-constrained environments. As regulatory frameworks evolve, developers will be increasingly accountable for ensuring ethical and inclusive practices. Ultimately, the success of multilingual AI will depend on sustained collaboration among researchers, technologists, communities, and policymakers.

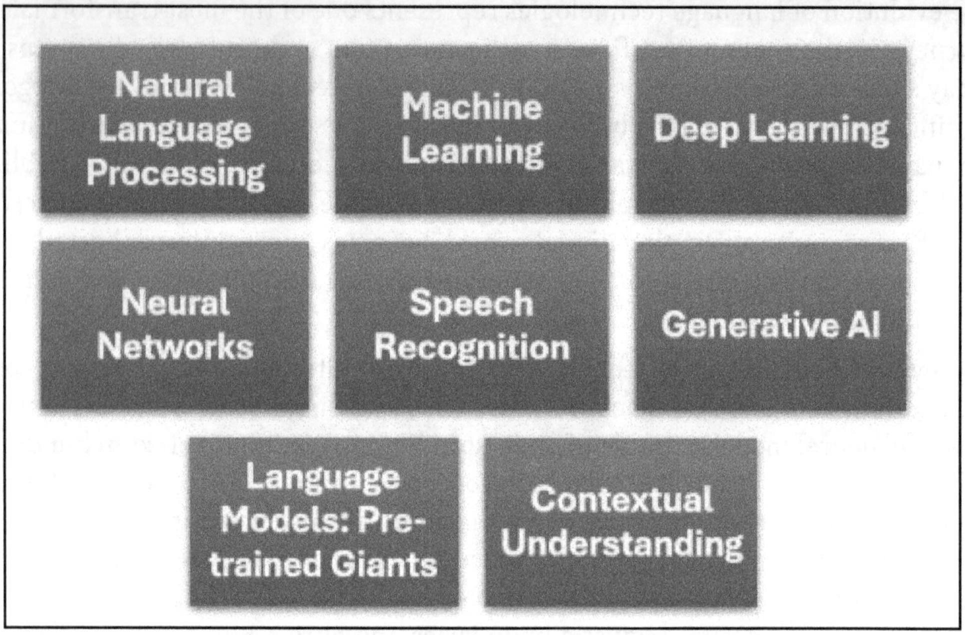

Fig: Building Multilingual AI Assistants

1.3.1 Early Stages of Language Technology Development

In the early stages, language technologies were limited in both scope and capability. Rule-based systems were the first attempts to encode grammar and vocabulary into machine-readable formats. These systems relied heavily on linguistic rules and handcrafted databases, requiring significant human expertise.

While they offered basic translation and grammatical analysis, they were rigid and failed to adapt to the complexities of natural human language. In the mid-to-late 20th century, statistical models began to replace rule-based systems. With the availability of bilingual corpora and aligned datasets, statistical machine translation (SMT) emerged, using probabilistic methods to predict the most likely translation based on word and phrase frequencies. However, SMT models were still constrained by the size and quality of available data, and their performance degraded significantly when dealing with languages that lacked sufficient training resources.

1.3.2 Rise of Neural Network Approaches

The introduction of neural network-based approaches in the 2010s marked a major turning point in language technology. Neural Machine Translation (NMT), which utilizes deep learning techniques, revolutionized how machines understand and generate language. Unlike previous systems, NMT models learn from vast datasets and capture contextual information, resulting in more fluent and accurate translations.

Recurrent Neural Networks (RNNs) and Long Short-Term Memory (LSTM) architectures laid the groundwork for early neural models. However, the breakthrough came with the development of the Transformer model in 2017. The Transformer architecture enabled more effective handling of long-range dependencies in text and significantly improved translation and comprehension tasks. This innovation led to the creation of multilingual models that could perform translation and understanding across several languages within a single model.

1.3.3 Development of Multilingual AI Models

Multilingual AI models have extended the capabilities of language technologies by enabling cross-lingual understanding. These models are trained on massive multilingual datasets, often covering hundreds of languages. By leveraging shared representation spaces, multilingual models can perform tasks in multiple languages without requiring separate training for each one.

Prominent examples include OpenAI's GPT models, Google's mT5, Meta's M2M-100, and XLM-R from Facebook AI. These models demonstrate impressive performance not only in translation but also in sentiment analysis, summarization, and question-answering across languages. A key strength of multilingual models is their ability to apply knowledge from high-resource languages to improve performance in low-resource languages, a process known as cross-lingual transfer.

1.3.4 Challenges in the Evolution of Multilingual AI

Despite these advancements, several challenges persist in the evolution of multilingual AI. One of the foremost issues is data inequality. High-resource languages such as English, Mandarin, and Spanish dominate available datasets, while many indigenous and regional languages remain underrepresented. This imbalance leads to performance disparities and limits the effectiveness of models in low-resource contexts. Furthermore, the structural diversity of languages poses difficulties for generalization. Differences in syntax, morphology, word order, and script require models to handle language-specific complexities. Multilingual models also struggle with code-switching, idiomatic expressions, and cultural nuances, which are integral to effective communication. Additionally, the high computational cost of training and maintaining large-scale models limits accessibility and raises concerns about environmental sustainability and inclusivity.

1.3.5 Applications and Impact

Multilingual AI has found extensive application across industries, transforming how businesses, governments, and individuals communicate and operate. In customer service, multilingual chatbots and virtual assistants provide real-time support to users in their native languages, enhancing user satisfaction and engagement. In healthcare, multilingual AI helps bridge language barriers between providers and patients, facilitating better diagnoses and care delivery. In education, AI-driven tools support language learning and make educational content accessible to students across linguistic backgrounds. Government services leverage multilingual AI for document translation, public information dissemination, and cross-border communication. Content creators and media organizations use AI to localize and subtitle videos, articles, and advertisements, reaching broader audiences. These applications highlight how multilingual AI promotes inclusivity, accessibility, and global connectivity.

1.3.6 Low-Resource Language Support and Preservation

A significant area of focus within the evolution of multilingual AI is the inclusion of low-resource languages. These languages often lack the digital presence necessary for AI models to perform well. Initiatives such as Masakhane, a grassroots effort to build NLP tools for African languages, and Mozilla's Common Voice, which collects speech data from underrepresented languages, aim to address this gap. These community-driven projects emphasize the importance of involving native speakers and linguists in the development process.

Advances in few-shot and zero-shot learning, as well as data augmentation techniques, are also being explored to extend multilingual AI capabilities to less-resourced languages. Supporting these languages not only ensures technological equity but also contributes to the preservation of linguistic and cultural heritage.

1.4 FROM RULE-BASED SYSTEMS TO TRANSFORMERS

The evolution from rule-based systems to transformer architectures represents one of the most significant advancements in artificial intelligence, particularly in the domain of language processing. This progression has enabled remarkable capabilities in multilingual applications, transforming global communication and information access. While challenges remain in addressing linguistic diversity and ethical considerations, the opportunities presented by these technologies are vast and transformative. As research continues to advance, multilingual AI will play an increasingly central role in connecting global communities, supporting cross-cultural understanding, and enabling more inclusive technological development. The journey from early computational linguistics to modern transformer-based models demonstrates the power of innovation in artificial intelligence and sets the stage for future breakthroughs in language technology. The development and deployment of multilingual AI systems raise important ethical considerations that must be addressed to ensure responsible innovation. Issues of bias and representation are particularly significant, as models trained predominantly on data from high-resource languages may perform poorly on languages with less digital representation. This disparity can reinforce existing inequalities in global information access and technological development. Ensuring diverse and representative training data is crucial for developing equitable AI systems that serve global populations.

Privacy concerns also emerge in multilingual applications, particularly when processing sensitive information across language boundaries. The potential for misuse or misinterpretation of translated content requires careful consideration of security and ethical guidelines. Additionally, the cultural context of language use demands attention to avoid misrepresentation or offense in cross-lingual applications. Developing ethical frameworks that address these concerns is essential for the responsible advancement of multilingual AI technologies.

Fig: From Rule-Based Systems to Transformers

The future of multilingual AI is marked by exciting possibilities for further advancement and application. Continued improvements in model architectures, particularly in the efficiency and scalability of transformer-based systems, will enable more sophisticated language processing capabilities. The integration of multimodal approaches that combine language with visual or auditory information presents new opportunities for comprehensive understanding and generation.

Advances in few-shot and zero-shot learning will enable models to adapt more effectively to low-resource languages and specialized domains. The development of more sophisticated evaluation metrics that capture the nuances of multilingual performance will support continued improvement in model development. Research into interpretability and explainability of AI decisions will enhance trust and adoption of these technologies in critical applications. As computational resources become more accessible, the potential for personalized and adaptive multilingual AI systems will expand, supporting more tailored and context-aware applications.

1.4.1 Era of Rule-Based Systems

The earliest approaches to language processing in AI relied on rule-based systems that operated through explicitly programmed linguistic rules and patterns. These systems were built on extensive lexicons and grammatical frameworks that attempted to capture the complexities of human language through predefined algorithms. While effective for simple tasks and controlled environments, rule-based systems struggled with the inherent ambiguity and variability of natural language. Their performance was particularly limited when dealing with languages that had complex morphological structures or when processing idiomatic expressions that deviated from standard grammatical rules.

Despite their limitations, rule-based systems played a crucial role in the early development of machine translation and natural language processing. They provided a foundation for understanding the challenges of computational linguistics and demonstrated the potential for automated language processing. However, the labor-intensive nature of creating and maintaining these systems, combined with their inability to scale effectively, ultimately led researchers to explore alternative approaches that could better handle the nuances of human language.

1.4.2 Statistical Machine Translation: A Probabilistic Approach

The transition from rule-based to statistical approaches marked a significant paradigm shift in language processing. Statistical machine translation emerged as a dominant methodology in the late 20th century, leveraging large bilingual corpora to learn translation patterns through probabilistic models. This approach represented a fundamental change in philosophy, moving away from explicit linguistic rules toward data-driven methods that could learn from examples.

Statistical machine translation systems operated by analyzing vast amounts of parallel texts in different languages, identifying patterns and correlations between source and target language segments. These systems used sophisticated statistical models to determine the most probable translation for a given input, considering both the likelihood of specific word sequences and the overall fluency of the output. While this approach significantly improved translation quality compared to rule-based systems, it still faced challenges with rare words, long-range dependencies, and maintaining contextual coherence across sentences.

The limitations of statistical machine translation became particularly apparent when dealing with language pairs that had limited parallel training data or when processing languages with significant structural differences. Despite these challenges, statistical approaches demonstrated the power of data-driven methods and set the stage for the neural revolution in language processing that would follow.

1.4.3 Neural Revolution: From Feedforward to Recurrent Networks

The introduction of neural networks to natural language processing represented a transformative development in the field. Early neural approaches utilized feedforward networks that processed language as sequences of words or characters, learning to map input patterns to output representations. These models showed promise in capturing complex relationships within language data but struggled with the sequential nature of text and the need to maintain context over long passages.

The development of recurrent neural networks (RNNs) addressed some of these limitations by incorporating memory mechanisms that allowed information to persist across time steps. Long Short-Term Memory (LSTM) networks and Gated Recurrent Units (GRUs) further refined this approach, enabling models to learn which information to retain or discard as they processed sequential data. These architectures demonstrated significant improvements in tasks such as language modeling and machine translation, particularly when combined with attention mechanisms that allowed models to focus on relevant parts of the input sequence.

While neural approaches outperformed statistical methods in many language tasks, they still faced challenges with very long sequences and maintaining coherence across extended contexts. The computational requirements of these models also presented practical limitations, particularly for real-time applications. Despite these challenges, neural networks established the foundation for the transformer architecture that would revolutionize the field.

1.4.4 Transformer Architecture: A Paradigm Shift

The introduction of the transformer architecture in 2017 marked a fundamental shift in natural language processing. Transformers addressed many of the limitations of previous approaches through their reliance on self-attention mechanisms rather than recurrent or convolutional operations. This innovation allowed models to process entire sequences simultaneously, capturing long-range dependencies more effectively and enabling parallelization that significantly improved training efficiency.

The transformer's self-attention mechanism computes relationships between all words in a sequence, regardless of their positional distance, allowing the model to build a more comprehensive understanding of context. This architecture, combined with techniques such as positional encoding and multi-head attention, enabled transformers to achieve state-of-the-art performance across a wide range of language tasks. The development of models like BERT (Bidirectional Encoder Representations from Transformers) and GPT (Generative Pre-trained Transformer) demonstrated the power of this approach, particularly when pre-trained on large corpora and fine-tuned for specific applications.

The transformer architecture's success extended to multilingual applications, where models could be trained on diverse language datasets to develop cross-lingual representations. This capability enabled more effective transfer learning across languages and improved performance on low-resource language tasks. The ability to process multiple languages within a unified framework represented a significant advancement in multilingual AI, opening new possibilities for global communication and information access.

1.4.5 Multilingual AI: Challenges and Opportunities

The development of effective multilingual AI systems presents unique challenges that extend beyond those encountered in monolingual applications. Languages vary significantly in their grammatical structures, vocabularies, and cultural contexts, requiring models to capture diverse linguistic patterns. The availability of training data varies dramatically across languages, with many languages having limited digital resources for model development. Additionally, the cultural and contextual nuances of language use demand sophisticated understanding that goes beyond simple vocabulary translation.

Despite these challenges, multilingual AI offers tremendous opportunities for global communication and information access. The ability to process and translate between multiple languages enables cross-cultural exchange, facilitates international business, and supports global collaboration in research and development. Multilingual models can also help preserve and promote less commonly spoken languages, supporting cultural diversity and linguistic heritage. The development of these systems has implications for education, healthcare, and governance, where language barriers can impede access to critical information and services.

1.5 KEY USE CASES: TRANSLATION, VOICE ASSISTANTS, CROSS-LANGUAGE SEARCH

The key use cases of multilingual AI—translation, voice assistants, and cross-language search—have redefined the way individuals and institutions engage with language in the digital age. These applications not only enhance convenience and efficiency but also foster greater inclusivity, breaking down the linguistic barriers that have historically limited access to information and opportunity. As multilingual AI continues to evolve, its integration into everyday technology will become more seamless, personalized, and equitable. By addressing the challenges of bias, representation, and ethical design, developers and stakeholders can ensure that multilingual AI serves as a tool for global understanding, empowerment, and connection.

1.5.1 Machine Translation: Breaking Down Language Barriers

One of the earliest and most transformative applications of multilingual AI is machine translation. From the days of phrase-based statistical models to today's deep learning-based neural machine translation systems, the evolution of translation technologies has opened up global access to information and enabled communication across borders.

Multilingual AI models such as Google's mT5, Facebook's M2M-100, and OpenAI's GPT-series have been trained on large-scale multilingual datasets, allowing them to translate between dozens or even hundreds of language pairs with high fluency and contextual accuracy. These models not only translate individual sentences but also retain meaning and coherence across entire documents, supporting translation in real-time for email, websites, social media, and academic or legal texts.

Fig: AI Translator—Breaking Language Barriers and Facilitating Global Communication

Multilingual AI has empowered users in both personal and professional settings. In education, students now have access to study materials in their native languages, even when those materials were originally written in another language. In healthcare, doctors and patients who do not speak the same language can rely on AI-based translation tools to convey medical histories and treatment plans. In business, multinational corporations use AI-driven translation to communicate with clients, translate product documentation, and localize marketing campaigns. Importantly, multilingual AI also facilitates the preservation and digitization of underrepresented languages, supporting efforts to make global content accessible to speakers of indigenous or endangered languages.

1.5.2 Voice Assistants: Enabling Multilingual Conversational Interfaces

Voice assistants have become a ubiquitous feature of modern life, found in smartphones, smart speakers, cars, and even home appliances. The rise of voice-enabled interfaces has redefined how people interact with machines, making communication more natural and intuitive. Multilingual AI plays a crucial role in the evolution of these assistants, allowing them to understand and respond in multiple languages.

Assistants like Amazon's Alexa, Google Assistant, Apple's Siri, and Microsoft's Cortana have incorporated multilingual speech recognition and natural language understanding models, enabling users to switch between languages seamlessly or interact in the language of their choice.

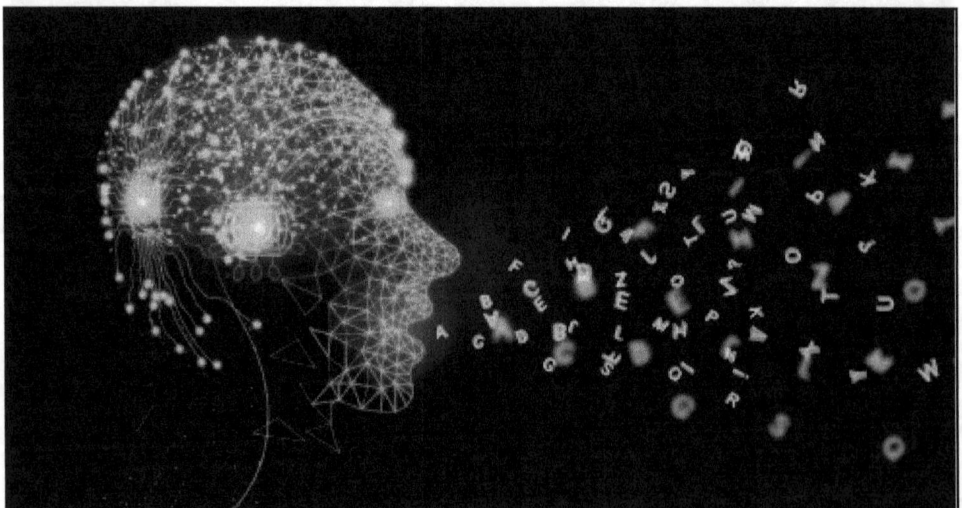

Fig: Voice Assistants

The capabilities of multilingual voice assistants extend beyond mere language switching. They are now able to detect code-switching within conversations, where users mix two or more languages within a single query. This is particularly common in bilingual or multilingual societies and requires sophisticated language models capable of contextual understanding. Furthermore, advances in multilingual AI have led to voice assistants that can interpret cultural nuances, idiomatic expressions, and local dialects, making them more responsive and relevant to diverse user bases.

In practical applications, multilingual voice assistants are transforming sectors such as customer service, healthcare, and accessibility. Call centers use AI-powered voice bots to handle inquiries in multiple languages, reducing wait times and improving user experience. In hospitals, voice-enabled systems help doctors retrieve patient data or input notes while multitasking, all in their preferred language. For users with disabilities, multilingual voice assistants offer new levels of independence, providing a hands-free way to control devices, search for information, and manage daily tasks in a language they are comfortable with.

1.5.3 Cross-Language Search: Accessing Global Knowledge

Another significant application of multilingual AI is cross-language search, which allows users to submit queries in one language and retrieve relevant results in another. This capability enhances the accessibility of global information resources and ensures that knowledge is not confined within language silos. Powered by multilingual embedding models and advanced information retrieval algorithms, cross-language search systems can understand the semantic intent behind a query and match it to documents, articles, or datasets written in different languages.

This functionality is especially valuable in academic research, journalism, and international law, where users need to access a wide range of sources that may be published in different languages. For example, a researcher looking for medical studies conducted in Japan can input their query in English and receive translated results from Japanese journals. Similarly, journalists investigating global issues can access reports from foreign news outlets without needing proficiency in the local language. Legal professionals working on cross-border cases can find precedents, regulations, or contracts that were originally written in other languages, ensuring that linguistic differences do not hinder the legal process.

Cross-language search is also critical in the context of crisis response and humanitarian aid. During natural disasters, conflicts, or pandemics, organizations must gather information from local communities to assess needs and deliver support effectively. Multilingual AI enables real-time monitoring of news, social media, and official updates in multiple languages, facilitating better decision-making and coordination. Moreover, by supporting query translation and multilingual indexing, these systems democratize access to knowledge and promote global collaboration.

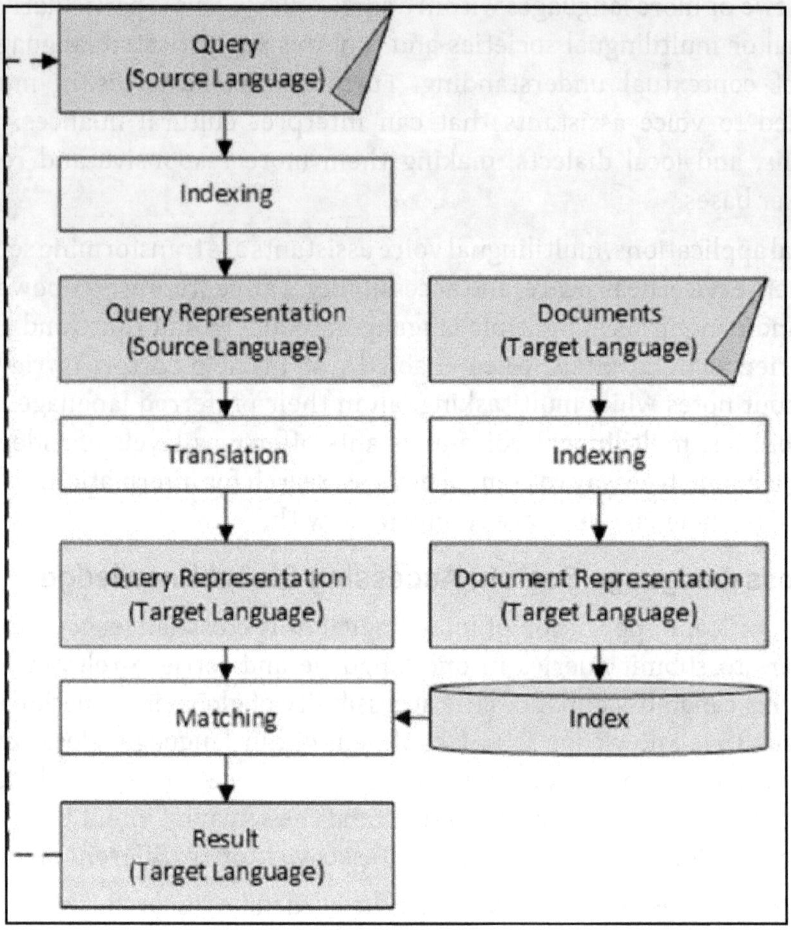

Fig: Cross-Language Search

1.5.4 Interconnectedness of Use Cases and Future Synergies

While translation, voice assistants, and cross-language search are distinct use cases, they often intersect and complement one another in practical applications. For instance, a voice assistant equipped with multilingual capabilities can perform real-time translation and also fetch cross-language search results in response to spoken queries. Similarly, translation tools can be embedded into search engines and content platforms, allowing users to interact with information without switching apps or interfaces. This convergence highlights the modular nature of multilingual AI, where core technologies such as natural language processing, speech recognition, and machine learning underpin a wide array of services.

The integration of these use cases is also driving innovation in Interlingua

. Multilingual chatbots that combine voice, text, and visual interaction are being developed to offer holistic user experiences. In virtual and augmented reality environments, users can navigate interfaces and interact with global users in their preferred language, supported by real-time translation and voice processing. Education platforms are incorporating multilingual voice tutors that can guide learners in various languages, adjusting to their pace and style of learning.

1.5.5 Challenges and Considerations

Despite significant progress, several challenges must be addressed to maximize the potential of multilingual AI in these use cases. Ensuring fairness and reducing bias in language models is critical, especially when translating sensitive or culturally significant content. The diversity of global languages, including those with complex grammar or limited digital resources, makes it difficult to achieve uniform performance across all languages. Real-time applications like voice assistants and cross-language search also demand low-latency, high-accuracy processing, which requires robust infrastructure and continuous optimization.

Ethical considerations also play an important role. As multilingual AI systems collect and process user data, ensuring privacy and informed consent becomes paramount. Moreover, overreliance on AI-based translation in high-stakes settings, such as legal or medical contexts, must be managed with human oversight to avoid misinterpretation and liability. Equally important is the involvement of native speakers and linguists in the development cycle to ensure that systems respect linguistic norms and cultural sensitivities.

CHAPTER 2

Linguistic Foundations and Challenges

2.1 DIVERSITY AND COMPLEXITY OF HUMAN LANGUAGES

Human language is among the most remarkable features of our species, serving not only as a communication tool but also as a carrier of culture, identity, and cognitive development. The sheer diversity and complexity of human languages reflect the vast range of human experience across different geographies, histories, and social contexts. There are currently over 7,000 spoken languages in the world, each with its unique structure, vocabulary, phonetics, and syntax. This linguistic richness presents both opportunities and challenges for linguists, educators, policymakers, and technologists.

The diversity and complexity of human languages stand as a testament to the adaptability, creativity, and interconnectedness of human societies. While this complexity poses significant challenges for linguists, educators, and technologists, it also offers rich opportunities for discovery, innovation, and cross-cultural understanding. Efforts to document, preserve, and understand the world's linguistic heritage must be prioritized, not only for academic reasons but also for their value to human dignity and cultural sustainability. Embracing the full range of human languages means embracing the full potential of human expression and knowledge, ensuring that no voice is left unheard in our increasingly globalized world.

2.1.1 Structural Complexity and Typological Variation

The complexity of human languages is evident in their structural diversity. Every language comprises several subsystems including phonology, morphology, syntax, semantics, and pragmatics. Phonology deals with the sound system, and even at this level, languages vary widely. Some languages, like Rotokas in Papua New Guinea, have as few as twelve phonemes, while others like !Xóõ, a Khoisan language, have more than a hundred. This variation affects everything from pronunciation to voice recognition systems and automatic speech synthesis. Morphology—the study of word formation—also demonstrates linguistic complexity. Some languages, like English, are considered analytic or isolating, using word order and helper words (like prepositions) to convey meaning. Others, like Turkish or Finnish, are agglutinative, creating long compound words through affixes. Still others, such as Russian or Latin, are fusional, where a single affix may convey several grammatical meanings at once. Polysynthetic languages, like Inuktitut, combine many morphemes to express entire sentences in a single word. These typological differences make it difficult to create one-size-fits-all linguistic models, especially for tasks such as machine translation or syntactic parsing.

Fig: Language Diversity

Syntax, which governs sentence structure, shows similar variation. While the basic Subject-Verb-Object (SVO) order is common across many languages, others use Subject-Object-Verb (SOV), Verb-Subject-Object (VSO), or even free word order depending on emphasis and context. Japanese, Hindi, and Korean use postpositions instead of prepositions, and their use of honorifics further complicates syntactic rules. These grammatical and syntactical diversities demand linguistic models that can adapt to multiple frameworks and understand the rules that underpin language use in different cultural contexts.

2.1.2 Linguistic Universals and Cognitive Constraints

Despite the vast differences among languages, many linguists have identified certain commonalities or linguistic universals. These are features or principles that appear to be shared by all human languages, such as the presence of nouns and verbs, the ability to form questions, and mechanisms for negation. The theory of Universal Grammar, proposed by Noam Chomsky, suggests that all human beings possess an innate set of grammatical principles that shape language acquisition. While this theory remains debated, it emphasizes the cognitive foundation of linguistic behavior.

Cognitive constraints also influence language structure. For instance, the limits of short-term memory affect how complex a sentence can be before it becomes difficult to understand. Similarly, the need for efficient communication leads to the creation of conventions that minimize ambiguity. Understanding these constraints helps researchers design more effective natural language processing systems and educational tools for language learning. However, the interaction between universal principles and cultural variation ensures that each language remains a unique and evolving system.

2.1.3 Endangered Languages and Cultural Preservation

One of the pressing issues related to linguistic diversity is the endangerment and extinction of many languages. Linguists estimate that one language disappears every two weeks, often as a result of globalization, colonization, migration, and language policy. With the loss of a language comes the disappearance of a worldview, oral traditions, ecological knowledge, and cultural heritage. Efforts to preserve and revitalize endangered languages involve community-led initiatives, digital archiving, and the integration of traditional knowledge into educational systems.

Technology can play a pivotal role in preservation efforts. Tools such as audio recorders, speech recognition software, and open-source dictionaries have been developed to document endangered languages. Multilingual AI systems trained on diverse linguistic data can help support the use and learning of minority languages. Nonetheless, these technological solutions must be developed in collaboration with native speakers and communities to ensure ethical, accurate, and respectful representation.

2.1.4 Challenges in Language Technology and AI

The complexity and diversity of human languages pose major challenges for computational linguistics and artificial intelligence. Most modern language technologies, including translation engines, chatbots, and voice assistants, are trained predominantly on data from high-resource languages such as English, Mandarin, Spanish, and French. As a result, the performance of these systems tends to be poor when applied to low-resource or morphologically complex languages.

Lack of annotated corpora, limited online content, and orthographic variations are major barriers to building effective AI tools for underrepresented languages.

Additionally, many languages are primarily oral and may lack a standardized writing system. Even among well-documented languages, dialectal variation and code-switching (mixing of two or more languages in a single discourse) present unique computational challenges. The emergence of multilingual pretrained models such as mBERT and XLM-R has provided a foundation for cross-lingual understanding, but they still struggle with fine-grained semantic distinctions and idiomatic expressions.

Bias is another major concern. Language models trained on biased data can inadvertently reinforce stereotypes or marginalize minority voices. This highlights the importance of ethical design in multilingual AI systems, including the diversification of training data, transparency in model development, and the involvement of linguists and community stakeholders in the design process.

2.1.5 Linguistic Identity and Social Implications

Language is not just a tool for communication; it is deeply tied to identity, power, and social inclusion. The dominance of certain languages in education, media, and governance can lead to the marginalization of speakers of minority languages. Policies that promote monolingualism often result in educational disparities, cultural alienation, and loss of heritage. Conversely, multilingual education and linguistic rights support social cohesion, cognitive development, and individual empowerment. The study of sociolinguistics reveals how language functions in diverse social settings. Issues such as language prestige, code-switching, diglossia, and linguistic discrimination reflect broader patterns of inequality. Recognizing the importance of linguistic diversity in social justice frameworks is essential to ensuring equitable access to resources and representation. Language planning and policy must balance the need for national unity with the rights of linguistic minorities, promoting both integration and diversity.

2.2 MORPHOLOGY, SYNTAX, AND SEMANTICS IN MULTILINGUAL CONTEXTS

2.2.1 Morphological Adaptations across Language Systems

In linguistics, morphology is the study of words, including the principles by which they are formed, and how they relate to one another within a language. Most approaches to morphology investigate the structure of words in terms of morphemes, which are the smallest units in a language with some independent meaning. Morphemes include roots that can exist as words by themselves, but also categories such as affixes that can only appear as part of a larger word. For example, in English the root catch and the suffix -ing are both morphemes; catch may appear as its own word, or it may be combined with -ing to form the new word catching. Morphology also analyzes how words behave as parts of speech, and how they may be inflected to express grammatical categories including number, tense, and aspect. Concepts such as productivity are concerned with how speakers create words in specific contexts, which evolves over the history of a language. The basic fields of linguistics broadly focus on language structure at different "scales". Morphology is considered to operate at a scale larger than phonology, which investigates the categories of speech sounds that are distinguished within a spoken language, and thus may constitute the difference between a morpheme and another. Conversely, syntax is concerned with the next-largest scale, and studies how words in turn form phrases and sentences. Morphological typology is a distinct field that categorises languages based on the morphological features they exhibit.

Lexemes and Word-Forms

The term "word" has no well-defined meaning. Instead, two related terms are used in morphology: lexeme and word-form. Generally, a lexeme is a set of inflected word-forms that is often represented with the citation form in small capitals. For instance, the lexeme eat includes the word-forms eat, eats, eaten, and ate. Eat and eats are therefore different word-forms of the same lexeme. In contrast, eat and eater are distinct lexemes, as they represent two different concepts.

Prosodic Word vs. Morphological Word

Here are examples from other languages of the failure of a single phonological word to coincide with a single morphological word form. In Latin, one way to express the concept of 'NOUN-PHRASE$_1$ and NOUN-PHRASE$_2$' (as in "apples and oranges") is to suffix '-que' to the second noun phrase: "apples oranges-and". An extreme level of the theoretical quandary posed by some phonological words is provided by the Kwak'wala language.

In Kwak'wala, as in a great many other languages, meaning relations between nouns, including possession and "semantic case", are formulated by affixes, instead of by independent "words". The three-word English phrase, "with his club", in which 'with' identifies its dependent noun phrase as an instrument and 'his' denotes a possession relation, would consist of two words or even one word in many languages. Unlike most other languages, Kwak'wala semantic affixes phonologically attach not to the lexeme they pertain to semantically but to the preceding lexeme. Consider the following example (in Kwak'wala, sentences begin with what corresponds to an English verb):

kwixʔid-i-da	*bəgwanəma$_i$-χ-a*	*q'asa-s-is$_i$*	*t'alwagwayu*
clubbed-PIVOT-DETERMINER	man-ACCUSATIVE-DETERMINER	otter-INSTRUMENTAL-3SG-POSSESSIVE	club

"the man clubbed the otter with his club."

That is, to a speaker of Kwak'wala, the sentence does not contain the "words" 'him-the-otter' or 'with-his-club' Instead, the markers -i-da (PIVOT-'the'), referring to "man", attaches not to the noun bəgwanəma ("man") but to the verb; the markers -χ-a (ACCUSATIVE-'the'), referring to otter, attach to bəgwanəma instead of to q'asa ('otter'), etc. In other words, a speaker of Kwak'wala does not perceive the sentence to consist of these phonological words:

kwixʔid	*i-da-bəgwanəma*	*χ-a-q'asa*	*s-is$_i$-t'alwagwayu*
clubbed	PIVOT-the-man$_i$	hit-the-otter	with-his$_i$-club

A central publication on this topic is the volume edited by Dixon and Aikhenvald (2002), examining the mismatch between prosodic-phonological and grammatical definitions of "word" in various Amazonian, Australian Aboriginal, Caucasian, Eskimo, Indo-European, Native North American, West African, and sign languages. Apparently, a wide variety of languages make use of the hybrid linguistic unit clitic, possessing the grammatical features of independent words but the prosodic-phonological lack of freedom of bound morphemes. The intermediate status of clitics poses a considerable challenge to linguistic theory.

Inflection vs. Word Formation

Given the notion of a lexeme, it is possible to distinguish two kinds of morphological rules. Some morphological rules relate to different forms of the same lexeme, but other rules relate to different lexemes. Rules of the first kind are inflectional rules, but those of the second kind are rules of word formation. The generation of the English plural dogs from dog is an inflectional rule, and compound phrases and words like dog catcher or dishwasher are examples of word formation. Informally, word formation rules form "new" words (more accurately, new lexemes), and inflection rules yield variant forms of the "same" word (lexeme).

The distinction between inflection and word formation is not at all clear-cut. There are many examples for which linguists fail to agree whether a given rule is inflection or word formation. The next section will attempt to clarify the distinction.

Word formation includes a process in which one combines two complete words, but inflection allows the combination of a suffix with a verb to change the latter's form to that of the subject of the sentence. For example: in the present indefinite, 'go' is used with subject I/we/you/they and plural nouns, but third-person singular pronouns (he/she/it) and singular nouns causes 'goes' to be used. The '-es' is therefore an inflectional marker that is used to match with its subject. A further difference is that in word formation, the resultant word may differ from its source word's grammatical category, but in the process of inflection, the word never changes its grammatical category.

Types of Word Formation

There is a further distinction between two primary kinds of morphological word formation: derivation and compounding. The latter is a process of word formation that involves combining complete word forms into a single compound form. Dog catcher, therefore, is a compound, as both dog and catcher are complete word forms in their own right but are subsequently treated as parts of one form. Derivation involves affixing bound (non-independent) forms to existing lexemes, but the addition of the affix derives a new lexeme. The word independent, for example, is derived from the word dependent by using the prefix in-, and dependent itself is derived from the verb depend.

There is also word formation in the processes of clipping in which a portion of a word is removed to create a new one, blending in which two parts of different words are blended into one, acronyms in which each letter of the new word represents a specific word in the representation (NATO for North Atlantic Treaty Organization), borrowing in which words from one language are taken and used in another, and coinage in which a new word is created to represent a new object or concept.

Paradigms and Morphosyntax

A linguistic paradigm is the complete set of related word forms associated with a given lexeme. The familiar examples of paradigms are the conjugations of verbs and the declensions of nouns. Also, arranging the word forms of a lexeme into tables, by classifying them according to shared inflectional categories such as tense, aspect, mood, number, gender or case, organizes such. For example, the personal pronouns in English can be organized into tables by using the categories of person (first, second, third); number (singular vs. plural); gender (masculine, feminine, neuter); and case (nominative, oblique, genitive).

The inflectional categories used to group word forms into paradigms cannot be chosen arbitrarily but must be categories that are relevant to stating the syntactic rules of the language. Person and number are categories that can be used to define paradigms in English because the language has grammatical agreement rules, which require the verb in a sentence to appear in an inflectional form that matches the person and number of the subject. Therefore, the syntactic rules of English care about the difference between dog and dogs because the choice between both forms determines the form of the verb that is used. However, no syntactic rule shows the difference between dog and dog catcher, or dependent and independent. The first two are nouns, and the other two are adjectives.

An important difference between inflection and word formation is that inflected word forms of lexemes are organized into paradigms that are defined by the requirements of syntactic rules, and there are no corresponding syntactic rules for word formation. The relationship between syntax and morphology, as well as how they interact, is called “morphosyntax”; the term is also used to underline the fact that syntax and morphology are interrelated. The study of morphosyntax concerns itself with inflection and paradigms, and some approaches to morphosyntax exclude from its domain the phenomena of word formation, compounding, and derivation. Within morphosyntax fall the study of agreement and government.

Allomorphy

Above, morphological rules are described as analogies between word forms: dog is to dogs as cat is to cats and dish is to dishes. In this case, the analogy applies both to the form of the words and to their meaning. In each pair, the first word means "one of X", and the second "two or more of X", and the difference is always the plural form -s (or -es) affixed to the second word, which signals the key distinction between singular and plural entities. One of the largest sources of complexity in morphology is that the one-to-one correspondence between meaning and form scarcely applies to every case in the language. In English, there are word form pairs like ox/oxen, goose/geese, and sheep/sheep whose difference between the singular and the plural is signaled in a way that departs from the regular pattern or is not signaled at all. Even cases regarded as regular, such as -s, are not so simple; the -s in dogs is not pronounced the same way as the -s in cats, and in plurals such as dishes, a vowel is added before the -s. Those cases, in which the same distinction is effected by alternative forms of a "word", constitute allomorphy.

Phonological rules constrain the sounds that can appear next to each other in a language, and morphological rules, when applied blindly, would often violate phonological rules by resulting in sound sequences that are prohibited in the language in question. For example, to form the plural of dish by simply appending an -s to the end of the word would result in the form *[dɪʃs], which is not permitted by the phonotactics of English. To "rescue" the word, a vowel sound is inserted between the root and the plural marker, and [dɪʃɪz] results. Similar rules apply to the pronunciation of the -s in dogs and cats: it depends on the quality (voiced vs. unvoiced) of the final preceding phoneme.

Lexical Morphology

Lexical morphology is the branch of morphology that deals with the lexicon that, morphologically conceived, is the collection of lexemes in a language. As such, it concerns itself primarily with word formation: derivation and compounding.

Models

There are three principal approaches to morphology and each tries to capture the distinctions above in different ways:

- Morpheme-based morphology, which makes use of an item-and-arrangement approach.

- Lexeme-based morphology, which normally makes use of an item-and-process approach.
- Word-based morphology, which normally makes use of a word-and-paradigm approach.

Morpheme-Based Morphology

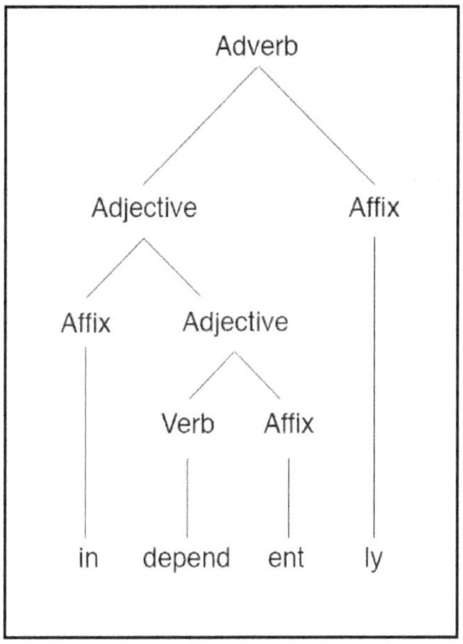

Fig: Morpheme-Based Morphology Tree of the Word "Independently"

In morpheme-based morphology, word forms are analyzed as arrangements of morphemes. A morpheme is defined as the minimal meaningful unit of a language. In a word such as independently, the morphemes are said to be in-, de-, pend, -ent, and -ly; pend is the (bound) root and the other morphemes are, in this case, derivational affixes. In words such as dogs, dog is the root and the -s is an inflectional morpheme. In its simplest and most naïve form, this way of analyzing word forms, called "item-and-arrangement", treats words as if they were made of morphemes put after each other ("concatenated") like beads on a string. More recent and sophisticated approaches, such as distributed morphology, seek to maintain the idea of the morpheme while accommodating non-concatenated, analogical, and other processes that have proven problematic for item-and-arrangement theories and similar approaches.

Morpheme-based morphology presumes three basic axioms:

- Baudouin's "single morpheme" hypothesis: Roots and affixes have the same status as morphemes.
- Bloomfield's "sign base" morpheme hypothesis: As morphemes, they are dualistic signs, since they have both (phonological) form and meaning.

- Bloomfield's "lexical morpheme" hypothesis: morphemes, affixes and roots alike are stored in the lexicon.

Morpheme-based morphology comes in two flavours, one Bloomfieldian and one Hockettian. For Bloomfield, the morpheme was the minimal form with meaning, but did not have meaning itself. For Hockett, morphemes are "meaning elements", not "form elements". For him, there is a morpheme plural using allomorphs such as -s, -en and -ren. Within much morpheme-based morphological theory, the two views are mixed in unsystematic ways so a writer may refer to "the morpheme plural" and "the morpheme -s" in the same sentence.

Lexeme-Based Morphology

Lexeme-based morphology usually takes what is called an item-and-process approach. Instead of analyzing a word form as a set of morphemes arranged in sequence, a word form is said to be the result of applying rules that alter a word-form or stem in order to produce a new one. An inflectional rule takes a stem, changes it as is required by the rule, and outputs a word form; a derivational rule takes a stem, changes it as per its own requirements, and outputs a derived stem; a compounding rule takes word forms, and similarly outputs a compound stem.

Word-Based Morphology

Word-based morphology is (usually) a word-and-paradigm approach. The theory takes paradigms as a central notion. Instead of stating rules to combine morphemes into word forms or to generate word forms from stems, word-based morphology states generalizations that hold between the forms of inflectional paradigms.

The major point behind this approach is that many such generalizations are hard to state with either of the other approaches. Word-and-paradigm approaches are also well-suited to capturing purely morphological phenomena, such as morphomes. Examples to show the effectiveness of word-based approaches are usually drawn from fusional languages, where a given "piece" of a word, which a morpheme-based theory would call an inflectional morpheme, corresponds to a combination of grammatical categories, for example, "third-person plural".

Morpheme-based theories usually have no problems with this situation since one says that a given morpheme has two categories. Item-and-process theories, on the other hand, often break down in cases like these because they all too often assume that there will be two separate rules here, one for third person, and the other for plural, but the distinction between them turns out to be artificial. The approaches treat these as whole words that are related to each other by analogical rules. Words can be categorized based on the pattern they fit into. This applies both to existing words and to new ones. Application of a pattern different from the one that has been used historically can give rise to a new word, such as older replacing elder (where older follows the normal pattern of adjectival comparatives) and cows replacing kine (where cows fits the regular pattern of plural formation).

Morphological Typology

In the 19th century, philologists devised a now classic classification of languages according to their morphology. Some languages are isolating, and have little to no morphology; others are agglutinative whose words tend to have many easily separable morphemes (such as Turkic languages); others yet are inflectional or fusional because their inflectional morphemes are "fused" together (like some Indo-European languages such as Pashto and Russian). That leads to one bound morpheme conveying multiple pieces of information. A standard example of an isolating language is Chinese. An agglutinative language is Turkish (and practically all Turkic languages). Latin and Greek are prototypical inflectional or fusional languages.

It is clear that this classification is not at all clearcut, and many languages (Latin and Greek among them) do not neatly fit any one of these types, and some fit in more than one way. A continuum of complex morphology of language may be adopted. The three models of morphology stem from attempts to analyze languages that more or less match different categories in this typology.

The item-and-arrangement approach fits very naturally with agglutinative languages. The item-and-process and word-and-paradigm approaches usually address fusional languages. As there is very little fusion involved in word formation, classical typology mostly applies to inflectional morphology. Depending on the preferred way of expressing non-inflectional notions, languages may be classified as synthetic (using word formation) or analytic (using syntactic phrases).

Examples

Pingelapese is a Micronesian language spoken on the Pingelap atoll and on two of the eastern Caroline Islands, called the high island of Pohnpei. Similar to other languages, words in Pingelapese can take different forms to add to or even change its meaning. Verbal suffixes are morphemes added at the end of a word to change its form. Prefixes are those that are added at the front. For example, the Pingelapese suffix –kin means 'with' or 'at.' It is added at the end of a verb.

ius = to use → ius-kin = to use with

mwahu = to be good → mwahu-kin = to be good at

sa- is an example of a verbal prefix. It is added to the beginning of a word and means 'not.'

pwung = to be correct → sa-pwung = to be incorrect

There are also directional suffixes that when added to the root word give the listener a better idea of where the subject is headed. The verb alu means to walk. A directional suffix can be used to give more detail.

-da = 'up' → aluh-da = to walk up

-di = 'down' → aluh-di = to walk down

-eng = 'away from speaker and listener' → aluh-eng = to walk away

Directional suffixes are not limited to motion verbs. When added to non-motion verbs, their meanings are a figurative one. The following table gives some examples of directional suffixes and their possible meanings.

Directional suffix	Motion verb	Non-motion verb
-da	up	Onset of a state
-di	down	Action has been completed
-la	away from	Change has caused the start of a new state
-doa	towards	Action continued to a certain point in time
-sang	from	Comparative

2.2.2 Syntactic Transfer and Convergence Phenomena

In linguistics, syntax is the study of how words and morphemes combine to form larger units such as phrases and sentences. Central concerns of syntax include word order, grammatical relations, hierarchical sentence structure (constituency), agreement, the nature of crosslinguistic variation, and the relationship between form and meaning (semantics). Diverse approaches, such as generative grammar and functional grammar, offer unique perspectives on syntax, reflecting its complexity and centrality to understanding human language.

- **Sequencing of Subject, Verb and Object:** One basic description of a language's syntax is the sequence in which the subject (S), verb (V), and object (O) usually appear in sentences. Over 85% of languages usually place the subject first, either in the sequence SVO or the sequence SOV. The other possible sequences are VSO, VOS, OVS, and OSV, the last three of which are rare. In most generative theories of syntax, the surface differences arise from a more complex clausal phrase structure, and each order may be compatible with multiple derivations. However, word order can also reflect the semantics or function of the ordered elements.
- **Grammatical Relations:** Another description of a language considers the set of possible grammatical relations in a language or in general and how they behave in relation to one another in the morphosyntactic

alignment of the language. The description of grammatical relations can also reflect transitivity, passivization, and head-dependent-marking or other agreement. Languages have different criteria for grammatical relations. For example, subjecthood criteria may have implications for how the subject is referred to from a relative clause or coreferential with an element in an infinite clause.

- **Constituency:** Constituency is the feature of being a constituent and how words can work together to form a constituent (or phrase). Constituents are often moved as units, and the constituent can be the domain of agreement. Some languages allow discontinuous phrases in which words belonging to the same constituent are not immediately adjacent but are broken up by other constituents. Constituents may be recursive, as they may consist of other constituents, potentially of the same type.

Early History

The Astadhyayi of Paṇini, from c. 4th century BC in Ancient India, is often cited as an example of a premodern work that approaches the sophistication of a modern syntactic theory since works on grammar had been written long before modern syntax came about. In the West, the school of thought that came to be known as "traditional grammar" began with the work of Dionysius Thrax.

For centuries, a framework known as grammaire générale, first expounded in 1660 by Antoine Arnauld and Claude Lancelot in a book of the same title, dominated work in syntax: as its basic premise the assumption that language is a direct reflection of thought processes and so there is a single most natural way to express a thought. However, in the 19th century, with the development of historical-comparative linguistics, linguists began to realize the sheer diversity of human language and to question fundamental assumptions about the relationship between language and logic. It became apparent that there was no such thing as the most natural way to express a thought and so logic could no longer be relied upon as a basis for studying the structure of language.

The Port-Royal grammar modeled the study of syntax upon that of logic. (Indeed, large parts of Port-Royal Logic were copied or adapted from the Grammaire générale.) Syntactic categories were identified with logical ones, and all sentences were analyzed in terms of "subject – copula – predicate". Initially, that view was adopted even by the early comparative linguists such as Franz Bopp. The central role of syntax within theoretical linguistics became clear only in the 20th century, which could reasonably be called the "century of syntactic theory" as far as linguistics is concerned.

Theories

There are a number of theoretical approaches to the discipline of syntax. One school of thought, founded in the works of Derek Bickerton, sees syntax as a branch of biology, since it conceives of syntax as the study of linguistic knowledge as embodied in the human mind. Other linguists (e.g., Gerald Gazdar) take a more Platonistic view since they regard syntax to be the study of an abstract formal system. Yet others (e.g., Joseph Greenberg) consider syntax a taxonomical device to reach broad generalizations across languages.

Syntacticians have attempted to explain the causes of word-order variation within individual languages and cross-linguistically. Much of such work has been done within the framework of generative grammar, which holds that syntax depends on a genetic endowment common to the human species. In that framework and in others, linguistic typology and universals have been primary explicanda.

Alternative explanations, such as those by functional linguists, have been sought in language processing. It is suggested that the brain finds it easier to parse syntactic patterns that are either right- or left-branching but not mixed. The most-widely held approach is the performance–grammar correspondence hypothesis by John A. Hawkins, who suggests that language is a non-innate adaptation to innate cognitive mechanisms. Cross-linguistic tendencies are considered as being based on language users' preference for grammars that are organized efficiently and on their avoidance of word orderings that cause processing difficulty.

Some languages, however, exhibit regular inefficient patterning such as the VO languages Chinese, with the adpositional phrase before the verb, and Finnish, which has postpositions, but there are few other profoundly exceptional languages. More recently, it is suggested that the left- versus right-branching patterns are cross-linguistically related only to the place of role-marking connectives (adpositions and subordinators), which links the phenomena with the semantic mapping of sentences.

Theoretical Syntactic Models

Dependency Grammar

Dependency grammar is an approach to sentence structure in which syntactic units are arranged according to the dependency relation, as opposed to the constituency relation of phrase structure grammars. Dependencies are directed links between words. The (finite) verb is seen as the root of all clause structure and all the other words in the clause are either directly or indirectly dependent on this root (i.e. the verb). Some prominent dependency-based theories of syntax are the following:

Recursive categorical syntax, or algebraic syntax.

- Functional generative description.
- Meaning-text theory.
- Operator grammar.
- Word grammar.

Lucien Tesniere (1893–1954) is widely seen as the father of modern dependency-based theories of syntax and grammar. He argued strongly against the binary division of the clause into subject and predicate that is associated with the grammars of his day (S → NP VP) and remains at the core of most phrase structure grammars. In place of that division, he positioned the verb as the root of all clause structure.

Categorial Grammar

Categorial grammar is an approach in which constituents combine as function and argument, according to combinatory possibilities specified in their syntactic categories. For example, other approaches might posit a rule that combines a noun phrase (NP) and a verb phrase (VP), but CG would posit a syntactic category NP and another NP\S, read as "a category that searches to the left (indicated by \) for an NP (the element on the left) and outputs a sentence (the element on the right)."

Thus, the syntactic category for an intransitive verb is a complex formula representing the fact that the verb acts as a function word requiring an NP as an input and produces a sentence level structure as an output. The complex category is notated as (NP\S) instead of V. The category of transitive verb is defined as an element that requires two NPs (its subject and its direct object) to form a sentence. That is notated as (NP/(NP\S)), which means, "A category that searches to the right (indicated by /) for an NP (the object) and generates a function (equivalent to the VP) which is (NP\S), which in turn represents a function that searches to the left for an NP and produces a sentence." Tree-adjoining grammar is a categorial grammar that adds in partial tree structures to the categories.

Functional Grammars

Functionalist models of grammar study the form–function interaction by performing a structural and a functional analysis.

- Functional discourse grammar (Dik).
- Prague linguistic circle.
- Role and reference grammar (RRG).
- Systemic functional grammar.

Generative Syntax

Generative syntax is the study of syntax within the overarching framework of generative grammar. Generative theories of syntax typically propose analyses of grammatical patterns using formal tools such as phrase structure grammars augmented with additional operations such as syntactic movement. Their goal in analyzing a particular language is to specify rules which generate all and only the expressions which are well-formed in that language. In doing so, they seek to identify innate domain-specific principles of linguistic cognition, in line with the wider goals of the generative enterprise. Generative syntax is among the approaches that adopt the principle of the autonomy of syntax by assuming that meaning and communicative intent is determined by the syntax, rather than the other way around.

Generative syntax was proposed in the late 1950s by Noam Chomsky, building on earlier work by Zellig Harris, Louis Hjelmslev, and others. Since then, numerous theories have been proposed under its umbrella:

- **Transformational Grammar (TG):** Original theory of generative syntax laid out by Chomsky in Syntactic Structures in 1957.
- **Government and Binding Theory (GB):** Revised theory in the tradition of TG developed mainly by Chomsky in the 1970s and 1980s.
- **Minimalist Program (MP):** A reworking of the theory out of the GB framework published by Chomsky in 1995.

Other theories that find their origin in the generative paradigm are:

- Arc pair grammar.
- Generalized phrase structure grammar (GPSG).
- Generative semantics.
- Head-driven phrase structure grammar (HPSG).
- Lexical functional grammar (LFG).
- Nanosyntax.
- Relational grammar (RG).
- Harmonic grammar (HG).

Cognitive and Usage-Based Grammars

The Cognitive Linguistics framework stems from generative grammar but adheres to evolutionary, rather than Chomskyan, linguistics. Cognitive models often recognise the generative assumption that the object belongs to the verb phrase. Cognitive frameworks include the following:

- Cognitive grammar.
- Construction grammar (CxG).
- Emergent grammar.

2.2.3 Semantic Mapping across Linguistic Boundaries

Semantics is the study of linguistic meaning. It examines what meaning is, how words get their meaning, and how the meaning of a complex expression depends on its parts. Part of this process involves the distinction between sense and reference. Sense is given by the ideas and concepts associated with an expression while reference is the object to which an expression points. Semantics contrasts with syntax, which studies the rules that dictate how to create grammatically correct sentences, and pragmatics, which investigates how people use language in communication. Semantics, together with syntactics and pragmatics, is a part of semiotics.

Lexical semantics is the branch of semantics that studies word meaning. It examines whether words have one or several meanings and in what lexical relations they stand to one another. Phrasal semantics studies the meaning of sentences by exploring the phenomenon of compositionality or how new meanings can be created by arranging words. Formal semantics relies on logic and mathematics to provide precise frameworks of the relation between language and meaning. Cognitive semantics examines meaning from a psychological perspective and assumes a close relation between language ability and the conceptual structures used to understand the world. Other branches of semantics include conceptual semantics, computational semantics, and cultural semantics.

Theories of meaning are general explanations of the nature of meaning and how expressions are endowed with it. According to referential theories, the meaning of an expression is the part of reality to which it points. Ideational theories identify meaning with mental states like the ideas that an expression evokes in the minds of language users. According to causal theories, meaning is determined by causes and effects, which behaviorist semantics analyzes in terms of stimulus and response. Further theories of meaning include truth-conditional semantics, verificationist theories, the use theory, and inferentialist semantics. The study of semantic phenomena began during antiquity but was not recognized as an independent field of inquiry until the 19th century. Semantics is relevant to the fields of formal logic, computer science, and psychology.

Definition

Semantics is the study of meaning in languages. It is a systematic inquiry that examines what linguistic meaning is and how it arises. It investigates how expressions are built up from different layers of constituents, like morphemes, words, clauses, sentences, and texts, and how the meanings of the constituents affect one another. Semantics can focus on a specific language, like English, but in its widest sense, it investigates meaning structures relevant to all languages. As a descriptive discipline, it aims to determine how meaning works without prescribing what meaning people should associate with particular expressions. Some of its key questions are "How do the meanings of words combine to create the meanings of sentences?", "How do meanings relate to the minds of language users, and to the things words refer to?", and "What is the connection between what a word means, and the contexts in which it is used?". The main disciplines engaged in semantics are linguistics, semiotics, and philosophy. Besides its meaning as a field of inquiry, semantics can also refer to theories within this field, like truth-conditional semantics, and to the meaning of particular expressions, like the semantics of the word fairy.

As a field of inquiry, semantics has both an internal and an external side. The internal side is interested in the connection between words and the mental phenomena they evoke, like ideas and conceptual representations. The external side examines how words refer to objects in the world and under what conditions a sentence is true. Many related disciplines investigate language and meaning. Semantics contrasts with other subfields of linguistics focused on distinct aspects of language. Phonology studies the different types of sounds used in languages and how sounds are connected to form words while syntax examines the rules that dictate how to arrange words to create sentences.

These divisions are reflected in the fact that it is possible to master some aspects of a language while lacking others, like when a person knows how to pronounce a word without knowing its meaning. As a subfield of semiotics, semantics has a more narrow focus on meaning in language while semiotics studies both linguistic and non-linguistic signs. Semiotics investigates additional topics like the meaning of non-verbal communication, conventional symbols, and natural signs independent of human interaction. Examples include nodding to signal agreement, stripes on a uniform signifying rank, and the presence of vultures indicating a nearby animal carcass.

Semantics further contrasts with pragmatics, which is interested in how people use language in communication. An expression like "That's what I'm talking about" can mean many things depending on who says it and in what situation. Semantics is interested in the possible meanings of expressions: what they can and cannot mean in general. In this regard, it is sometimes defined as the study of context-independent meaning.

Pragmatics examines which of these possible meanings is relevant in a particular case. In contrast to semantics, it is interested in actual performance rather than in the general linguistic competence underlying this performance. This includes the topic of additional meaning that can be inferred even though it is not literally expressed, like what it means if a speaker remains silent on a certain topic. A closely related distinction by the semiotician Charles W. Morris holds that semantics studies the relation between words and the world, pragmatics examines the relation between words and users, and syntax focuses on the relation between different words. Semantics is related to etymology, which studies how words and their meanings changed in the course of history. Another connected field is hermeneutics, which is the art or science of interpretation and is concerned with the right methodology of interpreting text in general and scripture in particular. Metasemantics examines the metaphysical foundations of meaning and aims to explain where it comes from or how it arises.

The word semantics originated from the Ancient Greek adjective semantikos, meaning 'relating to signs', which is a derivative of sēmeion, the noun for 'sign'. It was initially used for medical symptoms and only later acquired its wider meaning regarding any type of sign, including linguistic signs. The word semantics entered the English language from the French term semantique, which the linguist Michel Bréal first introduced at the end of the 19th century.

Meaning

Semantics studies meaning in language, which is limited to the meaning of linguistic expressions. It concerns how signs are interpreted and what information they contain. An example is the meaning of words provided in dictionary definitions by giving synonymous expressions or paraphrases, like defining the meaning of the term ram as adult male sheep. There are many forms of non-linguistic meaning that are not examined by semantics. Actions and policies can have meaning in relation to the goal they serve. Fields like religion and spirituality are interested in the meaning of life, which is about finding a purpose in life or the significance of existence in general.

Linguistic meaning can be analyzed on different levels. Word meaning is studied by lexical semantics and investigates the denotation of individual words. It is often related to concepts of entities, like how the word dog is associated with the concept of the four-legged domestic animal. Sentence meaning falls into the field of phrasal semantics and concerns the denotation of full sentences. It usually expresses a concept applying to a type of situation, as in the sentence "the dog has ruined my blue skirt".

The meaning of a sentence is often referred to as a proposition. Different sentences can express the same proposition, like the English sentence "the tree is green" and the German sentence „der Baum ist grün". Utterance meaning is studied by pragmatics and is about the meaning of an expression on a particular occasion. Sentence meaning and utterance meaning come apart in cases where expressions are used in a non-literal way, as is often the case with irony. Semantics is primarily interested in the public meaning that expressions have, like the meaning found in general dictionary definitions. Speaker meaning, by contrast, is the private or subjective meaning that individuals associate with expressions. It can diverge from the literal meaning, like when a person associates the word needle with pain or drugs.

Sense and Reference

Meaning is often analyzed in terms of sense and reference, also referred to as intension and extension or connotation and denotation. The referent of an expression is the object to which the expression points. The sense of an expression is the way in which it refers to that object or how the object is interpreted. For example, the expressions morning star and evening star refer to the same planet, just like the expressions 2 + 2 and 3 + 1 refer to the same number. The meanings of these expressions differ not on the level of reference but on the level of sense. Sense is sometimes understood as a mental phenomenon that helps people identify the objects to which an expression refers. Some semanticists focus primarily on sense or primarily on reference in their analysis of meaning. To grasp the full meaning of an expression, it is usually necessary to understand both to what entities in the world it refers and how it describes them.

The distinction between sense and reference can explain identity statements, which can be used to show how two expressions with a different sense have the same referent. For instance, the sentence "the morning star is the evening star" is informative and people can learn something from it. The sentence "the morning star is the morning star", by contrast, is an uninformative tautology since the expressions are identical not only on the level of reference but also on the level of sense.

Compositionality

Compositionality is a key aspect of how languages construct meaning. It is the idea that the meaning of a complex expression is a function of the meanings of its parts. It is possible to understand the meaning of the sentence "Zuzana owns a dog" by understanding what the words Zuzana, owns, a and dog mean and how they are combined. In this regard, the meaning of complex expressions like sentences is different from word meaning since it is normally not possible to deduce what a word means by looking at its letters and one needs to consult a dictionary instead.

Compositionality is often used to explain how people can formulate and understand an almost infinite number of meanings even though the amount of words and cognitive resources is finite. Many sentences that people read are sentences that they have never seen before and they are nonetheless able to understand them.

When interpreted in a strong sense, the principle of compositionality states that the meaning of a complex expression is not just affected by its parts and how they are combined but fully determined this way. It is controversial whether this claim is correct or whether additional aspects influence meaning. For example, context may affect the meaning of expressions; idioms like "kick the bucket" carry figurative or non-literal meanings that are not directly reducible to the meanings of their parts.

Truth and Truth Conditions

Truth is a property of statements that accurately present the world and true statements are in accord with reality. Whether a statement is true usually depends on the relation between the statement and the rest of the world. The truth conditions of a statement are the way the world needs to be for the statement to be true. For example, it belongs to the truth conditions of the sentence "it is raining outside" that raindrops are falling from the sky. The sentence is true if it is used in a situation in which the truth conditions are fulfilled, i.e., if there is actually rain outside.

Truth conditions play a central role in semantics and some theories rely exclusively on truth conditions to analyze meaning. To understand a statement usually implies that one has an idea about the conditions under which it would be true. This can happen even if one does not know whether the conditions are fulfilled.

Semiotic Triangle

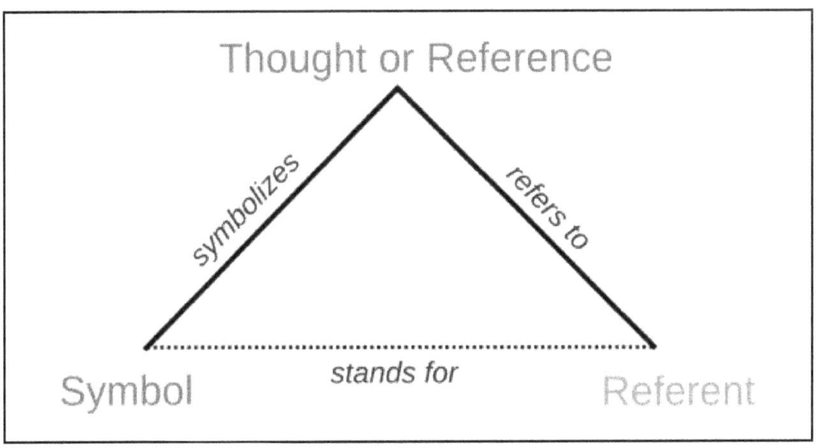

Fig: The Semiotic Triangle Aims to Explain how the Relation between Language (Symbol) and World (Referent) is Mediated by the Language Users (Thought or Reference)

The semiotic triangle, also called the triangle of meaning, is a model used to explain the relation between language, language users, and the world, represented in the model as Symbol, Thought or Reference, and Referent. The symbol is a linguistic signifier, either in its spoken or written form. The central idea of the model is that there is no direct relation between a linguistic expression and what it refers to, as was assumed by earlier dyadic models. This is expressed in the diagram by the dotted line between symbol and referent.

The model holds instead that the relation between the two is mediated through a third component. For example, the term apple stands for a type of fruit but there is no direct connection between this string of letters and the corresponding physical object.

The relation is only established indirectly through the mind of the language user. When they see the symbol, it evokes a mental image or a concept, which establishes the connection to the physical object. This process is only possible if the language user learned the meaning of the symbol before. The meaning of a specific symbol is governed by the conventions of a particular language. The same symbol may refer to one object in one language, to another object in a different language, and to no object in another language.

Others

Many other concepts are used to describe semantic phenomena. The semantic role of an expression is the function it fulfills in a sentence. In the sentence "the boy kicked the ball", the boy has the role of the agent who performs an action. The ball is the theme or patient of this action as something that does not act itself but is involved in or affected by the action. The same entity can be both agent and patient, like when someone cuts themselves. An entity has the semantic role of an instrument if it is used to perform the action, for instance, when cutting something with a knife then the knife is the instrument. For some sentences, no action is described but an experience takes place, like when a girl sees a bird. In this case, the girl has the role of the experiencer. Other common semantic roles are location, source, goal, beneficiary, and stimulus.

Lexical relations describe how words stand to one another. Two words are synonyms if they share the same or a very similar meaning, like car and automobile or buy and purchase. Antonyms have opposite meanings, such as the contrast between alive and dead or fast and slow. One term is a hyponym of another term if the meaning of the first term is included in the meaning of the second term. For example, ant is a hyponym of insect. A prototype is a hyponym that has characteristic features of the type it belongs to. A robin is a prototype of a bird but a penguin is not. Two words with the same pronunciation are homophones like flour and flower, while two words with the same spelling are homonyms, like a bank of a river in contrast to a bank as a financial institution. Hyponymy is closely related to meronymy, which describes the relation between part and whole. For instance, wheel is a meronym of car. An expression is ambiguous if it has more than one possible meaning. In some cases, it is possible to disambiguate them to discern the intended meaning. The term polysemy is used if the different meanings are closely related to one another, like the meanings of the word head, which can refer to the topmost part of the human body or the top-ranking person in an organization.

The meaning of words can often be subdivided into meaning components called semantic features. The word horse has the semantic feature animate but lacks the semantic feature human. It may not always be possible to fully reconstruct the meaning of a word by identifying all its semantic features.

A semantic or lexical field is a group of words that are all related to the same activity or subject. For instance, the semantic field of cooking includes words like bake, boil, spice, and pan.

The context of an expression refers to the situation or circumstances in which it is used and includes time, location, speaker, and audience. It also encompasses other passages in a text that come before and after it. Context affects the meaning of various expressions, like the deictic expression here and the anaphoric expression she.

A syntactic environment is extensional or transparent if it is always possible to exchange expressions with the same reference without affecting the truth value of the sentence. For example, the environment of the sentence "the number 8 is even" is extensional because replacing the expression "the number 8" with "the number of planets in the Solar System" does not change its truth value. For intensional or opaque contexts, this type of substitution is not always possible. For instance, the embedded clause in "Paco believes that the number 8 is even" is intensional since Paco may not know that the number of planets in the solar system is 8.

Semanticists commonly distinguish the language they study, called object language, from the language they use to express their findings, called metalanguage. When a professor uses Japanese to teach their student how to interpret the language of first-order logic then the language of first-order logic is the object language and Japanese is the metalanguage. The same language may occupy the role of object language and metalanguage at the same time. This is the case in monolingual English dictionaries, in which both the entry term belonging to the object language and the definition text belonging to the metalanguage are taken from the English language.

Branches

Lexical Semantics

Lexical semantics is the sub-field of semantics that studies word meaning. It examines semantic aspects of individual words and the vocabulary as a whole. This includes the study of lexical relations between words, such as whether two terms are synonyms or antonyms. Lexical semantics categorizes words based on semantic features they share and groups them into semantic fields unified by a common subject. This information is used to create taxonomies to organize lexical knowledge, for example, by distinguishing between physical and abstract entities and subdividing physical entities into stuff and individuated entities. Further topics of interest are polysemy, ambiguity, and vagueness. Lexical semantics is sometimes divided into two complementary approaches: semasiology and onomasiology. Semasiology starts from words and examines what their meaning is. It is interested in whether words have one or several meanings and how those meanings are related to one another. Instead of going from word to meaning, onomasiology goes from meaning to word. It starts with a concept and examines what names this concept has or how it can be expressed in a particular language.

Some semanticists also include the study of lexical units other than words in the field of lexical semantics. Compound expressions like being under the weather have a non-literal meaning that acts as a unit and is not a direct function of its parts. Another topic concerns the meaning of morphemes that make up words, for instance, how negative prefixes like in- and dis- affect the meaning of the words they are part of, as in inanimate and dishonest.

Phrasal Semantics

Phrasal semantics studies the meaning of sentences. It relies on the principle of compositionality to explore how the meaning of complex expressions arises from the combination of their parts. The different parts can be analyzed as subject, predicate, or argument. The subject of a sentence usually refers to a specific entity while the predicate describes a feature of the subject or an event in which the subject participates. Arguments provide additional information to complete the predicate. For example, in the sentence "Mary hit the ball", Mary is the subject, hit is the predicate, and the ball is an argument. A more fine-grained categorization distinguishes between different semantic roles of words, such as agent, patient, theme, location, source, and goal.

Verbs usually function as predicates and often help to establish connections between different expressions to form a more complex meaning structure. In the expression "Beethoven likes Schubert", the verb like connects a liker to the object of their liking. Other sentence parts modify meaning rather than form new connections. For instance, the adjective red modifies the color of another entity in the expression red car. A further compositional device is variable binding, which is used to determine the reference of a term. For example, the last part of the expression "the woman who likes Beethoven" specifies which woman is meant. Parse trees can be used to show the underlying hierarchy employed to combine the different parts. Various grammatical devices, like the gerund form, also contribute to meaning and are studied by grammatical semantics.

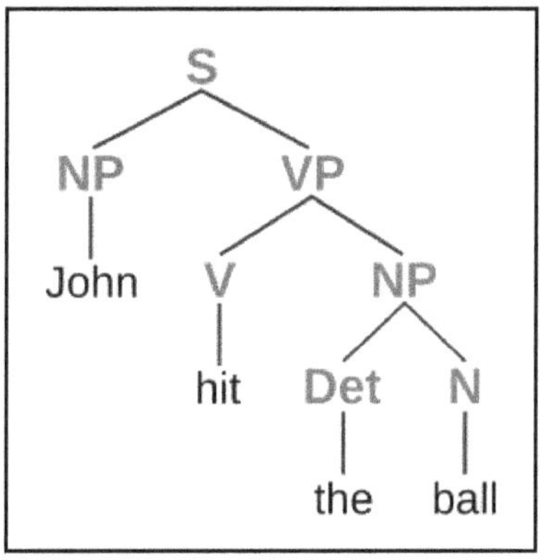

Fig: Parse Trees, like the Constituency-Based Parse Tree, Show how Expressions are Combined to Form Sentences

Formal Semantics

Formal semantics uses formal tools from logic and mathematics to analyze meaning in natural languages. It aims to develop precise logical formalisms to clarify the relation between expressions and their denotation. One of its key tasks is to provide frameworks of how language represents the world, for example, using ontological models to show how linguistic expressions map to the entities of that model. A common idea is that words refer to individual objects or groups of objects while sentences relate to events and states. Sentences are mapped to a truth value based on whether their description of the world is in correspondence with its ontological model.

Formal semantics further examines how to use formal mechanisms to represent linguistic phenomena such as quantification, intensionality, noun phrases, plurals, mass terms, tense, and modality. Montague semantics is an early and influential theory in formal semantics that provides a detailed analysis of how the English language can be represented using mathematical logic. It relies on higher-order logic, lambda calculus, and type theory to show how meaning is created through the combination of expressions belonging to different syntactic categories. Dynamic semantics is a subfield of formal semantics that focuses on how information grows over time. According to it, "meaning is context change potential": the meaning of a sentence is not given by the information it contains but by the information change it brings about relative to a context.

Cognitive Semantics

Cognitive semantics studies the problem of meaning from a psychological perspective or how the mind of the language user affects meaning. As a subdiscipline of cognitive linguistics, it sees language as a wide cognitive ability that is closely related to the conceptual structures used to understand and represent the world. Cognitive semanticists do not draw a sharp distinction between linguistic knowledge and knowledge of the world and see them instead as interrelated phenomena. They study how the interaction between language and human cognition affects the conceptual organization in very general domains like space, time, causation, and action.

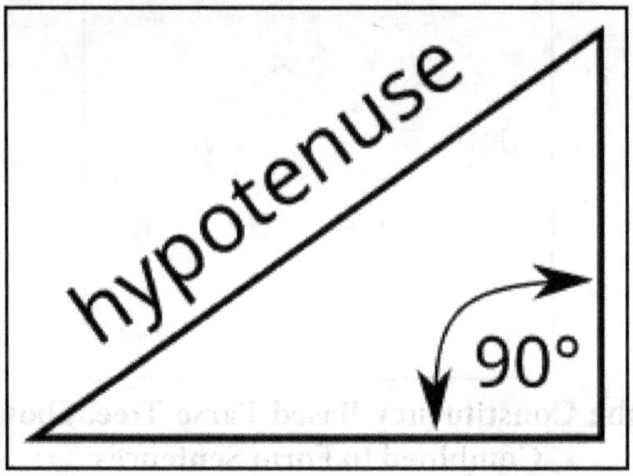

Fig: Cognitive Semantics is Interested in the Conceptual Structures Underlying Language, which can be Articulated through the Contrast between Profile and Base

The contrast between profile and base is sometimes used to articulate the underlying knowledge structure. The profile of a linguistic expression is the aspect of the knowledge structure that it brings to the foreground while the base is the background that provides the context of this aspect without being at the center of attention. For example, the profile of the word hypotenuse is a straight line while the base is a right-angled triangle of which the hypotenuse forms a part.

Cognitive semantics further compares the conceptual patterns and linguistic typologies across languages and considers to what extent the cognitive conceptual structures of humans are universal or relative to their linguistic background. Another research topic concerns the psychological processes involved in the application of grammar. Other investigated phenomena include categorization, which is understood as a cognitive heuristic to avoid information overload by regarding different entities in the same way, and embodiment, which concerns how the language user's bodily experience affects the meaning of expressions.

Frame semantics is an important subfield of cognitive semantics. Its central idea is that the meaning of terms cannot be understood in isolation from each other but needs to be analyzed on the background of the conceptual structures they depend on. These structures are made explicit in terms of semantic frames. For example, words like bride, groom, and honeymoon evoke in the mind the frame of marriage.

Others

Conceptual semantics shares with cognitive semantics the idea of studying linguistic meaning from a psychological perspective by examining how humans conceptualize and experience the world. It holds that meaning is not about the objects to which expressions refer but about the cognitive structure of human concepts that connect thought, perception, and action. Conceptual semantics differs from cognitive semantics by introducing a strict distinction between meaning and syntax and by relying on various formal devices to explore the relation between meaning and cognition. Computational semantics examines how the meaning of natural language expressions can be represented and processed on computers. It often relies on the insights of formal semantics and applies them to problems that can be computationally solved. Some of its key problems include computing the meaning of complex expressions by analyzing their parts, handling ambiguity, vagueness, and context-dependence, and using the extracted information in automatic reasoning. It forms part of computational linguistics, artificial intelligence, and cognitive science. Its applications include machine learning and machine translation.

Cultural semantics studies the relation between linguistic meaning and culture. It compares conceptual structures in different languages and is interested in how meanings evolve and change because of cultural phenomena associated with politics, religion, and customs. For example, address practices encode cultural values and social hierarchies, as in the difference of politeness of expressions like tu and usted in Spanish or du and Sie in German in contrast to English, which lacks these distinctions and uses the pronoun you in either case. Closely related fields are intercultural semantics, cross-cultural semantics, and comparative semantics.

Pragmatic semantics studies how the meaning of an expression is shaped by the situation in which it is used. It is based on the idea that communicative meaning is usually context-sensitive and depends on who participates in the exchange, what information they share, and what their intentions and background assumptions are. It focuses on communicative actions, of which linguistic expressions only form one part. Some theorists include these topics within the scope of semantics while others consider them part of the distinct discipline of pragmatics.

Theories of Meaning

Referential

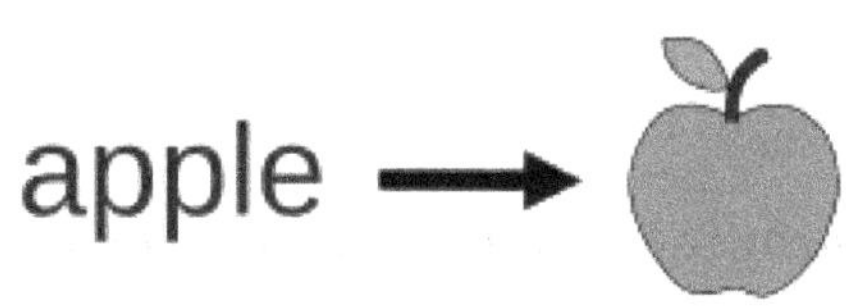

Fig: Referential Theories Identify Meaning with the Entities to which Expressions Point

Referential theories state that the meaning of an expression is the entity to which it points. The meaning of singular terms like names is the individual to which they refer. For example, the meaning of the name George Washington is the person with this name. General terms refer not to a single entity but to the set of objects to which this term applies. In this regard, the meaning of the term cat is the set of all cats. Similarly, verbs usually refer to classes of actions or events and adjectives refer to properties of individuals and events.

Simple referential theories face problems for meaningful expressions that have no clear referent. Names like Pegasus and Santa Claus have meaning even though they do not point to existing entities. Other difficulties concern cases in which different expressions are about the same entity. For instance, the expressions Roger Bannister and the first man to run a four-minute mile refer to the same person but do not mean exactly the same thing. This is particularly relevant when talking about beliefs since a person may understand both expressions without knowing that they point to the same entity. A further problem is given by expressions whose meaning depends on the context, like the deictic terms here and I.

To avoid these problems, referential theories often introduce additional devices. Some identify meaning not directly with objects but with functions that point to objects. This additional level has the advantage of taking the context of an expression into account since the same expression may point to one object in one context and to another object in a different context. For example, the reference of the word here depends on the location in which it is used.

A closely related approach is possible world semantics, which allows expressions to refer not only to entities in the actual world but also to entities in other possible worlds. According to this view, expressions like the first man to run a four-minute mile refer to different persons in different worlds. This view can also be used to analyze sentences that talk about what is possible or what is necessary: possibility is what is true in some possible worlds while necessity is what is true in all possible worlds.

Ideational

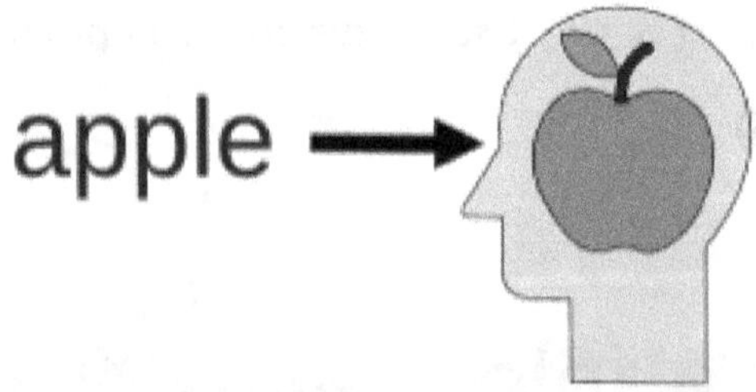

Fig: Ideational Theories Identify Meaning with the Mental States of Language Users

Ideational theories, also called mentalist theories, are not primarily interested in the reference of expressions and instead explain meaning in terms of the mental states of language users. One historically influential approach articulated by John Locke holds that expressions stand for ideas in the speaker's mind. According to this view, the meaning of the word dog is the idea that people have of dogs. Language is seen as a medium used to transfer ideas from the speaker to the audience. After having learned the same meaning of signs, the speaker can produce a sign that corresponds to the idea in their mind and the perception of this sign evokes the same idea in the mind of the audience. A closely related theory focuses not directly on ideas but on intentions. This view is particularly associated with Paul Grice, who observed that people usually communicate to cause some reaction in their audience. He held that the meaning of an expression is given by the intended reaction.

This means that communication is not just about decoding what the speaker literally said but requires an understanding of their intention or why they said it. For example, telling someone looking for petrol that "there is a garage around the corner" has the meaning that petrol can be obtained there because of the speaker's intention to help. This goes beyond the literal meaning, which has no explicit connection to petrol.

Causal

Causal theories hold that the meaning of an expression depends on the causes and effects it has. According to behaviorist semantics, also referred to as stimulus-response theory, the meaning of an expression is given by the situation that prompts the speaker to use it and the response it provokes in the audience.

For instance, the meaning of yelling "Fire!" is given by the presence of an uncontrolled fire and attempts to control it or seek safety. Behaviorist semantics relies on the idea that learning a language consists in adopting behavioral patterns in the form of stimulus-response pairs. One of its key motivations is to avoid private mental entities and define meaning instead in terms of publicly observable language behavior.

Another causal theory focuses on the meaning of names and holds that a naming event is required to establish the link between name and named entity. This naming event acts as a form of baptism that establishes the first link of a causal chain in which all subsequent uses of the name participate. According to this view, the name Plato refers to an ancient Greek philosopher because, at some point, he was originally named this way and people kept using this name to refer to him. This view was originally formulated by Saul Kripke to apply to names only but has been extended to cover other types of speech as well.

Others

Truth-conditional semantics analyzes the meaning of sentences in terms of their truth conditions. According to this view, to understand a sentence means to know what the world needs to be like for the sentence to be true. Truth conditions can themselves be expressed through possible worlds. For example, the sentence "Hillary Clinton won the 2016 American presidential election" is false in the actual world but there are some possible worlds in which it is true. The extension of a sentence can be interpreted as its truth value while its intension is the set of all possible worlds in which it is true. Truth-conditional semantics is closely related to verificationist theories, which introduce the additional idea that there should be some kind of verification procedure to assess whether a sentence is true. They state that the meaning of a sentence consists in the method to verify it or in the circumstances that justify it. For instance, scientific claims often make predictions, which can be used to confirm or disconfirm them using observation. According to verificationism, sentences that can neither be verified nor falsified are meaningless.

The use theory states that the meaning of an expression is given by the way it is utilized. This view was first introduced by Ludwig Wittgenstein, who understood language as a collection of language games. The meaning of expressions depends on how they are used inside a game and the same expression may have different meanings in different games. Some versions of this theory identify meaning directly with patterns of regular use. Others focus on social norms and conventions by additionally taking into account whether a certain use is considered appropriate in a given society.

Inferentialist semantics, also called conceptual role semantics, holds that the meaning of an expression is given by the role it plays in the premises and conclusions of good inferences. For example, one can infer from "x is a male sibling" that "x is a brother" and one can infer from "x is a brother" that "x has parents". According to inferentialist semantics, the meaning of the word brother is determined by these and all similar inferences that can be drawn.

2.2.4 Cognitive Implications of Multilingual Linguistic Processing

The cognitive management of multiple morphological, syntactic, and semantic systems has significant implications for our understanding of the human language faculty. Neurolinguistic research shows that multilinguals develop specialized neural pathways for handling competition between linguistic structures, with executive control mechanisms playing a crucial role in language selection and inhibition. The constant need to navigate between different grammatical and meaning systems appears to confer cognitive advantages in areas such as problem-solving and metalinguistic awareness. However, this cognitive flexibility comes with processing costs, as evidenced by slightly slower lexical access times in multilinguals compared to monolinguals. The study of aphasia in multilingual individuals provides unique insights into how morphological, syntactic, and semantic knowledge may be differentially impaired or preserved across languages, informing both linguistic theory and clinical practice.

2.2.5 Challenges in Computational Modeling of Multilingual Systems

Developing computational models that adequately capture the complexities of multilingual morphology, syntax, and semantics presents formidable challenges. Machine translation systems often struggle with morphological richness, particularly in agglutinative languages where single words may contain multiple meaning-bearing units.

Syntactic divergences between languages pose problems for parsing algorithms, especially when dealing with non-configurational languages or those with free word order. Semantic representation in AI systems frequently fails to capture the culture-specific nuances that multilingual humans effortlessly navigate. Current approaches in multilingual natural language processing, such as multilingual BERT and other transformer models, have made significant strides but still exhibit biases favoring high-resource languages. The development of truly robust multilingual systems requires better integration of linguistic theory with machine learning approaches, particularly for low-resource languages with different typological profiles.

2.2.6 Educational Implications for Language Teaching

Understanding the interactions between morphology, syntax, and semantics in multilingual contexts has direct applications in language pedagogy. Effective teaching strategies must address how learners transfer morphological awareness from their first language when acquiring additional languages. Syntactic instruction benefits from contrastive analysis that highlights both similarities and differences between the target language and learners' other languages. Semantic development requires special attention to false friends, lexical gaps, and culture-specific meanings that may not align across languages.

Multilingual classrooms present unique opportunities to leverage students' existing linguistic knowledge while being mindful of potential interference patterns. Recent pedagogical approaches emphasize metalinguistic awareness as a crucial skill, helping learners consciously navigate the morphological, syntactic, and semantic systems of their multiple languages. These insights are particularly valuable in heritage language education, where maintaining grammatical competence alongside semantic-cultural knowledge is essential.

2.2.7 Sociolinguistic Dimensions of Multilingual Structures

The use of multiple morphological, syntactic, and semantic systems is never purely cognitive but is deeply embedded in social and identity-related factors. Language choice and mixing patterns often serve as markers of in-group belonging, with specific morphological and syntactic features signaling social identities. Semantic shifts in contact situations frequently reflect power dynamics between language communities, with dominant languages influencing the semantic structure of minority languages. The study of urban multilingualism reveals how new morphological and syntactic patterns emerge in linguistically diverse communities, sometimes developing into stable vernacular varieties. These sociolinguistic processes demonstrate that the structural aspects of multilingualism cannot be divorced from their social contexts, as language contact always occurs within specific historical and cultural circumstances that shape linguistic outcomes.

2.3 TYPOLOGICAL VARIATION AND LOW-RESOURCE LANGUAGES

The study of typological variation and the challenges of low-resource languages represent crucial areas of linguistic research with significant implications for language technology. Understanding the systematic differences across languages provides valuable insights into the nature of human communication, while addressing the challenges of under-resourced languages supports global linguistic diversity. As research continues to advance, the integration of theoretical and computational approaches promises to enhance our understanding of language and develop more inclusive technologies. The future of this field is marked by opportunities for interdisciplinary collaboration and technological innovation that will support the documentation and preservation of the world's linguistic heritage.

The development of language technologies for low-resource languages raises important ethical considerations. Issues of representation and bias are particularly significant, as the lack of resources can lead to marginalization of these languages in technological applications. Ensuring equitable development and deployment of language technologies is crucial for supporting linguistic diversity. Community engagement and collaboration are essential for ethical language technology development. Working with native speaker communities ensures that technologies are culturally appropriate and meet the needs of language users. The development of ethical guidelines and best practices is necessary for responsible innovation in this domain.

The future of linguistic research on typological variation and low-resource languages is marked by exciting opportunities for advancement. The integration of computational methods with traditional linguistic analysis promises to enhance our understanding of language diversity. The development of more sophisticated models that can capture complex linguistic phenomena will support both theoretical and applied research. Interdisciplinary collaboration between linguists, computer scientists, and language communities will be essential for advancing this field. The creation of shared resources and infrastructure will support more comprehensive studies of linguistic variation. As technology continues to develop, the potential for preserving and promoting linguistic diversity will expand, supporting global communication and cultural heritage.

2.3.1 Linguistic Typology

Linguistic typology is the study of structural patterns that occur across languages, seeking to identify universal tendencies and constraints on linguistic variation. This field examines how languages can differ in their sound systems, word formation processes, sentence structures, and meaning systems while still conforming to certain fundamental principles of human language. Typological research has revealed that while languages exhibit remarkable diversity, they also share common underlying patterns that reflect cognitive and communicative universals.

One of the fundamental insights of linguistic typology is that languages can be classified based on shared structural features. For example, languages can be categorized according to their basic word order patterns, such as subject-verb-object (SVO) or subject-object-verb (SOV) sequences. Other typological dimensions include morphological complexity, where languages may be isolating (with minimal inflection), agglutinative (with clear morpheme boundaries), or fusional (with complex morpheme interactions). The study of these patterns provides valuable insights into the nature of human language and its cognitive foundations.

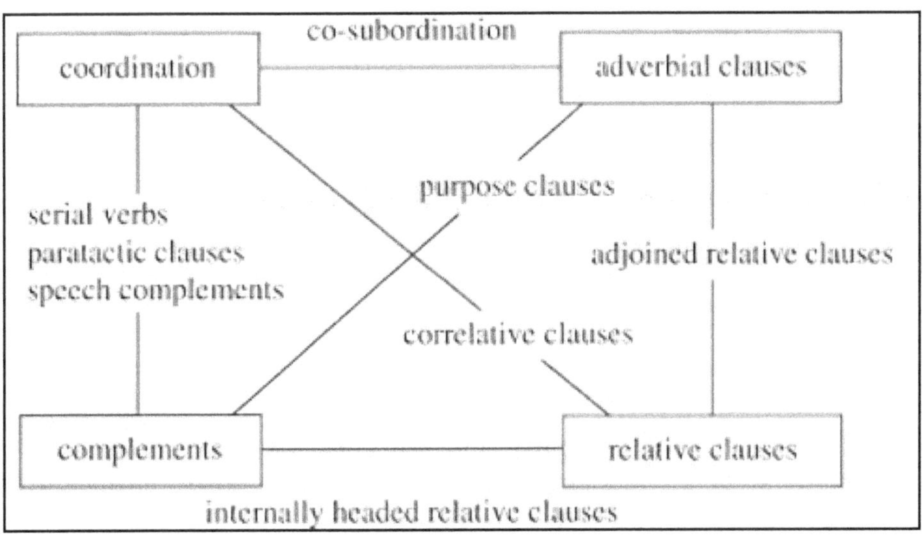

Fig: Linguistic Typolog

2.3.2 Phonological Variation across Languages

Phonological typology examines the systematic differences in sound systems across languages. This includes variations in consonant and vowel inventories, syllable structures, and prosodic patterns. Some languages have relatively simple phoneme inventories, while others exhibit complex systems with numerous distinctive sounds. The study of phonological typology reveals constraints on possible sound combinations and universal tendencies in sound patterns.

One significant area of phonological variation concerns tone systems, where pitch variations can distinguish lexical meaning. Tone languages, common in parts of Asia and Africa, present particular challenges for language processing technologies that were originally developed for non-tonal languages. The documentation and analysis of these phonological systems are crucial for developing speech technologies that can accurately process diverse language inputs.

2.3.3 Morphological Diversity and Complexity

Morphological typology focuses on how languages form words and express grammatical relationships through affixation and other morphological processes. Languages exhibit considerable variation in their morphological systems, from isolating languages with minimal inflection to polysynthetic languages that can express complex meanings in single words. The study of morphological typology reveals patterns in how languages balance the trade-off between synthetic complexity and analytic simplicity. A particularly challenging area for language technology is the processing of languages with complex morphological systems. These languages often require sophisticated algorithms to handle phenomena such as non-concatenative morphology, where word forms change in unpredictable ways, or templatic morphology, where affixes are inserted within root morphemes. The development of computational models that can accurately process these complex systems remains an active area of research in natural language processing.

2.3.4 Syntactic Variation and Word Order Patterns

Syntactic typology examines how languages organize words into phrases and sentences, revealing fundamental patterns in human language structure. The study of word order variation has shown that while languages exhibit considerable diversity in their basic sentence patterns, these variations are constrained by functional and processing considerations. The documentation of syntactic patterns across languages provides insights into the cognitive principles underlying human communication. One significant challenge in syntactic typology is the processing of languages with free word order or non-configurational structures. These languages, where word order is relatively flexible and determined more by pragmatic considerations than syntactic rules, present difficulties for parsing algorithms that rely on fixed word order patterns. The development of syntactic models that can handle this variability is crucial for advancing natural language understanding systems.

2.3.5 Semantic and Lexical Variation

Semantic typology explores how languages categorize and express meaning, revealing both universal tendencies and language-specific patterns in conceptual organization. The study of lexical semantics shows how languages can differ in how they divide conceptual space, with some languages having single words for concepts that require phrases in other languages. This variation presents challenges for cross-lingual applications such as machine translation and information retrieval.

A particularly interesting area of semantic variation concerns how languages express spatial and temporal relationships. The documentation of these semantic systems provides valuable insights into cognitive categorization and cultural conceptualization. The development of semantic models that can capture these cross-lingual variations is essential for creating more culturally aware language technologies.

2.3.6 Challenges of Low-Resource Languages

Low-resource languages present significant challenges for linguistic research and language technology development. These languages typically lack extensive digital corpora, standardized orthographies, or computational tools, making them difficult to process with conventional natural language processing techniques. The scarcity of resources creates a digital divide that limits access to language technologies for speakers of these languages. One of the primary challenges is the lack of annotated data for training machine learning models. Without sufficient labeled examples, it is difficult to develop accurate models for tasks such as part-of-speech tagging, parsing, or machine translation. This resource scarcity is compounded by the fact that many low-resource languages exhibit complex linguistic phenomena that require sophisticated models to process accurately.

2.3.7 Data Collection and Annotation

Addressing the challenges of low-resource languages requires innovative approaches to data collection and annotation. Field linguistics plays a crucial role in documenting these languages, providing the foundational data needed for computational processing. Collaborative efforts between linguists, native speakers, and computer scientists are essential for creating high-quality annotated datasets. Crowdsourcing and community-based approaches have shown promise for collecting and annotating data for low-resource languages. These methods leverage the knowledge of native speakers to create linguistic resources while empowering language communities. The development of efficient annotation tools and methodologies is crucial for scaling these efforts to create comprehensive datasets.

2.3.8 Transfer Learning and Cross-Lingual Approaches

Transfer learning and cross-lingual approaches represent promising strategies for addressing the challenges of low-resource languages. These methods leverage knowledge from high-resource languages to improve performance on languages with limited data. By training models on related languages or language families, it is possible to develop more accurate systems for low-resource settings. Multilingual models that learn shared representations across languages have shown particular promise for low-resource applications. These models can capture common linguistic patterns while adapting to language-specific variations. The development of effective transfer learning techniques is an active area of research in natural language processing.

2.4 CODE-SWITCHING AND MIXED-LANGUAGE INPUTS

The study of code-switching and mixed-language inputs represents a crucial area of research at the intersection of linguistics and computational science. These phenomena provide unique insights into bilingual language processing and the nature of human communication. While presenting significant challenges for analysis, the accurate processing of code-switched language is essential for developing more sophisticated models of language use and creating technologies that accommodate natural multilingual communication. As research continues to advance, the integration of theoretical and computational approaches promises to enhance our understanding of language mixing and develop more effective multilingual language technologies. The future of this field is marked by opportunities for interdisciplinary collaboration and technological innovation that will support the documentation and processing of the world's diverse linguistic practices.

The future of code-switching research is marked by exciting opportunities for advancing both linguistic theory and computational applications. The integration of large language models with linguistic analysis promises to enhance our understanding of mixed-language processing. The development of more sophisticated models that can capture the complex interactions between languages will support both theoretical and applied research. Interdisciplinary collaboration between linguists, cognitive scientists, and computer scientists will be essential for advancing this field. The creation of shared resources and standardized evaluation metrics will support more comprehensive studies of code-switching patterns. As technology continues to develop, the potential for creating more natural and effective multilingual communication systems will expand, supporting global communication and cultural exchange.

2.4.1 Nature of Code-Switching

Code-switching refers to the practice of alternating between two or more languages or language varieties within a single conversation or even within a single utterance. This linguistic phenomenon is particularly common among bilingual and multilingual speakers, reflecting the complex ways in which languages interact in the minds of speakers. Code-switching serves various communicative functions, including expressing cultural identity, signaling group membership, or adapting to different social contexts. The study of code-switching patterns reveals important information about the cognitive organization of multiple languages in the brain and the social dynamics of language use. Research has identified several types of code-switching, including inter-sentential switching (between sentences), intra-sentential switching (within sentences), and tag-switching (inserting single words or phrases from another language). Each type presents different linguistic characteristics and processing challenges. The analysis of these patterns provides insights into the syntactic, semantic, and pragmatic constraints that govern language mixing. Understanding these constraints is crucial for developing accurate models of bilingual language production and comprehension.

2.4.2 Psycholinguistic Perspectives on Code-Switching

From a psycholinguistic perspective, code-switching offers valuable insights into how bilingual speakers manage multiple linguistic systems. Studies have shown that code-switching is not random but follows specific grammatical and cognitive patterns, suggesting that bilingual speakers maintain separate yet interconnected linguistic systems. The processing of code-switched utterances involves complex interactions between the languages' phonological, morphological, and syntactic systems, challenging traditional models of language representation.

Neuroimaging studies have revealed that code-switching engages specific neural mechanisms that differ from those used in single-language processing. These findings suggest that bilingual speakers develop unique cognitive strategies for managing multiple languages simultaneously. The study of these neural processes provides important information about the brain's capacity for language control and the cognitive advantages associated with bilingualism. Understanding these processes is essential for developing accurate models of bilingual language processing.

2.4.3 Computational Challenges in Processing Mixed-Language Inputs

The computational processing of code-switched and mixed-language inputs presents significant challenges for natural language processing systems. Traditional models, which typically assume monolingual input, struggle to accurately analyze utterances that contain elements from multiple languages. The variability in switching patterns and the lack of large annotated datasets for training make this task particularly difficult. Developing systems that can effectively process code-switched language requires innovative approaches that can handle the complex interactions between different linguistic systems.

One of the primary challenges is identifying the language boundaries within mixed-language utterances. This task requires sophisticated algorithms that can recognize the linguistic features of each language and determine where switches occur. The development of language identification models that can operate at various levels of linguistic analysis (phonological, morphological, syntactic) is crucial for accurate processing. Additionally, the lack of standardized representations for code-switched data complicates the creation of training datasets for machine learning approaches.

2.4.4 Approaches to Modeling Code-Switching

Several computational approaches have been developed to address the challenges of processing code-switched language. Rule-based systems that incorporate linguistic constraints on switching patterns have shown some success in modeling certain types of code-switching. These approaches rely on predefined grammatical rules that govern where and how language switching can occur. While effective for some constrained scenarios, these systems often struggle with the variability and creativity inherent in natural code-switching.

Statistical and machine learning approaches have demonstrated more flexibility in handling the variability of code-switched language. These methods learn patterns from annotated datasets, identifying common switching points and linguistic features that characterize different languages. Recent advances in neural network architectures, particularly those incorporating attention mechanisms, have shown promise in capturing the complex interactions between languages in mixed utterances. The development of these models requires large, diverse datasets that represent the natural variability of code-switching patterns.

2.4.5 Data Collection and Annotation Challenges

The creation of datasets for studying code-switching presents significant challenges due to the natural variability of this linguistic phenomenon. Collecting representative samples of code-switched language requires careful consideration of social and contextual factors that influence switching patterns. The annotation of these datasets is particularly complex, as it requires identifying not only the language boundaries but also the linguistic features that characterize each segment.Crowdsourcing and community-based approaches have shown potential for collecting and annotating code-switched data.

These methods leverage the knowledge of bilingual speakers to create more natural and representative datasets. The development of annotation guidelines that capture the relevant linguistic features while accommodating natural variation is crucial for creating high-quality datasets. Additionally, the ethical considerations of data collection, particularly regarding speaker privacy and cultural sensitivity, must be carefully addressed.

2.4.6 Applications in Natural Language Processing

The accurate processing of code-switched language has important applications in various natural language processing tasks. In machine translation, understanding mixed-language inputs is crucial for developing systems that can handle the natural language use of bilingual speakers. Speech recognition systems that can process code-switched utterances would significantly improve voice interfaces for multilingual users. Sentiment analysis and other semantic processing tasks also benefit from models that can interpret the meaning of mixed-language expressions. The development of these applications requires not only accurate language identification but also an understanding of how meaning is constructed across language boundaries. The semantic interpretation of code-switched utterances involves complex interactions between the languages' lexical and grammatical systems. Creating models that can capture these interactions is essential for developing effective multilingual language technologies.

2.4.7 Social and Cognitive Implications of Code-Switching

The study of code-switching has important implications for understanding both social dynamics and cognitive processing in bilingual communities. From a sociolinguistic perspective, code-switching reflects the complex ways in which language use is tied to identity, power relations, and cultural practices. The patterns of language mixing can reveal information about social hierarchies, group membership, and individual identities within multilingual communities. Cognitively, the ability to code-switch provides insights into the mental organization of multiple languages. Studies suggest that bilingual speakers develop unique cognitive strategies for managing their linguistic repertoires, with potential advantages for executive function and metalinguistic awareness. Understanding these cognitive processes is important for developing educational approaches that support bilingual language development and for creating technologies that accommodate natural language use patterns.

2.5 LANGUAGE BIASES AND CULTURAL NUANCES

Language biases and cultural nuances are inherent aspects of human communication. They reflect the complexities of society and the diverse ways in which people understand and express the world around them. Recognizing and addressing these elements is crucial not only for effective communication but also for social justice, equality, and inclusion. Whether in human interaction, media representation, education, or artificial intelligence, mindful language use can promote respect, empower marginalized voices, and foster global understanding. As the world becomes increasingly interconnected, embracing linguistic and cultural diversity is not just an ethical imperative—it is a practical necessity for navigating the challenges and opportunities of the modern era.

2.5.1 Language Bias

Language bias refers to the tendency of language to reflect and reinforce stereotypes, power dynamics, and societal hierarchies. This bias can be intentional or unintentional and is often ingrained in everyday language. It may manifest through gendered expressions, racial connotations, class implications, or assumptions about ability and intelligence. For example, gender bias is evident in the use of male-oriented terms such as "mankind" or job titles like "fireman" and "chairman," which assume male as the default. Similarly, racial and ethnic bias can be observed in how certain communities are portrayed in the media or in the negative connotations attached to specific dialects or accents.

Language bias is not limited to individual words but extends to broader discourses. News coverage, educational materials, and policy documents may exhibit bias through selective framing, emphasis, or omission of details. For instance, descriptions of crime may differ depending on the ethnicity of the subject involved, subtly shaping public perceptions. Language also perpetuates ableism when it equates disability with weakness or limitation, often using phrases like "crippled economy" or "blind to the facts" that carry derogatory undertones. These biases may go unnoticed but have a profound impact on how individuals are perceived and treated in society.

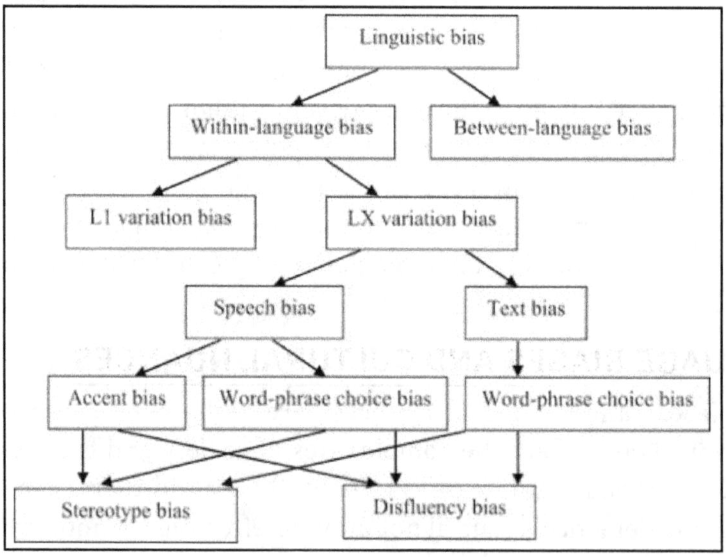

Fig: Language Bias

2.5.2 Cultural Nuances in Communication

Cultural nuances are the subtle yet significant differences in language use that are shaped by cultural norms, traditions, values, and communication styles. These nuances influence how people interpret gestures, intonation, word choice, and conversational expectations. For example, in high-context cultures like Japan or Saudi Arabia, much of the communication is implicit and relies on shared understanding, body language, and tone. In contrast, low-context cultures such as the United States or Germany favor direct, explicit communication where meaning is contained in the words themselves.

Language reflects these cultural differences in various ways. Honorifics and forms of address are critical in many Asian languages, where hierarchy and respect are deeply embedded in daily interaction. In contrast, Western languages may emphasize egalitarianism through the use of first names or informal speech even in professional settings. Humor, sarcasm, politeness strategies, and storytelling conventions also vary widely between cultures, affecting cross-cultural communication. Misunderstandings may arise when speakers from different cultures interpret language through their own cultural frameworks, leading to unintended offense or confusion.

2.5.3 Impacts of Bias and Nuance in Artificial Intelligence

In the realm of artificial intelligence and natural language processing, addressing language biases and cultural nuances is a growing challenge. AI systems, including translation engines, voice assistants, and content moderation tools, are trained on large datasets that often reflect existing societal biases. As a result, these systems can perpetuate harmful stereotypes or fail to recognize the intricacies of culturally specific language use. For instance, translation algorithms might default to male pronouns for professions like "doctor" and female pronouns for "nurse," reflecting historical biases rather than actual usage trends.

Similarly, voice assistants may struggle with recognizing accents or dialects that deviate from standardized norms, thereby marginalizing users from certain linguistic or cultural backgrounds. Automated content moderation systems may flag culturally appropriate expressions as offensive or fail to detect hate speech that is expressed through coded language. These limitations highlight the importance of inclusive and representative data, as well as the need for culturally aware design in AI development. It is not enough for systems to understand words—they must also grasp the social and cultural contexts in which those words are used.

2.5.4 Role of Media and Education

Media plays a powerful role in both reinforcing and challenging language biases. The way stories are told, who gets to speak, and what is left unsaid all contribute to the shaping of societal attitudes. Representation matters—not just in terms of visibility, but also in how characters, communities, and cultures are portrayed. Stereotypical portrayals of gender, race, ethnicity, and nationality in film, television, and journalism can normalize prejudice and limit public understanding. Conversely, media that highlights diverse voices and challenges linguistic stereotypes can foster greater empathy and awareness.

Education systems also play a critical role in addressing language bias and teaching cultural nuance. Curriculum content, language instruction, and classroom interaction all influence how students perceive language and culture. Teaching inclusive language practices, critical media literacy, and intercultural communication skills helps students recognize bias and develop respectful, effective communication strategies. Language education should emphasize not only grammar and vocabulary but also pragmatic use, cultural competence, and awareness of how language can reflect social inequality.

2.5.5 Promoting Linguistic Equity and Inclusion

Efforts to promote linguistic equity involve conscious strategies to make language use more inclusive, respectful, and representative. This includes adopting gender-neutral language, avoiding ableist and racially charged expressions, and recognizing the legitimacy of diverse dialects and language varieties. Inclusive language policies in workplaces, academic institutions, and public communication can help create environments where everyone feels acknowledged and respected.

Cultural competence training is another valuable approach, particularly in sectors such as healthcare, education, and international business. Understanding cultural nuances in communication can improve service delivery, enhance collaboration, and prevent misunderstandings. In a globalized world, intercultural communication is not optional—it is essential for building mutual respect and understanding across borders and communities.

Digital platforms and content creators also have a responsibility to consider language and cultural context. Algorithms must be carefully designed to avoid replicating systemic biases, and user interfaces should accommodate linguistic diversity through multilingual support, accessible formats, and culturally relevant content. Engaging with local communities and linguists can help ensure that technology serves a broader range of users more effectively.

CHAPTER 3

Architectures and Techniques in Multilingual AI

3.1 MULTILINGUAL WORD EMBEDDINGS (MBERT, XLM)

Multilingual word embeddings such as mBERT and XLM mark a pivotal advancement in the quest for truly multilingual AI. By enabling models to understand and generate language across linguistic boundaries, these technologies are democratizing access to powerful AI tools and fostering global communication. While challenges related to data imbalance, computational resources, and ethical concerns remain, the continued evolution of multilingual models promises a more inclusive, equitable, and linguistically diverse future for artificial intelligence. As researchers, technologists, and communities collaborate to bridge the remaining gaps, the vision of AI that speaks and understands all languages is gradually becoming a reality.

The future of multilingual word embeddings and AI points toward more inclusive and adaptive models. Research is increasingly focused on improving performance in low-resource settings by leveraging transfer learning, data augmentation, and synthetic data generation. Initiatives such as massively multilingual models, including mT5 and mGPT, are exploring scaling across hundreds of languages while maintaining performance parity. Additionally, approaches that integrate linguistic typology and phonological information are being explored to guide the alignment process more effectively. Ethical considerations are also taking center stage in multilingual AI research. There is growing recognition of the need for linguistic fairness and the responsible use of language technologies. Ensuring that models do not perpetuate harmful biases, respect cultural contexts, and are evaluated rigorously across all languages is essential. Moreover, community-driven efforts to collect and annotate data for underrepresented languages are gaining traction, highlighting the importance of inclusivity in AI development.

3.1.1 Word Embeddings and the Need for Multilinguality

Word embeddings are a foundational element of modern NLP, representing words as dense vector representations that capture semantic meanings. Traditional word embeddings like Word2Vec and GloVe encode meaning based on contextual similarity, allowing machines to understand relationships between words numerically. While effective in monolingual settings, these embeddings fall short in multilingual contexts, where the meaning of a concept may span different expressions and grammar structures across languages. As the demand for AI applications that operate across multiple languages grew—ranging from translation and summarization to sentiment analysis and question answering—the need for models that could understand and bridge these linguistic variations became more pronounced. Multilingual word embeddings address this challenge by learning representations that are aligned across different languages, ideally enabling cross-lingual transfer and knowledge sharing.

3.1.2 Multilingual BERT (mBERT): Architecture and Capabilities

Multilingual BERT, developed by Google, is a variant of the original BERT (Bidirectional Encoder Representations from Transformers) model. BERT itself revolutionized NLP by introducing deep bidirectional contextual understanding of language using the transformer architecture. mBERT extends this concept to multiple languages by training a single BERT model on the concatenated Wikipedia corpora of 104 languages using a shared WordPiece vocabulary. Importantly, mBERT is trained using the masked language modeling (MLM) objective, but without any explicit alignment or supervision across languages.

Despite lacking supervised cross-lingual alignment, mBERT displays remarkable zero-shot cross-lingual transfer capabilities. This means a model trained on tasks in one language—such as sentiment classification in English—can perform reasonably well on the same task in another language like Spanish or Hindi, without being explicitly retrained in the target language. This emergent behavior suggests that mBERT internally learns language-agnostic features that generalize across languages to some extent. However, this also implies limitations, especially for syntactically or morphologically distant languages, where alignment may be weaker due to the lack of direct supervision.

3.1.3 XLM: Cross-lingual Language Model Pretraining

XLM, short for Cross-lingual Language Model, represents a significant evolution in the development of multilingual AI. Developed by Facebook AI (now Meta AI), XLM introduces explicit cross-lingual objectives that enhance the alignment between different languages during pretraining. The key innovation in XLM lies in its training strategy, which includes both MLM and translation language modeling (TLM). While MLM is similar to the objective used in BERT and mBERT, TLM is unique to XLM and is designed to leverage parallel corpora—aligned sentences in different languages. During TLM pretraining, the model is exposed to parallel sentence pairs and tasked with predicting masked words using context from both languages, thereby strengthening the cross-lingual representations.

XLM models have been shown to outperform mBERT in various multilingual benchmarks, particularly in tasks involving cross-lingual understanding and machine translation. The use of parallel corpora in training allows XLM to develop a more fine-grained understanding of semantic equivalences between languages, especially beneficial in low-resource scenarios where the target language may lack sufficient monolingual training data. Additionally, XLM offers flexibility in model configurations and supports both monolingual and multilingual training regimes, making it a versatile choice for multilingual NLP applications.

3.1.4 Applications in Multilingual AI

The real-world applications of multilingual word embeddings like mBERT and XLM are vast and impactful. One of the most prominent areas is machine translation, where models such as XLM-R (a refined variant of XLM) contribute to high-quality translations across multiple language pairs, including those involving low-resource languages. These models also power cross-lingual information retrieval systems, where users can search in one language and retrieve relevant documents in another. In content moderation and sentiment analysis, multilingual models allow platforms to monitor and analyze user-generated content in various languages without building separate models for each linguistic community.

Furthermore, in the realm of education and accessibility, multilingual AI is critical. For example, virtual assistants and educational platforms that support multiple languages can cater to diverse populations more effectively. This inclusivity is particularly important in regions with high linguistic diversity or where English is not the dominant language. By providing support in native languages, these technologies help bridge the digital divide and promote greater participation in the digital economy.

3.1.5 Challenges and Limitations

Despite their impressive capabilities, mBERT and XLM face several challenges. One of the major limitations is the issue of language imbalance in training data. Since both models rely heavily on large-scale corpora like Wikipedia, languages with limited digital presence may be underrepresented, leading to suboptimal performance in those languages. This bias reinforces linguistic inequality, particularly disadvantaging communities speaking minority or indigenous languages.

Another concern lies in the generalization capability of these models. While zero-shot transfer works well for certain tasks and language pairs, it may fail when the target language is structurally very different from the source language or when domain-specific nuances are involved. Furthermore, multilingual models are typically larger and more computationally intensive than monolingual ones, posing challenges in terms of deployment, particularly on low-power devices or in bandwidth-constrained environments. In addition, there is an ongoing debate about the explainability and interpretability of these deep learning models. Understanding how multilingual models arrive at their decisions across languages remains a complex problem, which can hinder their adoption in sensitive domains such as healthcare, legal services, or public policy.

3.2 TRANSFORMER-BASED MODELS

3.2.1 mBERT

mBERT has emerged as a transformative model in the realm of multilingual NLP, offering a powerful tool for understanding and processing over 100 languages with a single neural network. While it does not incorporate cross-lingual alignment explicitly, its surprising ability to generalize across languages has paved the way for numerous applications in zero-shot learning and multilingual AI. Though challenges remain in terms of fairness, efficiency, and performance on low-resource languages, mBERT has set the foundation for a new era of inclusive language technologies. As the field continues to evolve, mBERT's legacy will remain vital in guiding future innovations toward a more linguistically diverse and equitable AI ecosystem.

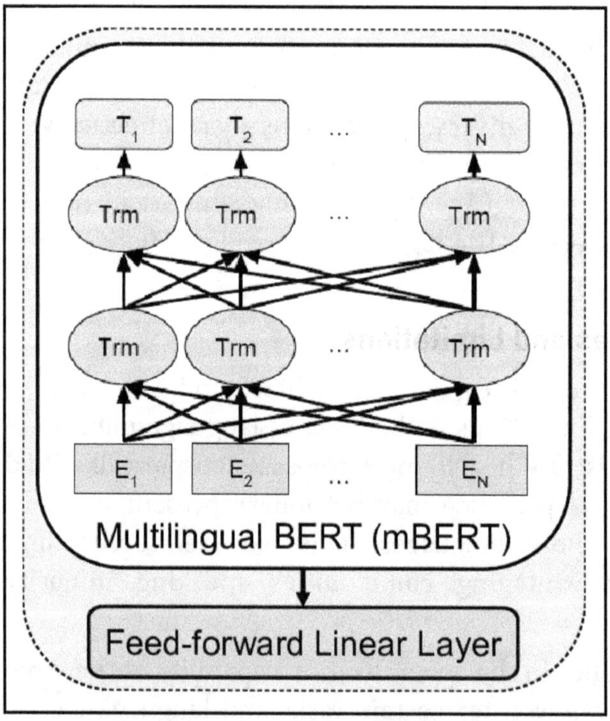

Fig: Multilingual BERT (mBERT) Model

Architecture and Training Methodology of mBERT

Multilingual BERT shares the same architectural design as the original BERT model. It is based on the transformer encoder architecture, which uses self-attention mechanisms to process input text bidirectionally. This allows mBERT to understand the context of each word not just from the left or right, but from both directions simultaneously, making its representations highly context-sensitive. The standard version of mBERT is derived from the BERT-Base configuration, consisting of 12 transformer layers, 12 attention heads, and 768 hidden dimensions, totaling approximately 110 million parameters. What distinguishes mBERT from its monolingual counterpart is its multilingual training corpus and shared subword vocabulary. The model is pretrained on the Wikipedia dumps of 104 languages, selected based on the availability of sufficient textual content. Instead of treating each language independently, mBERT uses a single shared WordPiece vocabulary of around 110,000 tokens, allowing it to encode text from all languages in a unified token space. The model is trained using the masked language modeling (MLM) objective, where a certain percentage of input tokens are randomly masked, and the model is trained to predict the original tokens based on the surrounding context. Unlike cross-lingual models like XLM, mBERT does not use any parallel data or translation-based objectives during training. This makes its multilingual ability even more intriguing, as the model learns language-agnostic patterns purely from large-scale monolingual corpora.

Zero-Shot and Cross-Lingual Transfer Learning

One of the most powerful and widely discussed features of mBERT is its ability to perform zero-shot transfer across languages. In practice, this means that a model fine-tuned on a downstream task such as named entity recognition (NER) or sentiment analysis in English can often generalize to other languages like Spanish, Hindi, or Arabic without needing additional labeled data in those languages. This cross-lingual ability is not a result of explicit alignment during training but emerges as a byproduct of shared vocabulary and training on a combined corpus. This phenomenon has inspired significant interest and research into understanding how mBERT develops such multilingual capabilities. Zero-shot learning with mBERT has proven useful in practical scenarios, particularly for low-resource languages where labeled data is scarce. For instance, organizations can train mBERT on a rich-resource language and apply it to linguistically related or even unrelated languages, depending on the task and domain. However, the performance of zero-shot transfer varies widely across language pairs, and several studies have pointed out that it works better when the source and target languages are typologically similar or share substantial vocabulary overlap.

Evaluation and Benchmarks

To assess the performance of mBERT, researchers have developed a variety of multilingual benchmarks. The XTREME and XGLUE benchmarks, for example, provide comprehensive evaluation suites for tasks such as cross-lingual question answering, part-of-speech tagging, sentence classification, and paraphrase identification across dozens of languages. In many of these tasks, mBERT achieves competitive performance, especially considering that it is a single model handling over a hundred languages simultaneously. Its performance, however, is typically lower than models that incorporate explicit cross-lingual alignment or are trained with translation data.

In semantic tasks like sentence classification and NER, mBERT performs reasonably well, particularly for high-resource languages. However, in syntactic tasks that depend heavily on word order or grammar, such as dependency parsing, its performance tends to degrade when transferring to typologically distant languages. Furthermore, mBERT often underperforms compared to monolingual BERT models when both are trained and tested on the same language. This is due to the fact that the shared capacity of mBERT is spread thin across many languages, limiting its ability to model each language in depth.

Advantages and Practical Use Cases

mBERT's main strength lies in its flexibility and wide applicability. A single model that can handle over a hundred languages is incredibly efficient from a deployment perspective. It simplifies infrastructure for multilingual applications, reduces storage requirements, and enables consistent behavior across languages. This is particularly valuable for global tech companies developing applications such as voice assistants, search engines, chatbots, and content moderation tools that need to operate in multilingual environments.

Moreover, mBERT has played a crucial role in democratizing access to language technologies. By providing reasonably good performance across many languages, including some that were previously underserved in NLP, it has opened the door to building tools and services in a broader range of linguistic contexts. For instance, NGOs and educational platforms have used mBERT to develop inclusive tools in regions with diverse language populations, supporting learning and communication in native languages.

Challenges and Limitations

Despite its many strengths, mBERT is not without significant limitations. One major issue is the imbalance in training data across languages. Languages like English, German, and French, which have large Wikipedia corpora, dominate the training process, while low-resource languages are underrepresented. As a result, mBERT's performance in underrepresented languages is often significantly lower, raising concerns about fairness and inclusivity in AI systems. Additionally, the shared vocabulary strategy, while efficient, may not be optimal for all languages. Morphologically rich languages such as Turkish or Finnish can suffer due to poor subword segmentation, where meaningful morphemes are broken into less useful fragments. This can lead to poor contextualization and reduced accuracy in downstream tasks. Furthermore, since mBERT lacks explicit cross-lingual alignment, it struggles with tasks requiring fine-grained semantic equivalence between languages, such as word translation or sentence alignment. Another challenge lies in the size and computational demands of the model. mBERT requires significant resources for both training and inference, making it less accessible for researchers and organizations with limited computational budgets. While distillation and pruning techniques can help reduce model size, they often come at the cost of performance.

Research Developments and Successor Models

Since the release of mBERT, the NLP research community has proposed several improved models that address some of its limitations. XLM and XLM-R (XLM-RoBERTa) introduced cross-lingual training with parallel data and larger, more balanced training corpora. These models achieve better performance in cross-lingual benchmarks due to their enhanced alignment strategies and better representation of low-resource languages. Other innovations like mT5, based on the Text-To-Text Transfer Transformer, expand multilingual capabilities to generative tasks such as translation, summarization, and question generation. Nonetheless, mBERT continues to serve as a benchmark and baseline in multilingual NLP research. Its simple yet powerful architecture, lack of reliance on parallel data, and wide availability through platforms like Hugging Face have made it a staple in both academic and industrial applications. Researchers continue to explore methods for improving mBERT's cross-lingual transfer capabilities through techniques such as adversarial training, language-specific adapters, and data augmentation.

3.2.2 XLM-R

XLM-R represents a significant advancement in the development of multilingual language models, offering new capabilities for cross-lingual understanding and natural language processing. The model's transformer-based architecture and extensive multilingual training enable sophisticated processing of diverse linguistic inputs, supporting applications in global communication and information access. While challenges remain in handling low-resource languages and computational requirements, the future of this technology is marked by opportunities for further innovation and application. As research continues to advance, models like XLM-R will play an increasingly central role in connecting global communities, supporting cross-cultural understanding, and enabling more inclusive language technologies. The evolution of multilingual language processing reflects the growing recognition of linguistic diversity and the importance of developing technologies that accommodate the rich spectrum of human communication.

The future of multilingual language models like XLM-R is marked by exciting opportunities for further advancement and application. Continued improvements in model architectures, particularly in the efficiency and scalability of transformer-based systems, will enable more sophisticated language processing capabilities. The integration of multimodal approaches that combine language with visual or auditory information presents new possibilities for comprehensive understanding and generation. Advances in few-shot and zero-shot learning will enhance the ability of models to adapt to new languages or domains with limited training data. The development of more sophisticated transfer learning techniques will improve performance on low-resource languages, addressing one of the persistent challenges in multilingual natural language processing. As computational resources become more accessible, the potential for personalized and adaptive language models will expand, supporting more tailored and context-aware applications. The creation of more diverse and representative training datasets will support continued improvement in model performance across the linguistic spectrum. Collaborative efforts to collect and annotate data from underrepresented languages will enhance the inclusivity and effectiveness of multilingual language technologies. The development of ethical guidelines and best practices will ensure the responsible advancement of these technologies, supporting global communication and cultural exchange.

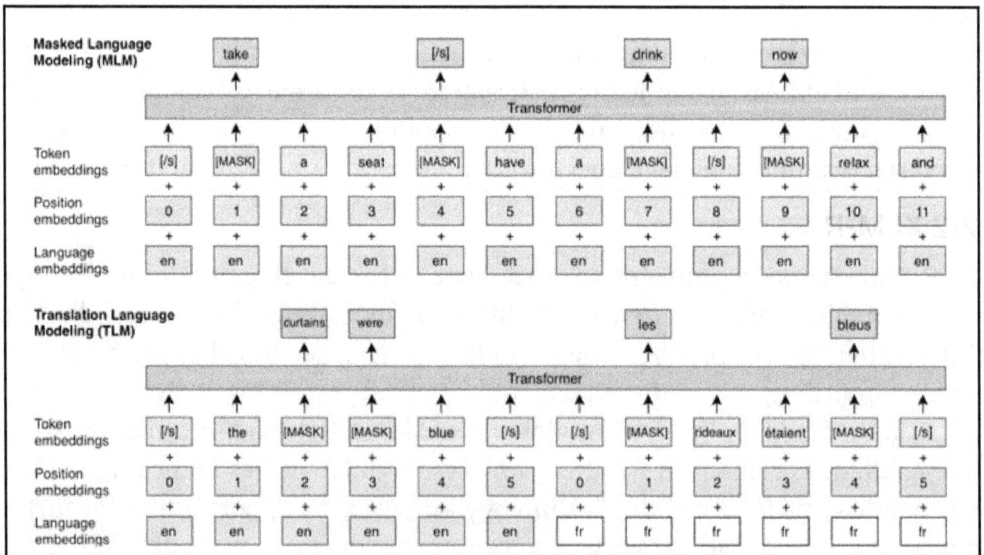

Fig: Cross Lingual Models(XLM-R)

3.2.3 mT5

mT5 represents a powerful advancement in the development of multilingual NLP models. By extending the text-to-text paradigm to over 100 languages, it enables a broad range of understanding and generation tasks in a unified framework. While challenges remain in terms of fairness, bias, and computational cost, the mT5 model lays a robust foundation for the next generation of inclusive and effective language technologies. Its contributions to multilingual AI will continue to shape the way language models are trained, evaluated, and deployed in a linguistically diverse world. The future of mT5 and multilingual models more generally lies in enhancing efficiency, inclusivity, and adaptability. Researchers are exploring approaches such as mixture-of-experts, modular training, and low-rank adaptation to reduce training cost and increase scalability. Further improvements in tokenization and subword modeling are also being investigated to better accommodate morphologically rich or agglutinative languages. Additionally, integrating multimodal inputs such as speech and images may extend the capabilities of mT5 to more complex real-world scenarios.

Foundation of the T5 Framework

Before delving into the specifics of mT5, it is essential to understand the principles behind the original T5 model. T5 treats every NLP task as a sequence-to-sequence problem. Whether the task is machine translation, sentiment classification, question answering, or summarization, the model receives a textual prompt and produces a textual response. For example, a sentiment classification task might have the input "classify sentiment: This movie was amazing," and the output would be "positive." This unified formulation simplifies the model design and enables transfer learning across tasks with minimal architectural adjustments. T5 was trained on the Colossal Clean Crawled Corpus (C4), a massive dataset derived from web scrapes filtered to ensure quality and relevance. The T5 model is based on the transformer architecture, specifically a standard encoder-decoder setup. This design allows it to handle both understanding (via the encoder) and generation (via the decoder) of natural language. T5 achieved state-of-the-art results on numerous benchmarks and set a precedent for adopting the text-to-text format in downstream applications.

Extending to Multilingual Settings: The Emergence of mT5

mT5 builds upon the T5 framework by adapting it for multilingual settings. The key innovation in mT5 is its training on mC4, the multilingual version of the C4 dataset. The mC4 corpus spans 101 languages, representing a vast and diverse range of linguistic structures and writing systems. The training corpus was collected from Common Crawl and filtered to remove low-quality content, resulting in a high-volume and high-variance dataset that serves as the backbone of mT5's multilingual capabilities. Like T5, mT5 uses a text-to-text format across tasks and languages. It is pre-trained using a denoising objective similar to the original T5 model, where spans of text are masked and the model is trained to reconstruct the original text. This span corruption objective is particularly effective for multilingual settings because it encourages the model to learn meaningful representations of language structure and semantics. Importantly, mT5 does not rely on parallel corpora or explicitly aligned translations during pretraining. Instead, it learns from independent monolingual data across many languages, making it more scalable and versatile.

3.2.4 BLOOM

The development of BLOOM represents a landmark achievement in the field of natural language processing, demonstrating the power of open collaboration in advancing language technology. As one of the largest open multilingual language models, BLOOM showcases impressive capabilities across diverse languages while setting new standards for transparency and accessibility in model development. The project's emphasis on ethical considerations and responsible development reflects the growing recognition of the need for careful stewardship in artificial intelligence research.

The success of BLOOM highlights the potential of collaborative approaches to address complex challenges in language technology. As the field continues to evolve, the principles embodied in this project—open science, ethical development, and international collaboration—will likely play an increasingly important role in shaping the future of natural language processing. The capabilities of models like BLOOM open up new possibilities for global communication and information access, supporting more inclusive and culturally aware language technologies. The ongoing development of such models promises to further advance our understanding of language and enhance the ability to process and generate text across the world's diverse linguistic landscape.

The future of projects like BLOOM is marked by exciting opportunities for further advancement through continued collaboration and innovation. The success of the BigScience workshop demonstrates the potential of large-scale collaborative efforts in advancing language technology. Future initiatives could build upon this model, incorporating even more diverse perspectives and expertise to address the challenges of multilingual language processing.

Advances in model architectures that improve efficiency and scalability will enable more accessible deployment of large language models. The development of techniques for continual learning and adaptation will support models that can update and improve over time, accommodating evolving language use. Research into evaluation methodologies that better capture the nuances of multilingual performance will enhance the ability to assess and improve these models. The open nature of BLOOM provides a foundation for these future developments, supporting collaborative efforts to advance language technology responsibly and inclusively.

3.2.5 SeamlessM4T

SeamlessM4T represents a monumental advancement in AI-powered multilingual communication, offering a unified solution for speech and text translation across numerous languages. Its ability to provide real-time, context-aware translations has far-reaching implications for business, education, healthcare, and everyday interactions. While challenges such as accuracy, bias, and computational demands remain, ongoing advancements in AI research promise to address these limitations.

As the world becomes increasingly interconnected, tools like SeamlessM4T will play a crucial role in breaking down language barriers and fostering global collaboration. By enabling seamless communication across cultures, this technology has the potential to create a more inclusive and united world, where language differences no longer hinder progress and understanding. The future of multilingual communication is here, and SeamlessM4T is leading the way. As AI technology continues to evolve, SeamlessM4T is expected to become even more sophisticated. Future iterations may incorporate enhanced neural networks, improved contextual understanding, and broader language coverage, further bridging communication gaps worldwide. Meta and other researchers are likely to focus on refining the model's accuracy, reducing biases, and expanding its accessibility to ensure it benefits a global audience. Another exciting prospect is the integration of SeamlessM4T with augmented reality (AR) and virtual reality (VR) platforms. Imagine wearing AR glasses that instantly translate street signs, menus, or conversations in real time, creating a truly immersive multilingual experience. Such innovations could redefine how people interact in foreign environments, making language barriers a thing of the past.Moreover, collaborations with governments, educational institutions, and humanitarian organizations could amplify the impact of SeamlessM4T. By deploying the technology in refugee support programs, international diplomacy, and global crisis response, AI-driven translation can play a pivotal role in fostering understanding and cooperation across cultures.

How SeamlessM4T Works

SeamlessM4T leverages advanced AI techniques, including large-scale transformer models and self-supervised learning, to achieve its multilingual capabilities. The model is trained on vast amounts of multilingual data, encompassing both text and speech from numerous languages. This extensive training allows it to understand context, idiomatic expressions, and linguistic nuances, resulting in more natural and accurate translations. One of the key innovations of SeamlessM4T is its multimodal architecture, which enables it to process and generate translations across different formats. For example, it can directly translate spoken words in one language into written text in another or convert speech in one language into speech in another without intermediate steps. This end-to-end approach minimizes errors that can occur when multiple translation systems are chained together. Additionally, the model supports automatic speech recognition (ASR), machine translation (MT), and text-to-speech (TTS) synthesis, making it a versatile tool for various applications.

Key Features

SeamlessM4T offers several cutting-edge features that set it apart from conventional translation systems. One of its most notable capabilities is its ability to handle multiple languages in a single model. Unlike traditional translation tools that are often limited to a few language pairs, SeamlessM4T supports a wide range of languages, allowing users to communicate across diverse linguistic backgrounds effortlessly.

Another important feature is its real-time translation capability. Whether translating spoken conversations or written text, the model provides near-instantaneous results, making it ideal for live interactions. This is particularly useful in scenarios such as international business meetings, customer support, and travel, where quick and accurate translations are essential.

Furthermore, SeamlessM4T incorporates advanced contextual understanding, allowing it to produce translations that are not only grammatically correct but also culturally appropriate. By analyzing the broader context of conversations, the model can avoid literal translations that may sound unnatural or confusing. This contextual awareness enhances the overall user experience, making interactions more fluid and intuitive.

Applications

The potential applications of SeamlessM4T are vast, spanning multiple industries and use cases. In the business world, the model can facilitate international trade and collaboration by enabling seamless communication between partners who speak different languages. Companies can use it for real-time translation during video conferences, customer service interactions, and document translations, improving efficiency and reducing misunderstandings.

In education, SeamlessM4T can serve as a powerful tool for language learning and accessibility. Students studying foreign languages can use it to practice listening and speaking skills, while educators can leverage it to deliver lessons in multiple languages. Additionally, the model can assist non-native speakers in academic settings by providing instant translations of lectures, research papers, and study materials. Another significant application is in healthcare, where clear communication is critical. Medical professionals can use SeamlessM4T to communicate with patients who speak different languages, ensuring accurate diagnoses and treatment plans. This can be particularly valuable in multicultural societies and regions with diverse populations. Beyond professional settings, SeamlessM4T can enhance everyday communication for travelers, expatriates, and immigrants. Tourists can use the model to navigate foreign countries, read signs, and converse with locals, while immigrants can rely on it for essential services such as banking, legal consultations, and social interactions.

Challenges

Despite its impressive capabilities, SeamlessM4T is not without challenges. One of the primary concerns is the accuracy of translations, especially for less commonly spoken languages. While the model performs well with major languages, its effectiveness may vary for dialects and languages with limited training data. Ensuring high-quality translations across all supported languages remains an ongoing challenge for developers. Another limitation is the potential for bias in translations. AI models like Seamles

sM4T learn from vast datasets that may contain cultural or linguistic biases, leading to skewed or inappropriate translations in certain contexts. Addressing these biases requires continuous refinement of training data and algorithmic adjustments to promote fairness and inclusivity.Additionally, real-time translation demands significant computational power, which may pose challenges for users with limited access to high-performance devices or stable internet connections. Optimizing the model for low-resource environments will be crucial for widespread adoption, particularly in developing regions.

3.3 ZERO-SHOT AND FEW-SHOT CROSS-LINGUAL TRANSFER

In recent years, the field of natural language processing (NLP) has seen a significant shift toward building models that can operate across multiple languages. With the development of large-scale multilingual pre-trained models, such as mBERT, XLM-R, and mT5, the concept of zero-shot and few-shot cross-lingual transfer has emerged as a powerful method for extending NLP capabilities to underrepresented and low-resource languages.

These approaches enable models to perform tasks in languages for which little or no annotated training data is available, effectively transferring knowledge from high-resource to low-resource languages. As global communication becomes increasingly multilingual, the ability of language models to understand and process multiple languages with minimal supervision is critical for developing inclusive and accessible AI technologies. Zero-shot and few-shot cross-lingual transfer techniques represent a transformative advancement in multilingual NLP, offering practical solutions to the challenge of extending AI capabilities to a broader array of languages. By enabling models to generalize from high-resource to low-resource settings with little or no labeled data, these methods pave the way for more inclusive, efficient, and equitable language technologies. While challenges remain in terms of performance disparity, data imbalance, and linguistic diversity, ongoing research and innovation are steadily overcoming these hurdles. As the global demand for multilingual AI systems continues to rise, zero-shot and few-shot learning will remain central to the future of natural language understanding and generation across languages.

As zero-shot and few-shot cross-lingual transfer becomes more widely adopted, ethical considerations must also be addressed. One concern is the potential for linguistic bias and uneven model performance, which could marginalize speakers of less supported languages. Transparency in model training data, representation strategies, and performance evaluation is essential to ensure equitable outcomes.

There is also the issue of cultural sensitivity. Models trained on internet data may reproduce stereotypes or misunderstand culturally specific expressions, leading to inaccurate or even offensive outputs. Incorporating culturally-aware training practices and involving native speakers in model evaluation and deployment can help mitigate these risks. Looking ahead, the field is likely to move toward more personalized and adaptable models that can learn from minimal input while respecting linguistic and cultural diversity. Advances in unsupervised learning, cross-lingual alignment, and model compression will continue to drive progress, making it feasible to bring high-quality language technology to every corner of the globe. Collaboration between researchers, communities, and policymakers will be essential to ensure that these innovations benefit all users, regardless of the language they speak.

3.3.1 Zero-Shot Cross-Lingual Transfer

Zero-shot cross-lingual transfer refers to the ability of a model to perform a task in a target language without having seen any labeled data in that language during training. In this setting, a multilingual model is typically trained or fine-tuned on a particular task using labeled data from a source language, usually English, and then evaluated directly on the same task in a different language. The success of zero-shot transfer relies on the model's ability to generalize its learned representations across languages. This is made possible by training the model on multilingual corpora using shared vocabularies and unified representations, which allow it to learn language-agnostic features. One of the key mechanisms enabling zero-shot transfer is the use of shared subword tokenization techniques, such as

SentencePiece, which break down text into smaller units that often overlap across languages. These shared units help align the internal representations of words and phrases in different languages. Moreover, pretraining objectives like masked language modeling and span corruption, when applied to multilingual datasets, allow the model to learn syntactic and semantic patterns common to multiple languages. As a result, the model can apply the reasoning and classification capabilities learned in one language to another, even if it has never seen labeled examples in the target language.

3.3.2 Few-Shot Cross-Lingual Transfer and Its Importance

Few-shot cross-lingual transfer is a closely related concept in which a model is exposed to a very small amount of labeled data in the target language before being evaluated. This is especially useful when zero-shot performance is inadequate due to linguistic distance between source and target languages or lack of adequate representation in the model's pretraining data. Few-shot learning helps bridge this gap by allowing the model to adapt to the nuances of the target language using only limited supervision. Even a handful of examples can significantly improve performance by aligning the model's internal representations more closely with the specific task and linguistic features of the new language.

Few-shot transfer is particularly important in real-world scenarios where collecting large-scale labeled datasets for every language is impractical. In many parts of the world, there is limited access to annotated resources, yet there is a strong need for AI applications in local languages. Few-shot methods, often combined with meta-learning or prompt tuning, provide a practical solution to rapidly adapt pre-trained models for new languages with minimal data. This makes it feasible to deploy intelligent systems in a broader range of linguistic contexts, enhancing global reach and impact.

3.3.3 Applications and Use Cases

Zero-shot and few-shot cross-lingual transfer techniques have enabled progress across a variety of NLP tasks, including text classification, sentiment analysis, machine translation, question answering, and named entity recognition. For instance, a sentiment classifier trained on English movie reviews can be applied to Spanish, French, or Arabic reviews with no or minimal additional training, enabling companies to monitor customer feedback across multiple regions.

In the realm of question answering, models like XLM-R and mT5 trained on English QA datasets such as SQuAD can answer questions in languages like Hindi or Swahili without being explicitly trained on QA data in those languages. Another notable application is in information retrieval and cross-lingual search systems. Users can input queries in one language and retrieve relevant documents written in another, facilitating access to information that might otherwise remain linguistically isolated. This capability is especially valuable for journalists, researchers, and humanitarian organizations working in multilingual contexts where access to comprehensive information is essential. Zero-shot and few-shot transfer also play a key role in speech technologies, such as multilingual speech recognition and speech-to-text translation, when paired with language models. These techniques enable voice assistants and transcription tools to support a wider range of languages and dialects, making them more inclusive and accessible to diverse populations.

3.3.4 Challenges

Despite their promise, zero-shot and few-shot cross-lingual transfer methods face several challenges. One of the most significant is the imbalance in training data. Multilingual models are typically trained on large-scale corpora such as Wikipedia or Common Crawl, where high-resource languages like English, French, and German are heavily represented, while many other languages receive minimal exposure. This leads to disparities in model performance, with the best results often confined to the most widely spoken or digitized languages.

Another challenge lies in the linguistic diversity of world languages. Languages differ significantly in syntax, morphology, script, and vocabulary, which can hinder transferability. For example, transferring knowledge from English to Chinese or Arabic is more difficult than between English and Spanish due to greater linguistic distance. Additionally, models trained without parallel corpora may struggle to establish strong semantic alignments across languages, particularly for low-resource languages with unique grammatical structures or writing systems.

Evaluation and benchmarking also present difficulties. Many benchmarks are dominated by a small set of languages, limiting our understanding of model behavior in underrepresented languages. This gap makes it harder to diagnose failure cases, design targeted improvements, or ensure fairness in multilingual applications.

3.3.5 Strategies for Improving Cross-Lingual Transfer

Researchers are exploring several strategies to address these limitations and enhance cross-lingual transfer performance. One common approach is to use language adapters or lightweight fine-tuning modules that allow the model to specialize in specific languages or tasks without retraining the entire model. These adapters can be inserted into the layers of a pre-trained model and trained on small amounts of data, making them efficient and scalable.

Another technique involves using data augmentation and synthetic data generation to increase the diversity of training examples in low-resource languages. For instance, back-translation can be used to create pseudo-parallel corpora, helping the model learn better cross-lingual mappings. Transfer learning approaches that leverage typological similarities between languages, such as training on linguistically related language pairs, have also shown promise. Prompt-based learning and in-context learning, especially with large language models like GPT-3 and its successors, represent another frontier in few-shot learning. These models can adapt to new tasks and languages with minimal examples by conditioning on task descriptions and demonstrations, rather than requiring explicit gradient-based fine-tuning.

3.4 LANGUAGE-ADAPTIVE FINE-TUNING (LAFT)

Language-Adaptive Fine-Tuning represents a significant leap forward in making AI systems truly multilingual. By tailoring the fine-tuning process to the unique characteristics of each language, LAFT enhances the accuracy, fairness, and usability of machine translation, virtual assistants, and other language technologies. While challenges such as data scarcity, computational costs, and bias mitigation persist, ongoing research and innovation promise to overcome these obstacles. As the demand for inclusive and high-performing AI grows, LAFT will play an increasingly vital role in bridging linguistic divides. Whether enabling seamless cross-language communication, preserving endangered languages, or improving global access to information, adaptive fine-tuning ensures that AI serves as a tool for connection rather than exclusion. The continued evolution of LAFT will undoubtedly shape the future of human-machine interaction in our multilingual world.

The future of LAFT lies in further refining its adaptability and scalability. One promising direction is the development of zero-shot and few-shot learning techniques, where models can generalize to new languages with minimal additional training data. This would be particularly transformative for endangered or underrepresented languages, allowing them to be integrated into AI systems without extensive datasets.

Another area of exploration is the integration of LAFT with multimodal AI systems that process text, speech, and visual inputs simultaneously. For example, a model fine-tuned with LAFT could improve automatic subtitling for videos in multiple languages or enhance real-time sign language translation by adapting to regional variations in gesture-based communication.

Collaborations between linguists and AI researchers will also be crucial in advancing LAFT. By incorporating deeper linguistic insights into fine-tuning algorithms, models can achieve a more nuanced understanding of language structures, dialects, and pragmatics. Such interdisciplinary efforts could lead to breakthroughs in preserving linguistic diversity through technology.

3.4.1 Need

The rapid expansion of AI-driven language technologies has highlighted the limitations of one-size-fits-all fine-tuning approaches. While large language models (LLMs) like GPT-4 and BERT exhibit impressive multilingual capabilities, their performance can vary significantly across languages due to differences in grammar, word order, and available training data. For instance, a model fine-tuned primarily on English may struggle with agglutinative languages like Turkish or Finnish, where words are formed by combining multiple morphemes. LAFT addresses these disparities by incorporating language-specific adjustments during the fine-tuning phase. This ensures that the model not only understands general linguistic patterns but also adapts to the idiosyncrasies of individual languages. Additionally, LAFT is particularly beneficial for low-resource languages—those with limited digital text corpora—by leveraging transfer learning from high-resource languages while preserving unique linguistic traits. As a result, AI systems become more inclusive, offering reliable performance across a broader spectrum of languages.

3.4.2 How Language-Adaptive Fine-Tuning Works

LAFT builds upon the foundation of transfer learning, where a pre-trained model is further trained (fine-tuned) on a specific dataset to enhance its performance in a particular domain. However, unlike conventional fine-tuning, LAFT introduces language-specific parameters that dynamically adjust based on the input language. This process involves several key steps, beginning with the identification of linguistic features that influence model behavior, such as word segmentation rules, syntactic structures, and morphological complexity.

Once these features are identified, the fine-tuning process incorporates adaptive mechanisms that modify the model's attention mechanisms, tokenization strategies, or even layer-wise learning rates depending on the target language. For example, languages with rich inflectional systems might require different tokenization approaches compared to isolating languages like Mandarin Chinese. Some implementations of LAFT also employ auxiliary language identification modules or adapter layers—small, language-specific neural network components inserted into the base model—to enhance adaptability without extensive retraining.

Another crucial aspect of LAFT is its use of multilingual datasets that include parallel corpora (texts translated into multiple languages) and monolingual data. By exposing the model to diverse linguistic inputs during fine-tuning, LAFT ensures balanced performance across languages rather than favoring those with the most training data. This approach is especially important for maintaining fairness and reducing bias in AI-generated outputs.

3.4.3 Applications

The versatility of LAFT makes it applicable across a wide range of AI-driven language technologies. One of the most prominent applications is in machine translation systems, where maintaining translation quality across language pairs is essential. By fine-tuning models adaptively, translation services like Google Translate and DeepL can provide more accurate and natural-sounding outputs for less commonly supported languages. Another significant application is in multilingual virtual assistants, such as Siri, Alexa, and Google Assistant. These systems must comprehend and generate responses in multiple languages while accounting for regional dialects and colloquialisms. LAFT enables these assistants to switch seamlessly between languages, offering contextually appropriate interactions. For instance, a user might ask a question in Spanish and receive a response in English without a drop in coherence or fluency.

LAFT also plays a vital role in content moderation and sentiment analysis across global social media platforms. Automated systems must detect hate speech, misinformation, and other harmful content in dozens of languages, each with its own slang and cultural context. Adaptive fine-tuning ensures that these systems do not overlook subtle linguistic cues that vary from one language to another, improving both accuracy and fairness in content filtering.

3.4.4 Challenges and Limitations

Despite its advantages, LAFT faces several challenges that researchers and developers must address. One major hurdle is the scarcity of high-quality training data for many languages, particularly those spoken by smaller populations. Without sufficient data, fine-tuning may fail to capture the full complexity of a language, leading to subpar performance. Efforts to crowdsource or synthetically generate training data can help mitigate this issue but may introduce noise or inaccuracies.

Another challenge is computational efficiency. Adaptive fine-tuning often requires additional parameters or modular components, increasing the model's complexity and resource demands. This can be a barrier for organizations with limited computational infrastructure, particularly when deploying LAFT-enhanced models in real-time applications. Optimizing these models for efficiency without sacrificing performance remains an active area of research.

Additionally, ensuring that LAFT does not inadvertently reinforce biases present in the training data is critical. Language models can inherit and amplify societal biases, such as gender stereotypes or cultural prejudices, especially when fine-tuning is not carefully monitored. Researchers must implement robust bias detection and mitigation strategies to prevent discriminatory outcomes in multilingual AI systems.

3.5 TOKENIZATION STRATEGIES (BYTE-PAIR ENCODING, SENTENCEPIECE)

Tokenization strategies such as Byte-Pair Encoding and SentencePiece represent fundamental advancements in natural language processing, enabling more sophisticated handling of diverse linguistic inputs. These methods have significantly improved the ability of language models to process text data efficiently while capturing complex morphological and semantic relationships. As the field continues to evolve, the development of more advanced tokenization approaches will support the creation of language technologies that can better understand and generate human language across its rich diversity. The ongoing research in tokenization reflects the growing recognition of its crucial role in language processing pipelines. Future advancements in this area promise to enhance the capabilities of language models, supporting more accurate and culturally aware applications. The continued evolution of tokenization strategies will remain essential for advancing natural language processing, particularly as language technologies expand to accommodate the world's diverse linguistic landscape. Through innovative approaches and interdisciplinary collaboration, tokenization research will continue to push the boundaries of what is possible in language understanding and generation.

The future of tokenization strategies is marked by exciting opportunities for further advancement and innovation. The integration of linguistic knowledge with data-driven approaches promises to enhance the quality of subword representations, capturing morphological and semantic relationships more effectively. The development of adaptive tokenization methods that can adjust to different languages or domains would support more flexible language processing systems. Advances in neural architectures that incorporate tokenization as part of the learning process represent a promising direction. These approaches could enable models to develop more sophisticated representations of language structure during training. Research into more efficient tokenization algorithms that reduce computational requirements while maintaining linguistic integrity would support deployment in resource-constrained environments.

The creation of more comprehensive evaluation frameworks for tokenization strategies will enhance the ability to assess their impact on language processing tasks. These frameworks should account for the diverse linguistic characteristics of different languages and the specific requirements of various applications. As language models continue to evolve, the development of tokenization methods that can accommodate their growing complexity and diversity will remain a crucial area of research in natural language processing.

3.5.1 Evolution of Tokenization in NLP

The development of tokenization methods has evolved alongside advancements in natural language processing, reflecting the growing complexity of language models and the diversity of linguistic data they must handle. Early approaches to tokenization relied on simple word-based segmentation, which worked reasonably well for languages with clear word boundaries like English but struggled with agglutinative languages or those with complex morphological structures. As language models grew more sophisticated and began processing larger and more diverse datasets, these simple approaches proved inadequate for capturing the nuances of human language.

The introduction of subword tokenization methods marked a significant advancement in the field, addressing many limitations of word-based approaches. These methods break words into smaller, more manageable units that can better represent the morphological and semantic relationships within language. Subword tokenization has become particularly valuable for handling rare words, morphological variations, and the open vocabulary problem where new words continually emerge in language use. The development of Byte-Pair Encoding and SentencePiece represents the culmination of this evolution, offering sophisticated solutions to the challenges of modern language processing.

3.5.2 Byte-Pair Encoding: A Data-Driven Approach

Byte-Pair Encoding emerged as a groundbreaking tokenization strategy that addresses several limitations of previous methods. Originally developed for data compression, BPE was adapted for natural language processing to create a flexible vocabulary that can handle the diversity of linguistic structures. The algorithm operates by iteratively merging the most frequent pairs of bytes or characters in the training data, building a vocabulary of subword units that optimally represents the language patterns.

The BPE process begins with a vocabulary of individual characters and progressively combines the most common adjacent pairs until a predetermined vocabulary size is reached. This data-driven approach results in a vocabulary that reflects the statistical properties of the training corpus, capturing common morphological patterns and word formations. The method's strength lies in its ability to handle rare words by breaking them into known subword units, thus avoiding the out-of-vocabulary problem that plagues word-based tokenization. BPE has become particularly valuable for processing languages with rich morphology or complex word formation rules, where traditional tokenization methods struggle to maintain linguistic integrity.

3.5.3 SentencePiece: Unifying Tokenization across Languages

SentencePiece represents an evolution of subword tokenization strategies, offering a unified approach that can handle multiple languages and scripts within a single framework. Developed to address the limitations of language-specific tokenizers, SentencePiece operates directly on raw text without requiring pre-tokenization, making it particularly suitable for multilingual applications. This approach treats the entire input as a sequence of Unicode characters, learning a vocabulary that can represent diverse linguistic structures.

The SentencePiece algorithm employs either Byte-Pair Encoding or unigram language modeling to build its vocabulary. The unigram approach differs from BPE by modeling the probability of subword units directly, allowing for more flexible vocabulary construction. This method can better handle languages with different scripts or those that don't use spaces between words, such as Chinese or Japanese. The unified nature of SentencePiece makes it particularly valuable for multilingual models, where a single tokenizer must accommodate diverse linguistic inputs. Its ability to learn a vocabulary that captures common patterns across languages has made it a preferred choice for modern language models that process text from multiple linguistic sources.

3.5.4 Comparative Analysis of Tokenization Strategies

The comparison of Byte-Pair Encoding and SentencePiece reveals both shared principles and distinct advantages that make each approach suitable for different applications. Both methods employ subword tokenization to address the limitations of word-based approaches, capturing morphological patterns and handling rare words more effectively. They share the fundamental concept of building vocabularies based on the statistical properties of training data, resulting in representations that reflect actual language use patterns. However, the methods differ in their implementation and specific capabilities. BPE operates on a more traditional tokenization pipeline, requiring initial segmentation of text into words or characters before applying the merging algorithm. SentencePiece, by contrast, works directly on raw text, making it more flexible for handling diverse scripts and languages without spaces. This difference makes SentencePiece particularly advantageous for multilingual applications where a unified tokenizer is desirable. The choice between these methods often depends on the specific requirements of the language processing task and the characteristics of the languages involved.

3.5.5 Implementation Considerations and Practical Applications

The practical implementation of tokenization strategies involves several important considerations that affect their performance and suitability for different applications. The size of the vocabulary represents a crucial parameter, as larger vocabularies can capture more linguistic nuances but require more computational resources. The training corpus used to build the vocabulary significantly impacts the resulting tokenization, with domain-specific data producing representations better suited to particular applications. For Byte-Pair Encoding, the initial segmentation of text and the number of merge operations affect the resulting vocabulary and its ability to represent language patterns. The algorithm's performance depends on the quality and representativeness of the training data, which should reflect the linguistic characteristics of the target application. SentencePiece implementations require careful consideration of the Unicode handling and the specific language scripts involved, as the method's strength lies in its ability to process diverse textual inputs uniformly. In practical applications, the choice of tokenization strategy affects downstream language processing tasks. Models trained with different tokenization approaches may exhibit varying performance on specific tasks, reflecting how the vocabulary construction influences the representation of linguistic information. The evaluation of tokenization methods should consider not only their impact on model performance but also their computational efficiency and memory requirements, particularly for deployment in resource-constrained environments.

3.5.6 Challenges and Limitations of Current Approaches

Despite their significant advantages over previous tokenization methods, Byte-Pair Encoding and SentencePiece still face several challenges that reflect the ongoing difficulties in language processing. One persistent issue is the handling of rare or out-of-vocabulary words, which while improved by subword approaches, can still present difficulties for language models. The segmentation of words into subword units may sometimes disrupt meaningful linguistic patterns, particularly for languages with complex morphological structures.

The computational requirements of these tokenization methods present practical limitations, especially for deployment in mobile or edge devices. The memory footprint of large vocabularies and the processing overhead of subword segmentation can impact system performance. Additionally, the training of these tokenizers requires substantial computational resources, which may not be available in all research or development environments.

The evaluation of tokenization strategies remains challenging, as standard metrics may not adequately capture their impact on downstream language tasks. The quality of tokenization affects all subsequent processing steps, making its assessment crucial but complex. Developing comprehensive evaluation frameworks that account for linguistic diversity and task-specific requirements represents an ongoing area of research in natural language processing.

CHAPTER

Machine Translation Systems 4

4.1 STATISTICAL VS. NEURAL MACHINE TRANSLATION

The transition from statistical to neural machine translation marks a major paradigm shift in computational linguistics and natural language processing. While SMT laid the groundwork for data-driven translation and proved the feasibility of large-scale automated language conversion, NMT has elevated translation quality to a new level by leveraging deep learning and contextual modeling. Each approach has unique strengths, and the choice between them depends on factors such as resource availability, domain specificity, and quality requirements. In modern practice, NMT dominates due to its superior fluency and adaptability, yet the legacy of SMT remains significant as both a historical milestone and a foundation for future hybrid innovations.

4.1.1 Statistical Machine Translation: An Overview

Statistical machine translation (SMT) is a machine translation approach where translations are generated on the basis of statistical models whose parameters are derived from the analysis of bilingual text corpora. The statistical approach contrasts with the rule-based approaches to machine translation as well as with example-based machine translation, that superseded the previous rule-based approach that required explicit description of each and every linguistic rule, which was costly, and which often did not generalize to other languages. The first ideas of statistical machine translation were introduced by Warren Weaver in 1949, including the ideas of applying Claude Shannon's information theory. Statistical machine translation was re-introduced in the late 1980s and early 1990s by researchers at IBM's Thomas J. Watson Research Center. Before the introduction of neural machine translation, it was by far the most widely studied machine translation method.

Basis

The idea behind statistical machine translation comes from information theory. A document is translated according to the probability distribution $p(e \mid f)$ that a string e e in the target language (for example, English) is the translation of a string f in the source language (for example, French). The problem of modeling the probability distribution $p(e|f)$ has been approa-ched in a number of ways. One approach which lends itself well to computer implementation is to apply Bayes' theorem, that is $p(e|f) \propto p(f|e)p(e)$, where the translation model $p(f|e)$ is the probability that the source string is the translation of the target string, and the language model $p(e)$ is the probability of seeing that target language string. This decomposition is attractive as it splits the problem into two subproblems. Finding the best translation $\tilde{e}$ is done by picking up the one that gives the highest probability:

$$\tilde{e} = arg\max_{e \in e^*} p(e|f) = arg\max_{e \in e^*} p(f|e)p(e)$$

For a rigorous implementation of this one would have to perform an exhaustive search by going through all strings e^* in the native language. Performing the search efficiently is the work of a machine translation decoder that uses the foreign string, heuristics and other methods to limit the search space and at the same time keeping acceptable quality. This trade-off between quality and time usage can also be found in speech recognition.

As the translation systems are not able to store all native strings and their translations, a document is typically translated sentence by sentence. Language models are typically approximated by smoothed n-gram models, and similar approaches have been applied to translation models, but this introduces additional complexity due to different sentence lengths and word orders in the languages.

Statistical translation models were initially word based (Models 1-5 from IBM Hidden Markov model from Stephan Vogel and Model 6 from Franz-Joseph Och), but significant advances were made with the introduction of phrase based models. Later work incorporated syntax or quasi-syntactic structures.

Benefits

The most frequently cited benefits of statistical machine translation (SMT) over rule-based approach are:

- More efficient use of human and data resources:
  - There are many parallel corpora in machine-readable format and even more monolingual data.
  - Generally, SMT systems are not tailored to any specific pair of languages.
- More fluent translations owing to use of a language model.

Shortcomings

Corpus creation can be costly.

- Specific errors are hard to predict and fix.
- Results may have superficial fluency that masks translation problems.
- Statistical machine translation usually works less well for language pairs with significantly different word order.

The benefits obtained for translation between Western European languages are not representative of results for other language pairs, owing to smaller training corpora and greater grammatical differences.

Word-Based Translation

In word-based translation, the fundamental unit of translation is a word in some natural language. Typically, the number of words in translated sentences are different, because of compound words, morphology and idioms. The ratio of the lengths of sequences of translated words is called fertility, which tells how many foreign words each native word produces. Necessarily it is assumed by information theory that each covers the same concept. In practice this is not really true. For example, the English word corner can be translated in Spanish by either rincón or esquina, depending on whether it is to mean its internal or external angle.

Simple word-based translation cannot translate between languages with different fertility. Word-based translation systems can relatively simply be made to cope with high fertility, such that they could map a single word to multiple words, but not the other way about. For example, if we were translating from English to French, each word in English could produce any number of French words—sometimes none at all. But there is no way to group two English words producing a single French word.

An example of a word-based translation system is the freely available GIZA++ package (GPLed), which includes the training program for IBM models and HMM model and Model 6. The word-based translation is not widely used today; phrase-based systems are more common. Most phrase-based systems are still using GIZA++ to align the corpus. The alignments are used to extract phrases or deduce syntax rules. And matching words in bi-text is still a problem actively discussed in the community. Because of the predominance of GIZA++, there are now several distributed implementations of it online.

Phrase-Based Translation

In phrase-based translation, the aim is to reduce the restrictions of word-based translation by translating whole sequences of words, where the lengths may differ. The sequences of words are called blocks or phrases. These are typically not linguistic phrases, but phrasemes that were found using statistical methods from corpora. It has been shown that restricting the phrases to linguistic phrases (syntactically motivated groups of words) decreased the quality of translation. The chosen phrases are further mapped one-to-one based on a phrase translation table, and may be reordered. This table could be learnt based on word-alignment, or directly from a parallel corpus. The second model is trained using the expectation maximization algorithm, similarly to the word-based IBM model.

Syntax-Based Translation

Syntax-based translation is based on the idea of translating syntactic units, rather than single words or strings of words (as in phrase-based MT), i.e. (partial) parse trees of sentences/utterances. Until the 1990s, with advent of strong stochastic parsers, the statistical counterpart of the old idea of syntax-based translation did not take off. Examples of this approach include DOP-based MT and later synchronous context-free grammars.

Hierarchical Phrase-Based Translation

Hierarchical phrase-based translation combines the phrase-based and syntax-based approaches to translation. It uses synchronous context-free grammar rules, but the grammars can be constructed by an extension of methods for phrase-based translation without reference to linguistically motivated syntactic constituents. This idea was first introduced in Chiang's Hiero system (2005).

Language Models

A language model is an essential component of any statistical machine translation system, which aids in making the translation as fluent as possible. It is a function that takes a translated sentence and returns the probability of it being said by a native speaker. A good language model will for example assign a higher probability to the sentence "the house is small" than to "small the is house". Other than word order, language models may also help with word choice: if a foreign word has multiple possible translations, these functions may give better probabilities for certain translations in specific contexts in the target language.

Challenges with Statistical Machine Translation

- **Sentence Alignment:** Single sentences in one language can be found translated into several sentences in the other and vice versa. Long sentences may be broken up, while short sentences may be merged. There are even languages that use writing systems without clear indication of a sentence end, such as Thai. Sentence aligning can be performed through the Gale-Church alignment algorithm. Efficient search and retrieval of the highest scoring sentence alignment is possible through this and other mathematical models.
- **Word Alignment:** Sentence alignment is usually either provided by

the corpus or obtained by the aforementioned Gale-Church alignment algorithm. To learn e.g. the translation model, however, we need to know which words align in a source-target sentence pair. The IBM-Models or the HMM-approach were attempts at solving this challenge. Function words that have no clear equivalent in the target language are another issue for the statistical models. For example, when translating from English to German, in the sentence "John does not live here", the word "does" has no clear alignment in the translated sentence "John wohnt hier nicht". Through logical reasoning, it may be aligned with the words "wohnt" (as it contains grammatical information for the English word "live") or "nicht" (as it only appears in the sentence because it is negated) or it may be unaligned.

- **Statistical Anomalies:** An example of such an anomaly is the phrase "I took the train to Berlin" being mistranslated as "I took the train to Paris" due to the statistical abundance of "train to Paris" in the training set.
- **Idiom and Register:** Depending on the corpora used, the use of idiom and linguistic register might not receive a translation that accurately represents the original intent. For example, the popular Canadian Hansard bilingual corpus primarily consists of parliamentary speech examples, where "Hear, Hear!" is frequently associated with "Bravo!" Using a model built on this corpus to translate ordinary speech in a conversational register would lead to incorrect translation of the word hear as Bravo! This problem is connected with word alignment, as in very specific contexts the idiomatic expression aligned with words that resulted in an idiomatic expression of the same meaning in the target language. However, it is unlikely, as the alignment usually does not work in any other contexts. For that reason, idioms could only be subjected to phrasal alignment, as they could not be decomposed further without losing their meaning. This problem was specific for word-based translation.
- **Different Word Orders:** Word order in languages differ. Some classification can be done by naming the typical order of subject (S), verb (V) and object (O) in a sentence and one can talk, for instance, of SVO or VSO languages. There are also additional differences in word orders, for instance, where modifiers for nouns are located, or where the same words are used as a question or a statement. In speech recognition, the speech signal and the corresponding textual representation can be mapped to each other in blocks in order. This is not always the case

with the same text in two languages. For SMT, the machine translator can only manage small sequences of words, and word order has to be thought of by the program designer. Attempts at solutions have included re-ordering models, where a distribution of location changes for each item of translation is guessed from aligned bi-text. Different location changes can be ranked with the help of the language model and the best can be selected.

- **Out of Vocabulary (OOV) Words:** SMT systems typically store different word forms as separate symbols without any relation to each other, and word forms or phrases that were not in the training data cannot be translated. This might be because of the lack of training data, changes in the human domain where the system is used, or differences in morphology.

4.1.2 Neural Machine Translation: An Overview

Neural machine translation (NMT) is an approach to machine translation that uses an artificial neural network to predict the likelihood of a sequence of words, typically modeling entire sentences in a single integrated model. It is the dominant approach today and can produce translations that rival human translations when translating between high-resource languages under specific conditions. However, there still remain challenges, especially with languages where less high-quality data is available, and with domain shift between the data a system was trained on and the texts it is supposed to translate. NMT systems also tend to produce fairly literal translations.

In the translation task, a sentence $\mathbf{x} = x_{1,I}$ (consisting of I tokens x_i) in the source language is to be translated into a sentence $\mathbf{y} = x_{1,J}$ (consisting of J tokens x_j) in the target language. The source and target tokens (which in the simple event are used for each other in order for a particular game vectors, so they can be processed mathematically. NMT models assign a probability $P(y \mid x)$ to potential translations y and then search a subset of potential translations for the one with the highest probability. Most NMT models are auto-regressive: They model the probability of each target token as a function of the source sentence and the previously predicted target tokens. The probability of the whole translation then is the product of the probabilities of the individual predicted tokens:

$$P(y \mid x) = \prod_{j=1}^{J} P(y_j \mid y_{1,i-1}, \mathbf{x})$$

NMT models differ in how exactly they model this function P, but most use some variation of the encoder-decoder architecture: They first use an encoder network to process x and encode it into a vector or matrix representation of the source sentence. Then they use a decoder network that usually produces one target word at a time, taking into account the source representation and the tokens it previously produced. As soon as the decoder produces a special end of sentence token, the decoding process is finished. Since the decoder refers to its own previous outputs during, this way of decoding is called auto-regressive.

History

Early Approaches

In 1987, Robert B. Allen demonstrated the use of feed-forward neural networks for translating auto-generated English sentences with a limited vocabulary of 31 words into Spanish. In this experiment, the size of the network's input and output layers was chosen to be just large enough for the longest sentences in the source and target language, respectively, because the network did not have any mechanism to encode sequences of arbitrary length into a fixed-size representation. In his summary, Allen also already hinted at the possibility of using auto-associative models, one for encoding the source and one for decoding the target.

Lonnie Chrisman built upon Allen's work in 1991 by training separate recursive auto-associative memory (RAAM) networks (developed by Jordan B. Pollack) for the source and the target language. Each of the RAAM networks is trained to encode an arbitrary-length sentence into a fixed-size hidden representation and to decode the original sentence again from that representation. Additionally, the two networks are also trained to share their hidden representation; this way, the source encoder can produce a representation that the target decoder can decode. Forcada and Ñeco simplified this procedure in 1997 to directly train a source encoder and a target decoder in what they called a recursive hetero-associative memory.

Also in 1997, Castaño and Casacuberta employed an Elman's recurrent neural network in another machine translation task with very limited vocabulary and complexity. Even though these early approaches were already similar to modern NMT, the computing resources of the time were not sufficient to process datasets large enough for the computational complexity of the machine translation problem on real-world texts. Instead, other methods like statistical machine translation rose to become the state of the art of the 1990s and 2000s.

Hybrid Approaches

During the time when statistical machine translation was prevalent, some works used neural methods to replace various parts in the statistical machine translation while still using the log-linear approach to tie them together. For example, in various works together with other researchers, Holger Schwenk replaced the usual n-gram language model with a neural one and estimated phrase translation probabilities using a feed-forward network.

seq2seq

In 2013 and 2014, end-to-end neural machine translation had their breakthrough with Kalchbrenner & Blunsom using a convolutional neural network (CNN) for encoding the source and both Cho et al. and Sutskever et al. using a recurrent neural network (RNN) instead. All three used an RNN conditioned on a fixed encoding of the source as their decoder to produce the translation. However, these models performed poorly on longer sentences.

This problem was addressed when Bahdanau et al. introduced attention to their encoder-decoder architecture: At each decoding step, the state of the decoder is used to calculate a source representation that focuses on different parts of the source and uses that representation in the calculation of the probabilities for the next token. Based on these RNN-based architectures, Baidu launched the "first large-scale NMT system" in 2015, followed by Google Neural Machine Translation in 2016. From that year on, neural models also became the prevailing choice in the main machine translation conference Workshop on Statistical Machine Translation.

Gehring et al. combined a CNN encoder with an attention mechanism in 2017, which handled long-range dependencies in the source better than previous approaches and also increased translation speed because a CNN encoder is parallelizable, whereas an RNN encoder has to encode one token at a time due to its recurrent nature. In the same year, "Microsoft Translator released AI-powered online neural machine translation (NMT). DeepL Translator, which was at the time based on a CNN encoder, was also released in the same year and was judged by several news outlets to outperform its competitors. It has also been seen that OpenAI's GPT-3 released in 2020 can function as a neural machine translation system. Some other machine translation systems, such as Microsoft translator and SYSTRAN can be also seen to have integrated neural networks into their operations.

Transformer

Another network architecture that lends itself to parallelization is the transformer, which was introduced by Vaswani et al. also in 2017. Like previous models, the transformer still uses the attention mechanism for weighting encoder output for the decoding steps. However, the transformer's encoder and decoder networks themselves are also based on attention instead of recurrence or convolution: Each layer weighs and transforms the previous layer's output in a process called self-attention.

Since the attention mechanism does not have any notion of token order, but the order of words in a sentence is obviously relevant, the token embeddings are combined with an explicit encoding of their position in the sentence. Since both the transformer's encoder and decoder are free from recurrent elements, they can both be parallelized during training. However, the original transformer's decoder is still auto-regressive, which means that decoding still has to be done one token at a time during inference.

The transformer model quickly became the dominant choice for machine translation systems and was still by far the most-used architecture in the Workshop on Statistical Machine Translation in 2022 and 2023.

Usually, NMT models' weights are initialized randomly and then learned by training on parallel datasets. However, since using large language models (LLMs) such as BERT pre-trained on large amounts of monolingual data as a starting point for learning other tasks has proven very successful in wider NLP, this paradigm is also becoming more prevalent in NMT. This is especially useful for low-resource languages, where large parallel datasets do not exist. An example of this is the mBART model, which first trains one transformer on a multilingual dataset to recover masked tokens in sentences, and then fine-tunes the resulting autoencoder on the translation task.

- **Generative LLMs:** Instead of fine-tuning a pre-trained language model on the translation task, sufficiently large generative models can also be directly prompted to translate a sentence into the desired language. This approach was first comprehensively tested and evaluated for GPT 3.5 in 2023 by Hendy et al. They found that "GPT systems can produce highly fluent and competitive translation outputs even in the zero-shot setting especially for the high-resource language translations". The WMT23 evaluated the same approach (but using GPT-4) and found that it was on par with the state of the art when translating into English, but not quite when translating into lower-resource languages. This is plausible considering that GPT models are trained mainly on English text.

Comparison with Statistical Machine Translation

NMT has overcome several challenges that were present in statistical machine translation (SMT):

- NMT's full reliance on continuous representation of tokens overcame sparsity issues caused by rare words or phrases. Models were able to generalize more effectively.
- The limited n-gram length used in SMT's n-gram language models caused a loss of context. NMT systems overcome this by not having a hard cut-off after a fixed number of tokens and by using attention to choosing which tokens to focus on when generating the next token.
- End-to-end training of a single model improved translation performance and also simplified the whole process.

The huge n-gram models (up to 7-gram) used in SMT required large amounts of memory, whereas NMT requires less.

Translation by Prompt Engineering LLMs

As outlined in the history section above, instead of using an NMT system that is trained on parallel text, one can also prompt a generative LLM to translate a text. These models differ from an encoder-decoder NMT system in a number of ways:

Generative language models are not trained on the translation task, let alone on a parallel dataset. Instead, they are trained on a language modeling objective, such as predicting the next word in a sequence drawn from a large dataset of text. This dataset can contain documents in many languages, but is in practice dominated by English text. After this pre-training, they are fine-tuned on another task, usually to follow instructions.

Since they are not trained on translation, they also do not feature an encoder-decoder architecture. Instead, they just consist of a transformer's decoder. In order to be competitive on the machine translation task, LLMs need to be much larger than other NMT systems. E.g., GPT-3 has 175 billion parameters, while mBART has 680 million and the original transformer-big has "only" 213 million. This means that they are computationally more expensive to train and use.

A generative LLM can be prompted in a zero-shot fashion by just asking it to translate a text into another language without giving any further examples in the prompt. Or one can include one or several example translations in the prompt before asking to translate the text in question. This is then called one-shot or few-shot learning, respectively. For example, the following prompts were used by Hendy et al. (2023) for zero-shot and one-shot translation:

```
### Translate this sentence from [source language] to [target language], Source:
    [source sentence]
### Target:
    Translate this into 1. [target language]:
    [shot 1 source]
1. [shot 1 reference]
Translate this into 1. [target language]:
    [input]
```

4.1.3 Key Differences in Architecture and Approach

One of the most fundamental differences between SMT and NMT lies in how they process language. SMT relies heavily on discrete statistical patterns derived from phrase or word alignments. It explicitly models translation probabilities and language fluency through separate components. This modular approach means that errors in one component, such as poor phrase alignment, can propagate and negatively affect the final translation.

In contrast, NMT uses continuous vector representations for words and sentences, enabling it to learn semantic relationships between words beyond direct co-occurrence in training data. The encoder–decoder model with attention allows NMT to dynamically focus on relevant source words while generating each target word. This holistic training process results in better handling of word order variations, polysemy, and contextual meaning. However, NMT models are also more computationally demanding and require larger datasets to achieve optimal performance compared to SMT.

4.1.4 Performance and Translation Quality

When evaluating translation quality, NMT generally outperforms SMT in terms of fluency, naturalness, and accuracy in preserving meaning. SMT outputs often appear rigid, with a tendency to produce literal translations that may sound unnatural to native speakers. This is because phrase-based SMT struggles with reordering words appropriately for the target language, especially when the grammatical structures differ significantly.

NMT, by contrast, is better at producing sentences that read as if they were originally written in the target language. It is more adept at handling idiomatic expressions and long sentences where dependencies span multiple words or clauses. Nevertheless, NMT can sometimes produce overly confident but incorrect translations, known as hallucinations, particularly when dealing with low-resource languages or highly technical content. SMT, though less fluent, can occasionally outperform NMT in domains with highly repetitive and formulaic language where statistical patterns are sufficient for accurate translation.

4.1.5 Data Requirements and Training

Both SMT and NMT require large bilingual corpora for training, but the scale and quality of data required by NMT are significantly greater. SMT systems can function reasonably well with moderately sized datasets because they primarily rely on matching observed phrase pairs and combining them with a language model trained on monolingual data. NMT, however, needs vast amounts of high-quality, domain-relevant parallel data to learn effective sentence representations and translation mappings.

Another distinction lies in adaptability. SMT systems can be tuned to specific domains by simply adding new phrase tables or retraining components on domain-specific data. NMT systems, while also adaptable, often require retraining or fine-tuning the entire network, which can be computationally expensive. However, advances in transfer learning and multilingual models have made NMT adaptation more efficient in recent years.

4.1.6 Computational Complexity and Efficiency

From a computational standpoint, SMT is less demanding in both training and inference compared to NMT. Training SMT models involves statistical estimation of translation and language model parameters, which can be accomplished with relatively modest computing resources. Inference in SMT is also relatively fast, as it involves looking up phrase translations and combining them according to the model's scoring function. NMT, on the other hand, requires significant computational power due to the deep learning architectures involved.

Training NMT models often demands powerful GPUs or TPUs and can take days or weeks, depending on dataset size and model complexity. Inference, while faster with modern hardware, still involves complex neural computations that are more resource-intensive than SMT lookups. Despite these costs, the improved translation quality offered by NMT often justifies the additional computational burden.

4.1.7 Strengths and Limitations of SMT and NMT

SMT's strengths include interpretability, modularity, and lower computational requirements. Its phrase tables and alignment models are transparent, allowing researchers and engineers to inspect and adjust specific translation patterns.

It is also relatively robust when trained on smaller datasets, making it suitable for low-resource settings. However, SMT struggles with fluency, context understanding, and the translation of unseen or rare words. NMT's strengths lie in its fluency, contextual awareness, and ability to generalize beyond exact matches in training data. The end-to-end nature of NMT allows it to optimize translation as a single task, resulting in more natural outputs. Its limitations include higher computational demands, greater susceptibility to hallucinations, and a heavy reliance on large, high-quality datasets.

4.1.8 Applications and Use Cases

In practice, NMT has largely replaced SMT in major commercial systems such as Google Translate, Microsoft Translator, and DeepL due to its superior performance in most language pairs. However, SMT remains relevant in scenarios where computational resources are limited or where interpretability and domain-specific control are essential. Hybrid systems that combine SMT's reliability with NMT's fluency have also been explored to leverage the strengths of both approaches.

NMT has expanded beyond sentence-level translation to applications such as document-level translation, multilingual systems, and even zero-shot translation where the system translates between language pairs it has never directly seen during training. These capabilities are fueled by architectures like the transformer, which enable effective modeling of relationships across long sequences and multiple languages simultaneously.

4.2 MULTILINGUAL NMT MODELS AND TRAINING PARADIGMS

Multilingual NMT models represent a significant leap forward in the quest for universal language translation. By training a single system to handle multiple languages, these models offer benefits in scalability, efficiency, and performance for low-resource languages. While challenges such as capacity dilution and negative transfer remain, innovations in architecture, data handling, and training paradigms continue to push the boundaries of what is possible. As the technology matures, multilingual NMT will become an indispensable tool for fostering cross-cultural understanding and global connectivity.

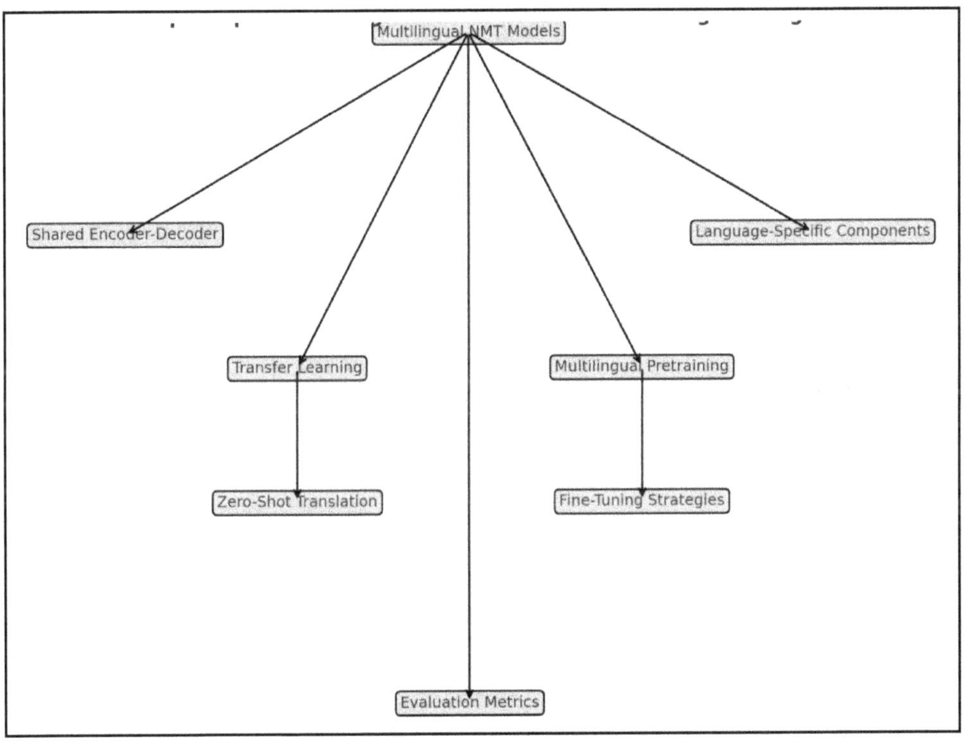

Fig: Clinical Otolaryngology—ENT Disorders

The future of multilingual NMT will likely involve models with even greater scalability and adaptability. Advances in sparse architectures and mixture-of-experts models may allow for extremely large multilingual systems that maintain high performance for all languages without overwhelming computational resources. Additionally, improved data collection and curation methods will be essential for expanding coverage to truly low-resource and endangered languages. Research into culturally aware translation, where models account for regional variations and sociolinguistic factors, will also enhance the utility of multilingual systems. Finally, ethical considerations such as bias mitigation, fairness, and equitable language representation will become increasingly important as multilingual NMT continues to influence global communication.

4.2.1 Foundations

The core principle behind multilingual NMT is to train a single neural network capable of mapping between multiple source and target languages. This is achieved by combining parallel corpora from different language pairs into a joint training dataset. The model learns shared language representations, enabling it to transfer knowledge from resource-rich language pairs to resource-poor ones. A key innovation in multilingual NMT is the use of language tags, where each input sentence is prepended with a token indicating the desired target language. This guides the model to produce translations in the correct output language while still using a common set of parameters for all languages.

Multilingual NMT systems are generally built using sequence-to-sequence architectures, with the Transformer model being the most widely adopted due to its efficiency and scalability. The shared encoder-decoder structure allows the model to learn universal patterns in sentence structure, word order, and semantics that are applicable across languages. This shared learning process fosters cross-lingual transfer, where the model's understanding of one language can enhance translation quality for another language.

4.2.2 Advantages

One of the most significant advantages of multilingual NMT is its capacity for zero-shot translation. In zero-shot scenarios, the model can translate between two languages it has never seen directly paired in the training data, using a third pivot language as a bridge. This capability emerges naturally from the model's shared representation space, where sentences from different languages are mapped into similar vector embeddings. This not only reduces the need for large amounts of parallel data for each language pair but also broadens the scope of supported translations without additional training.

Another advantage is the efficiency in deployment and maintenance. A single multilingual model can replace numerous bilingual models, reducing storage requirements and simplifying updates. For large-scale services such as Google Translate or Facebook's M2M-100, this unified approach allows for consistent quality improvements across all supported languages whenever the central model is upgraded. Additionally, multilingual training often improves low-resource language performance by allowing these languages to benefit from patterns learned in high-resource languages, a phenomenon known as transfer learning.

4.2.3 Challenges

Despite its many benefits, multilingual NMT faces several challenges. One major issue is the so-called capacity dilution problem, where a single model must divide its representational capacity among many languages. As the number of languages increases, the model may struggle to maintain high performance for all language pairs, especially for high-resource pairs that could otherwise achieve better results in dedicated bilingual systems. Balancing performance across languages requires careful tuning of model size, training data distribution, and optimization strategies.

Another challenge is the risk of negative transfer, where learning one language adversely affects performance in another. This often occurs when two languages are structurally dissimilar or when their training data is imbalanced, leading the model to overfit to the more dominant language patterns. Furthermore, multilingual models can sometimes produce mixed-language outputs, particularly when handling closely related languages with overlapping vocabularies. Addressing these issues often involves architectural modifications, data balancing techniques, or adaptive training schedules.

4.2.4 Training Paradigms

The training of multilingual NMT models generally follows a few established paradigms. The most common is the many-to-many paradigm, where the model is trained to translate between any combination of languages in the dataset. This approach maximizes the potential for cross-lingual transfer and zero-shot translation but can be computationally demanding due to the large number of possible translation directions.

Another approach is the many-to-one or one-to-many paradigm. In many-to-one training, the model is designed to translate from multiple source languages into a single target language, often English. This is useful for multilingual content aggregation or cross-lingual information retrieval. Conversely, one-to-many models translate from a single source language into multiple target languages, which is valuable for disseminating information to multilingual audiences. These restricted paradigms simplify the training process and often yield better performance for the targeted directions but limit the general applicability of the model.

4.2.5 Data Preparation and Tokenization

Effective training of multilingual NMT models depends heavily on robust data preparation and tokenization strategies. Since languages vary widely in script, morphology, and syntax, creating a shared vocabulary that can efficiently represent all languages is a key step. Subword tokenization techniques, such as

Byte Pair Encoding (BPE) or SentencePiece, are commonly used to break words into smaller units that can be shared across languages. This reduces the vocabulary size while allowing the model to handle rare words and inflected forms. Data balancing is also crucial. Without careful sampling, high-resource languages can dominate the training process, leading to poor performance for low-resource languages. Techniques such as temperature-based sampling or oversampling of low-resource data can help create a more equitable training distribution. Data augmentation methods, including back-translation and synthetic data generation, are often employed to boost the amount of training material for underrepresented languages.

4.2.6 Architectural Innovations

While the standard Transformer architecture is the backbone of most multilingual NMT models, various modifications have been proposed to enhance performance. Some approaches involve language-specific encoders or decoders, which allow the model to specialize in certain languages while still sharing parameters for cross-lingual transfer. Others use adapter modules—small, trainable layers inserted into the shared architecture—that can be tuned for individual languages without retraining the entire model. Multilingual NMT systems have also explored dynamic parameter allocation, where parts of the network are activated depending on the language pair being translated. This can improve efficiency and reduce interference between unrelated languages. Additionally, research into multilingual pretraining—using large-scale unsupervised language modeling across many languages before fine-tuning for translation—has shown promise in improving both high- and low-resource translation quality.

4.2.7 Applications

Multilingual NMT has a wide range of applications, from global communication platforms to cross-border e-commerce and multilingual customer service. In humanitarian contexts, these models are used to facilitate communication in crisis situations where multiple languages may be spoken. In academic and research settings, multilingual translation enables the dissemination of knowledge across linguistic boundaries. The flexibility of multilingual systems also makes them suitable for integration into speech-to-text and text-to-speech pipelines, enabling real-time multilingual communication. As multilingual NMT continues to improve, it is expected to play an even greater role in bridging linguistic divides and supporting inclusive access to information.

4.3 EVALUATION METRICS (BLEU, TER, CHRF++)

Evaluation metrics such as BLEU, TER, and ChrF++ are essential tools in natural language processing, providing objective measures to assess machine-generated text. While BLEU focuses on n-gram precision, TER measures edit distance, and

ChrF++ incorporates character-level matches. Each metric has strengths and weaknesses, and the choice of metric depends on the specific requirements of the task. Future advancements may lead to more sophisticated metrics that better capture semantic and syntactic nuances, but for now, these metrics remain foundational in evaluating automated text generation systems.

4.3.1 BLEU (Bilingual Evaluation Understudy)

BLEU is one of the most popular automatic evaluation metrics for machine translation. Introduced by Papineni et al. in 2002, it measures the similarity between a machine-generated translation and one or more reference translations provided by humans. The core idea behind BLEU is to compare n-grams (contiguous sequences of words) between the candidate and reference texts.

The BLEU score is calculated using a modified n-gram precision metric, where the number of matching n-grams in the candidate text is divided by the total number of n-grams in the candidate. To prevent excessively short translations from receiving artificially high scores, BLEU incorporates a brevity penalty that penalizes outputs significantly shorter than the reference. The final BLEU score ranges from 0 to 1, with higher scores indicating better translation quality.

Despite its widespread adoption, BLEU has several limitations. It does not account for semantic meaning, syntactic correctness, or fluency, focusing solely on surface-level n-gram matches. Additionally, BLEU may not perform well when evaluating languages with rich morphology or flexible word order. Nevertheless, due to its simplicity and strong correlation with human judgment in many cases, BLEU remains a standard benchmark in machine translation research.

Algorithm

Table: Example of poor machine translation output with high precision

Candidate	the	the	the	the	the	the	the
Reference 1	the	cat	is	on	the	mat	
Reference 2	there	is	a	cat	on	the	mat

Of the seven words in the candidate translation, all of them appear in the reference translations. Thus the candidate text is given a unigram precision of,

$$P = \frac{m}{w_t} = \frac{7}{7} = 1$$

where m is number of words from the candidate that are found in the reference, and w_t is the total number of words in the candidate. This is a perfect score, despite the fact that the candidate translation above retains little of the content of either of the references. The modification that BLEU makes is fairly straightforward. For each word in the candidate translation, the algorithm takes its maximum total count, m_{max}, in any of the reference translations. In the example above, the word "the" appears twice in reference 1, and once in reference 2. Thus $m_{max = 2}$. For the candidate translation, the count m w m_w of each word is clipped to a maximum of m_{max} for that word. In this case, "the" has $m_w = 7$ and $m_{max} = 2$, thus m_w is clipped to 2. These clipped counts m_w are then summed over all distinct words in the candidate. This sum is then divided by the total number of unigrams in the candidate translation. In the above example, the modified unigram precision score would be:

$$P = \frac{2}{7}$$

In practice, however, using individual words as the unit of comparison is not optimal. Instead, BLEU computes the same modified precision metric using n-grams. The length which has the "highest correlation with monolingual human judgements" was found to be four. The unigram scores are found to account for the adequacy of the translation, how much information is retained. The longer n-gram scores account for the fluency of the translation, or to what extent it reads like "good English".

Table: Comparing Metrics for Candidate "The The Cat"

Model	Set of grams	Score
Unigram	"the", "the", "cat"	$\frac{1+1+1}{3} = 1$
Grouped Unigram	"the"*2, "cat"*1	$\frac{1+1}{2+1} = \frac{2}{3}$
Bigram	"the the", "the cat"	$\frac{0+1}{2} = \frac{1}{2}$

An example of a candidate translation for the same references as above might be:

the cat

In this example, the modified unigram precision would be,

$$P = \frac{1}{2} + \frac{1}{2} = \frac{2}{2}$$

as the word 'the' and the word 'cat' appear once each in the candidate, and the total number of words is two. The modified bigram precision would be 1/1 as the bigram, "the cat" appears once in the candidate. It has been pointed out that precision is usually twinned with recall to overcome this problem, as the unigram recall of this example would be 3/6 or 2/7. The problem being that as there are multiple reference translations, a bad translation could easily have an inflated recall, such as a translation which consisted of all the words in each of the references.

To produce a score for the whole corpus, the modified precision scores for the segments are combined using the geometric mean multiplied by a brevity penalty to prevent very short candidates from receiving too high a score. Let r be the total length of the reference corpus, and c the total length of the translation corpus. If $c \leq r$, the brevity penalty applies, defined to be $e^{(1-r/c)}$. (In the case of multiple reference sentences, r is taken to be the sum of the lengths of the sentences whose lengths are closest to the lengths of the candidate sentences. However, in the version of the metric used by NIST evaluations prior to 2009, the shortest reference sentence had been used instead.)

iBLEU is an interactive version of BLEU that allows a user to visually examine the BLEU scores obtained by the candidate translations. It also allows comparing two different systems in a visual and interactive manner which is useful for system development.

Performance

BLEU has frequently been reported as correlating well with human judgement, and remains a benchmark for the assessment of any new evaluation metric. There are however a number of criticisms that have been voiced. It has been noted that, although in principle capable of evaluating translations of any language, BLEU cannot, in its present form, deal with languages lacking word boundaries. Designed to be used for several reference translation, in practice it's used with only the single one. BLEU is infamously dependent on the tokenization technique, and scores achieved with different ones are incomparable (which is often overlooked); in order to improve reproducibility and comparability, SacreBLEU variant was designed.

It has been argued that although BLEU has significant advantages, there is no guarantee that an increase in BLEU score is an indicator of improved translation quality.

4.3.2 TER (Translation Edit Rate)

TER is another important evaluation metric designed to measure the amount of editing required to transform a machine-generated translation into a human reference translation. Unlike BLEU, which relies on n-gram matches, TER is based on edit distance, specifically the number of insertions, deletions, substitutions, and shifts needed to make the candidate text identical to the reference. The TER score is computed as the ratio of the total number of edits to the average length of the reference translations. A lower TER score indicates better translation quality, as fewer edits are needed to match the reference. One advantage of TER is its ability to capture reordering errors, which BLEU may overlook.

This makes TER particularly useful in evaluating translations where word order plays a critical role. However, TER also has limitations. Since it is based on edit operations, it may not always align with human judgments, especially in cases where multiple valid translations exist. Additionally, TER does not explicitly consider semantic or syntactic correctness, focusing instead on surface-level modifications. Despite these drawbacks, TER is widely used in machine translation evaluation, particularly when assessing post-editing effort or comparing different translation systems.

4.3.3 ChrF++ (Character n-gram F-score)

ChrF++ is a more recent evaluation metric that addresses some of the shortcomings of BLEU and TER by incorporating character-level n-grams into the evaluation process. Proposed by Popović in 2015, ChrF++ is designed to be more robust across languages, particularly those with complex morphology or non-Latin scripts. The ChrF++ score is based on the harmonic mean of precision and recall for character n-grams, typically ranging from 1-gram to 6-grams. By considering character-level matches, ChrF++ can better handle morphological variations, spelling differences, and word segmentation issues. The inclusion of recall ensures that the metric penalizes omissions, making it more sensitive to completeness in translations.

One of the key advantages of ChrF++ is its language independence. Unlike BLEU, which may struggle with agglutinative languages like Finnish or Turkish, ChrF++ performs consistently across different linguistic structures. Additionally, ChrF++ has shown strong correlation with human judgments in various evaluation campaigns, making it a reliable alternative to traditional metrics. However, ChrF++ is not without limitations. Since it operates at the character level, it may sometimes over-penalize minor spelling variations that do not significantly impact readability. Furthermore, like other automatic metrics, ChrF++ does not assess semantic adequacy or fluency directly. Despite these challenges, ChrF++ has gained popularity in machine translation and other text-generation tasks due to its robustness and versatility.

4.3.4 Comparative Analysis of BLEU, TER, and ChrF++

Each of these evaluation metrics offers unique perspectives on translation quality, and their effectiveness depends on the specific use case. BLEU remains a standard due to its simplicity and historical prevalence, but it may not be ideal for morphologically rich languages or tasks requiring semantic evaluation. TER provides a more granular view of translation errors by measuring edit operations, making it useful for post-editing scenarios. However, its reliance on exact matches can be restrictive when multiple valid translations exist. ChrF++ bridges some of these gaps by leveraging character-level n-grams, offering better performance across diverse languages. Its ability to handle morphological variations makes it particularly valuable in multilingual settings. However, no single metric is perfect, and researchers often use a combination of these metrics to obtain a more comprehensive assessment of translation quality.

4.4 DOMAIN ADAPTATION AND CUSTOM TRANSLATION ENGINES

Domain adaptation and custom translation engines represent a major step forward in bridging the gap between generic translation capabilities and specialized communication needs. By aligning translation models with domain-specific terminology, style, and context, these approaches deliver higher accuracy, consistency, and usability. As technology evolves, their role will become even more essential in enabling precise, culturally appropriate, and contextually aware translations across industries. For organizations seeking to communicate effectively in specialized fields, investing in domain adaptation and custom translation solutions offers both immediate quality improvements and long-term strategic benefits.

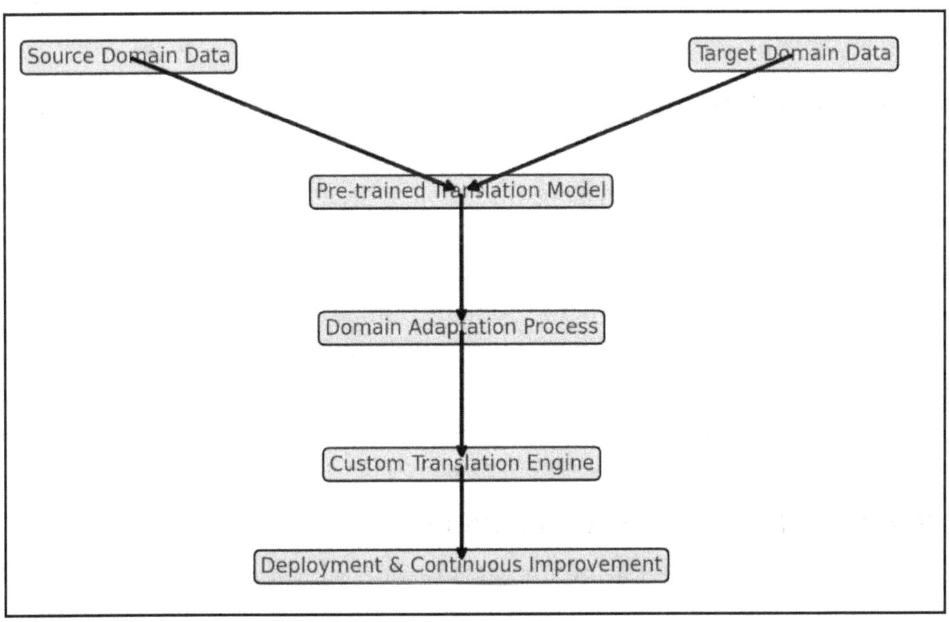

Fig: Domain Adaptation and Custom Translation Engines Workflow

The future of domain adaptation and custom translation engines lies in greater automation, improved adaptability, and tighter integration with human translation workflows. Advances in unsupervised and few-shot learning could reduce the dependency on large parallel corpora, making it easier to adapt models for niche domains. Real-time adaptive MT, where the system learns from user corrections on the fly, is likely to become more widespread. Furthermore, integration with other natural language processing tools, such as summarization and sentiment analysis, will create richer and more versatile multilingual communication systems. As artificial intelligence continues to advance, the boundary between human and machine translation will become increasingly blurred, leading to more collaborative and efficient translation processes.

4.4.1 Limitations of General Machine Translation

General-purpose machine translation engines are usually trained on large, mixed-domain corpora sourced from multiple text types such as news articles, social media, literature, and academic writing. While this diversity allows them to handle a wide range of input, it also means that they lack the specialized knowledge needed for high-quality translations in narrow professional fields. For instance, a general MT system may mistranslate legal terms because it is unfamiliar with specific contractual phrasing or jurisdictional nuances. Similarly, in the medical field, certain terms may have precise and context-dependent meanings that require domain expertise. Without adaptation, a translation engine might choose an inaccurate or ambiguous equivalent, potentially leading to misunderstandings or even harmful consequences. These limitations have made domain adaptation an essential process in professional translation workflows.

4.4.2 Domain Adaptation

Domain adaptation refers to the process of modifying a machine translation model so that it performs optimally in a specific subject area. This is achieved by training or fine-tuning the system with domain-specific bilingual or monolingual corpora. Through this process, the model learns the preferred vocabulary, idiomatic expressions, and stylistic norms of the domain. Domain adaptation can be performed using several techniques, including fine-tuning neural machine translation models, employing domain-specific lexicons, and incorporating terminology databases. The ultimate goal is to bridge the gap between the general training of the model and the specialized requirements of the domain in which it will be applied.

4.4.3 Role of Data in Domain Adaptation

The success of domain adaptation depends heavily on the availability and quality of relevant training data. Domain-specific parallel corpora, where source and target language texts are aligned, provide the most direct way to fine-tune a model. For example, in the legal field, a dataset might consist of bilingual versions of contracts, laws, and case summaries. In the healthcare domain, it might include patient information leaflets, medical journal articles, and clinical trial reports. When parallel corpora are not available, monolingual corpora can still be used to adapt the target language output by training language models that guide translation fluency and consistency. Data cleaning, preprocessing, and alignment are critical steps, as poor-quality training data can introduce errors and reduce the effectiveness of the adaptation process.

4.4.4 Custom Translation Engines

Custom translation engines are specialized MT systems that are built or adapted to meet the precise needs of an organization or user group. Unlike generic models, they are designed around specific linguistic preferences, terminological constraints, and functional requirements. This customization can range from minor adjustments, such as enforcing the consistent use of a client's glossary, to the creation of entirely new models trained on proprietary datasets. Custom engines often include mechanisms to maintain brand voice, comply with regulatory language standards, and ensure the proper handling of sensitive information. They can be deployed in cloud-based, on-premises, or hybrid environments depending on security, speed, and accessibility needs.

4.4.5 Process of Building a Custom Translation Engine

Developing a custom translation engine typically begins with a needs assessment, in which the target domain, languages, and functional requirements are identified. Next comes the collection and preparation of training data, including the integration of client-specific terminology and style guidelines. This data is then used to fine-tune or retrain a base machine translation model. After training, the system undergoes rigorous evaluation, often involving human linguists who assess translation quality and ensure compliance with domain-specific norms. Feedback from these evaluations is used to iteratively improve the system. Once deployed, custom engines may continue to evolve through ongoing learning, incorporating new domain materials as they become available.

4.4.6 Benefits of Domain Adaptation and Custom Translation Engines

The primary benefit of domain adaptation and custom translation engines is improved accuracy in specialized contexts. They produce translations that are more faithful to the source text's meaning while maintaining the appropriate terminology and style. This is particularly important in industries where mistranslations can have serious consequences, such as healthcare, law, and engineering.

Additionally, custom engines enhance productivity by reducing the need for extensive post-editing, allowing human translators to focus on quality control rather than correcting basic errors. They also enable organizations to maintain a consistent brand voice across multiple languages, fostering clearer communication with international audiences.

4.4.7 Challenges and Considerations

While domain adaptation and custom translation engines offer significant advantages, they also present challenges. Acquiring high-quality domain-specific training data can be difficult and costly, especially for less commonly used language pairs. Another challenge is preventing overfitting, where the model becomes too specialized and loses its ability to handle more general text. Additionally, customization processes require skilled computational linguists and machine learning engineers, which can make them resource-intensive. Security and confidentiality are also concerns when dealing with sensitive or proprietary training data, necessitating secure handling and storage protocols.

4.4.8 Role of Neural Machine Translation in Adaptation

The advent of neural machine translation (NMT) has greatly enhanced the potential of domain adaptation and custom engines. NMT models, especially those based on transformer architectures, have a remarkable ability to learn contextual relationships between words and phrases, making them highly adaptable to specific domains. Techniques such as fine-tuning, domain tagging, and multi-domain training allow NMT systems to integrate specialized knowledge while retaining general language understanding. The flexibility and scalability of NMT make it the preferred choice for most modern custom translation solutions.

4.5 OPEN-SOURCE TOOLS AND DATASETS (OPUS, TATOEBA, FLORES-101)

Open-source tools and datasets such as OPUS, Tatoeba, and FLORES-101 have revolutionized the fields of NLP and machine translation. These resources provide researchers and developers with the necessary data to build, train, and evaluate language models, fostering innovation and collaboration. OPUS offers a comprehensive collection of parallel corpora, Tatoeba provides crowdsourced sentence-level translations, and FLORES-101 serves as a benchmark for multilingual evaluation. The impact of these datasets extends beyond academic research, influencing industries and applications that rely on language technology.

However, challenges such as data quality and the representation of low-resource languages must be addressed to ensure their continued relevance. By embracing open-source principles and encouraging community contributions, the NLP field can continue to advance, making language technology more accessible and effective for users worldwide. Despite their numerous advantages, open-source datasets such as OPUS, Tatoeba, and FLORES-101 face several challenges. One of the primary concerns is data quality and consistency. Crowdsourced datasets like Tatoeba may contain errors or inconsistencies due to the varying expertise of contributors. While community moderation helps mitigate this issue, ensuring high-quality data remains an ongoing challenge. Another challenge is the representation of low-resource languages. While datasets like FLORES-101 aim to address this issue by including a diverse range of languages, many languages still lack sufficient data for training robust models. Efforts to expand coverage and improve data quality for these languages are essential for advancing multilingual NLP research.

The future of open-source datasets lies in continued collaboration and innovation. Initiatives such as data augmentation, where existing datasets are expanded through techniques like back-translation or synthetic data generation, can help address the scarcity of data for low-resource languages. Additionally, advancements in automated quality assessment tools can enhance the reliability of crowdsourced datasets. As the field of NLP continues to evolve, the role of open-source datasets will become increasingly important. Researchers and developers must work together to maintain and expand these resources, ensuring that they remain relevant and useful for future applications. By fostering a culture of openness and collaboration, the NLP community can continue to push the boundaries of language technology and make significant strides in multilingual research.

4.5.1 OPUS: A Comprehensive Collection of Parallel Corpora

OPUS is one of the largest and most widely used open-source collections of parallel corpora, providing multilingual datasets for machine translation and linguistic research. Developed and maintained by researchers at the University of Helsinki, OPUS aggregates data from various sources, including government documents, literary works, and web content. The primary goal of OPUS is to facilitate the training and evaluation of machine translation systems by offering diverse and high-quality bilingual and multilingual datasets.

The strength of OPUS lies in its extensive coverage of language pairs, making it a valuable resource for both high-resource and low-resource languages. The dataset includes translations from sources such as the European Parliament proceedings, United Nations documents, and open subtitles, ensuring a wide range of linguistic styles and domains. Researchers can access OPUS through its web interface or download the datasets for offline processing, making it highly accessible for academic and commercial use.

One of the key advantages of OPUS is its continuous updates and expansions. As new parallel corpora become available, they are integrated into the collection, ensuring that the dataset remains relevant and comprehensive. Additionally, OPUS provides tools for preprocessing and filtering data, allowing researchers to customize datasets based on specific requirements. This flexibility makes OPUS an essential tool for developing robust machine translation models and conducting cross-lingual research.

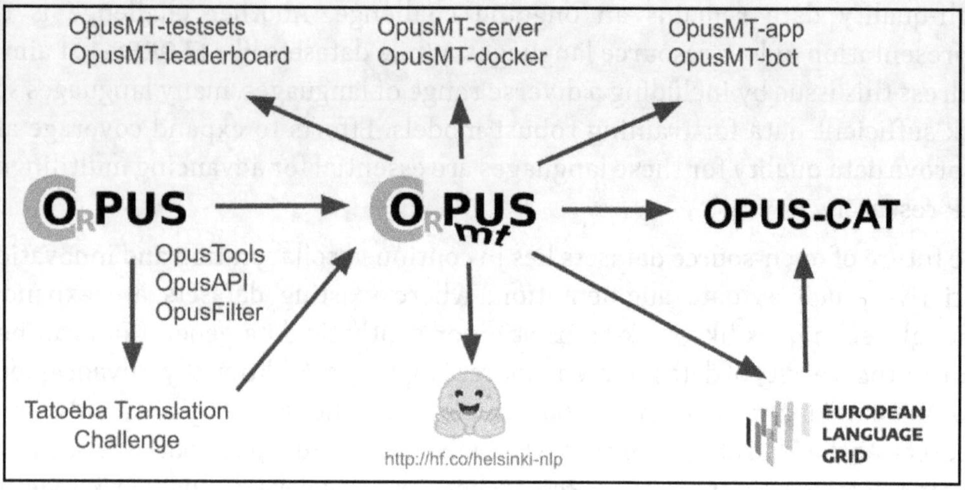

Fig: OPUS-MT and its Connections to other Components, Platforms and Application

4.5.2 Tatoeba: A Crowdsourced Multilingual Sentence Database

Tatoeba is a unique open-source dataset that focuses on sentence-level translations, making it particularly useful for phrase-based machine translation and language learning applications. Unlike OPUS, which primarily consists of large parallel corpora, Tatoeba relies on crowdsourced contributions from volunteers worldwide. This collaborative approach ensures a diverse and constantly growing collection of sentences in multiple languages.

The primary purpose of Tatoeba is to provide a repository of example sentences that demonstrate grammatical structures, vocabulary usage, and idiomatic expressions. Each sentence in Tatoeba is accompanied by translations in one or more languages, allowing users to compare linguistic patterns across different languages. This feature is particularly beneficial for language learners and educators who seek authentic examples of language usage.

Tatoeba's open and collaborative nature encourages contributions from native speakers, ensuring the accuracy and naturalness of the translations. The dataset is freely available for download and can be integrated into various NLP applications, including machine translation, language modeling, and educational tools. Additionally, Tatoeba's API allows developers to access the dataset programmatically, facilitating the creation of language-related applications and services. Despite its reliance on crowdsourcing, Tatoeba maintains a high standard of quality through community moderation and validation processes. Users can flag incorrect translations or suggest improvements, ensuring that the dataset remains reliable and up-to-date. This combination of accessibility, diversity, and quality makes Tatoeba a valuable resource for both researchers and language enthusiasts.

Graph TD

SentenceA[French Sentence: "Bonjour, comment allez-vous?"] → Link1(Translated to) → SentenceB[English Sentence: "Hello, how are you?"]

SentenceB → Link2(Translated to) → SentenceC[Spanish Sentence: "Hola, ¿cómo estás?"]

SentenceC → Link3(Translated to) → SentenceD[German Sentence: "Hallo, wie geht es Ihnen?"]

SentenceD → Link4(Translated to) → SentenceE[Italian Sentence: "Ciao, come stai?"]

4.5.3 FLORES-101: A Benchmark Dataset for Multilingual Evaluation

FLORES-101 is a specialized open-source dataset designed for evaluating the performance of machine translation systems across a wide range of languages. Developed by researchers at Facebook AI, FLORES-101 stands out for its focus on low-resource languages, which are often underrepresented in traditional evaluation benchmarks. The dataset consists of professionally translated sentences covering 101 languages, making it one of the most comprehensive multilingual evaluation tools available.

- The primary objective of FLORES-101 is to provide a standardized benchmark for assessing the quality of machine translation models, particularly in languages with limited resources. Unlike other datasets that may focus on high-resource languages such as English, Spanish, or Chinese, FLORES-101 includes languages from diverse linguistic families, ensuring a more inclusive evaluation framework. This approach helps researchers identify the strengths and weaknesses of translation models across different language pairs.
- FLORES-101 is structured to support both automatic and human evaluation methods. The dataset includes reference translations that can be used to compute metrics such as BLEU, TER, and chrF, which are commonly used to measure translation quality. Additionally, the dataset's design allows for fine-grained analysis of translation performance, enabling researchers to pinpoint specific linguistic challenges, such as handling idiomatic expressions or rare grammatical structures.
- The availability of FLORES-101 has significantly advanced the field of machine translation by providing a reliable and comprehensive evaluation tool. Researchers and developers can use the dataset to compare different translation models, assess the impact of training

data, and identify areas for improvement. Furthermore, the open-source nature of FLORES-101 encourages collaboration and innovation, as researchers can build upon existing work and contribute to the dataset's expansion.

4.5.4 Applications and Impact of Open-Source Datasets

The open-source datasets discussed—OPUS, Tatoeba, and FLORES-101—have had a profound impact on various aspects of NLP and machine translation. Their availability has democratized access to high-quality linguistic data, enabling researchers and developers from diverse backgrounds to contribute to the field. These datasets have been instrumental in training state-of-the-art machine translation models, improving language learning tools, and advancing cross-lingual research.

One of the most significant applications of these datasets is in the development of neural machine translation (NMT) systems. Models such as Transformer-based architectures rely on large amounts of parallel data to achieve high translation accuracy. OPUS, with its extensive collection of parallel corpora, has been widely used to train and fine-tune NMT models. Similarly, FLORES-101 provides a robust evaluation framework, allowing researchers to assess the performance of these models across multiple languages.

In addition to machine translation, these datasets have been utilized in other NLP tasks, such as text classification, sentiment analysis, and language generation. Tatoeba, for instance, has been employed in language learning applications, where its sentence-level translations help learners understand grammatical structures and vocabulary usage. The dataset's crowdsourced nature ensures that it reflects real-world language usage, making it a valuable resource for educational purposes.

The impact of these open-source datasets extends beyond academic research. Companies and organizations developing language-related technologies benefit from the availability of high-quality, freely accessible data. This reduces the cost and effort required to build and evaluate language models, fostering innovation and competition in the industry. Furthermore, the open-source nature of these datasets encourages transparency and reproducibility, which are essential for scientific progress.

CHAPTER 5

Speech and Voice Technologies

5.1 MULTILINGUAL SPEECH RECOGNITION (ASR)

Multilingual Speech Recognition represents a significant step toward breaking down linguistic barriers in human-computer interaction. By enabling a single system to understand and transcribe multiple languages, it fosters inclusivity, accessibility, and global communication. The field continues to evolve with advances in deep learning, data collection, and computational efficiency, promising even greater capabilities in the near future. However, to fully realize its potential, ongoing work must address challenges such as data scarcity, code-switching, and equitable representation of all languages. It has the potential to transform the way we interact with technology and with each other across linguistic boundaries. Here's a simplified block diagram illustrating a common approach:

```
Graph TD
InputAudio[Input Audio (Multiple Languages)] → |Feature Extraction| FeatureVectors[Acoustic Features (e.g., MFCCs)]
FeatureVectors → LanguageID[Language Identification (LID) Module (Optional)]
LanguageID → AcousticModel[Multilingual Acoustic Model (Neural Network)]
AcousticModel → |Output Phonemes/Subwords| Decoding[Decoding (Search Algorithm)]
Decoding → LanguageModel[Language Model(s) (Language-Specific or Shared)]
LanguageModel → Lexicon[Pronunciation Lexicon(s) (Language-Specific)]
Decoding → OutputText[Transcribed Text (Detected Language)]
subgraph Training Phase
SpeechCorpus[Multilingual Speech Corpus (Audio + Transcripts)] → FeatureExtractionTraining[Feature Extraction]
FeatureExtractionTraining → TrainAcousticModel[Train Multilingual Acoustic Model]
TextCorpora[Multilingual Text Corpora] → TrainLanguageModels[Train Language Models]
LexiconCreation[Create Pronunciation Lexicons]
end
```

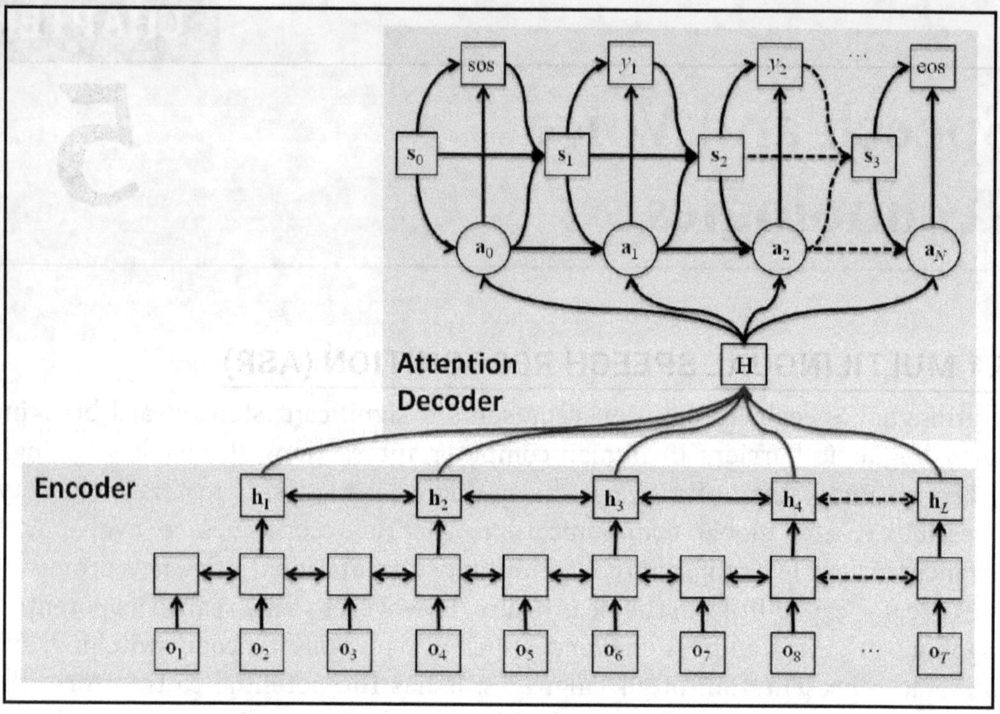

Fig: Multilingual End-to-end ASR for Incomplete Data

5.1.1 Evolution of ASR to Multilingual Capabilities

The early development of ASR systems was focused on monolingual environments, primarily in English, because of the availability of large datasets and computational resources. Over time, researchers recognized the limitations of this approach, especially in multilingual countries and regions where multiple languages are spoken daily. This led to efforts in building bilingual systems and later fully multilingual systems.

The evolution was supported by advancements in deep learning, particularly the use of neural network architectures such as Recurrent Neural Networks (RNNs), Long Short-Term Memory networks (LSTMs), and more recently Transformer-based models. These innovations allowed for better representation of linguistic diversity, enabling the system to learn common phonetic features across languages and transfer this knowledge from high-resource to low-resource languages.

5.1.2 Core Principles

At the heart of multilingual ASR lies the idea of shared representation. Speech signals from different languages share certain acoustic and phonetic similarities, even though vocabulary and grammar may differ. By creating a shared acoustic model that captures these similarities, it becomes possible to develop a single

ASR system capable of handling multiple languages. Another core principle is language identification, where the system can automatically detect the language being spoken before or during transcription. This is particularly useful in code-switching contexts. Additionally, multilingual ASR often relies on shared lexicons or subword units, such as phonemes or byte-pair encodings, to efficiently model multiple languages without excessive computational demands.

5.1.3 Challenges

Despite the potential of multilingual ASR, there are several challenges that researchers and engineers must overcome. One major challenge is the scarcity of training data for many languages, particularly those considered low-resource. While high-resource languages like English, Mandarin, or Spanish have abundant datasets, many regional languages lack sufficient recorded and transcribed speech.

Another challenge is handling code-switching, where speakers rapidly switch between languages mid-sentence. This requires the system not only to recognize both languages but also to seamlessly transition between them without loss of accuracy. Accents, dialectal variations, and background noise also add complexity. Furthermore, balancing the performance of the system across all supported languages can be difficult, as models often perform better on languages with more training data.

5.1.4 Data Requirements and Preparation

The quality and quantity of training data play a decisive role in the performance of multilingual ASR systems. For optimal results, the data must cover a wide variety of speakers, accents, and speaking conditions. Preparing multilingual datasets involves collecting audio samples, annotating them with accurate transcriptions, and ensuring proper alignment between speech and text. In many cases, speech data is augmented using techniques like speed perturbation, pitch shifting, and background noise injection to improve robustness. Another critical consideration is the use of phonetic transcriptions and language-specific dictionaries, which help map acoustic signals to the correct words across different languages.

5.1.5 Model Architectures for Multilingual ASR

Modern multilingual ASR systems typically rely on deep learning models trained on large-scale speech datasets. End-to-end architectures, such as sequence-to-sequence models with attention mechanisms or Transformer-based models like wav2vec 2.0, have become popular because they can jointly learn acoustic and language modeling. These models often employ a shared encoder that processes the audio input, followed by a decoder that generates transcriptions. Some systems use language embedding vectors to inform the model about the target language, improving accuracy in multilingual contexts. Transfer learning is also frequently applied, where a model pre-trained on high-resource languages is fine-tuned on lower-resource languages to achieve better performance.

5.1.6 Handling Code-Switching in ASR

Code-switching, a common phenomenon in multilingual societies, poses unique challenges for ASR. In such cases, the ASR system must not only detect changes in language but also process each segment accurately without confusion. Traditional ASR systems trained on monolingual datasets often fail in these scenarios, as they may misinterpret words from one language as belonging to another.

Multilingual ASR models address this issue by incorporating mixed-language training data and employing language identification modules. Some approaches use joint modeling of multiple languages within a single lexicon, while others train language models capable of predicting likely word sequences across languages.

5.1.7 Applications

Multilingual ASR has a wide range of applications in today's globalized communication landscape. In customer service, it allows call centers to handle clients in their preferred languages without switching between different systems. In education, it can assist in language learning and support multilingual classrooms by providing real-time transcription and translation.

Multilingual ASR also plays a role in accessibility, offering subtitles and closed captions in multiple languages for people with hearing impairments. In voice assistants and smart devices, multilingual ASR enables seamless interaction across languages, making technology more inclusive. Moreover, it is essential for media transcription, international conferencing, and multilingual content creation.

5.2 TEXT-TO-SPEECH (TTS) IN DIVERSE LANGUAGES

Text-to-Speech technology has made remarkable strides in supporting diverse languages, yet significant challenges remain in achieving universal, high-quality synthesis. Linguistic diversity, data scarcity, and ethical considerations necessitate continuous innovation in neural TTS models, multilingual training techniques, and inclusive data collection practices.

As research progresses, the potential for TTS to bridge communication gaps, preserve languages, and enhance accessibility will only grow, making it a cornerstone of global voice-enabled technologies. The future of multilingual TTS lies in creating systems that are not only technically advanced but also culturally and linguistically inclusive.

The future of multilingual TTS lies in improving generalization, reducing data dependency, and enhancing cross-lingual adaptability. One promising direction is the integration of large language models (LLMs) like GPT-4 into TTS systems, enabling more context-aware and expressive speech synthesis. By leveraging the linguistic knowledge embedded in LLMs, TTS systems could better handle code-switching (mixing multiple languages in speech) and idiomatic expressions.

Another area of exploration is emotional and expressive TTS, where synthesized speech conveys not just words but also emotions, tones, and speaking styles appropriate for different cultural contexts. Advances in prosody modeling and adaptive voice cloning will play a crucial role in achieving this goal.

5.2.1 Linguistic Challenges in Multilingual TTS Systems

Languages differ significantly in their phonetic structures, tonal features, and grammatical rules, making it difficult to develop a universal TTS system that performs equally well across all languages. For instance, tonal languages like Mandarin and Thai require precise pitch modulation to convey meaning, whereas stress-timed languages like English rely on syllable emphasis.

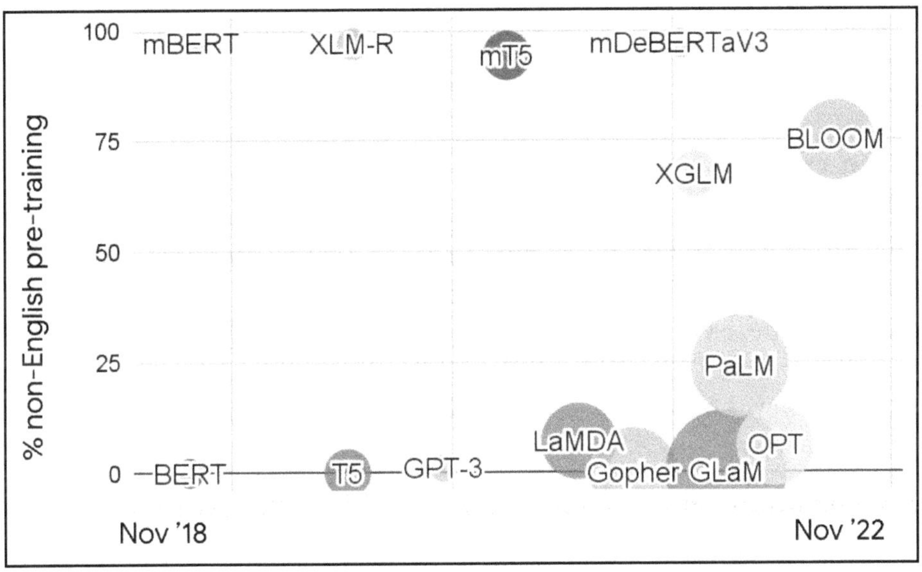

Fig: The State of Multilingual AI

Additionally, agglutinative languages such as Turkish and Finnish pose challenges due to their complex word formations and extensive use of suffixes. Another challenge is the representation of grapheme-to-phoneme (G2P) conversion, where written text must be accurately transformed into phonetic sequences. Some languages, like Spanish, have relatively consistent spelling-to-sound rules, while others, such as English and French, exhibit irregular pronunciations. Furthermore, dialects and regional accents introduce variability, requiring TTS systems to either generalize across variations or support multiple accent-specific models.The availability of training data also varies widely across languages. While large, high-quality speech corpora exist for widely spoken languages, many low-resource languages lack sufficient labeled audio data. This data scarcity hinders the development of robust TTS models for these languages, often necessitating techniques such as transfer learning, multilingual training, or synthetic data generation.

5.2.2 Advancements in Neural TTS for Multilingual Support

Recent advancements in deep learning have revolutionized TTS systems, with neural network architectures such as Tacotron, WaveNet, and FastSpeech enabling more natural and adaptable speech synthesis. End-to-end TTS models, which directly generate speech waveforms from text inputs, have reduced the reliance on handcrafted linguistic features, making it easier to extend these systems to new languages.

Multilingual TTS models leverage shared representations across languages, allowing a single system to synthesize speech in multiple languages without requiring separate models for each. Techniques such as meta-learning and cross-lingual transfer learning enable TTS systems to adapt to new languages with minimal training data. For example, a model trained on English, Spanish, and French can generalize some phonetic and prosodic patterns to a related language like Italian, even with limited Italian training samples.

Another significant development is the use of self-supervised learning models like wav2vec and Whisper, which can learn speech representations from unlabeled audio data. These models are particularly beneficial for low-resource languages, as they reduce dependency on large annotated datasets. Additionally, zero-shot and few-shot learning approaches allow TTS systems to mimic a speaker's voice or adapt to a new language using only a few audio samples, further enhancing flexibility.

5.2.3 Applications and Societal Impact of Multilingual TTS

The ability to synthesize speech in diverse languages has far-reaching implications across various domains. In education, multilingual TTS facilitates language learning by providing accurate pronunciation models for students. In healthcare, it enables medical devices and apps to communicate with patients in their native languages, improving accessibility and understanding. Businesses leverage multilingual TTS for customer service chatbots and interactive voice response (IVR) systems, ensuring seamless communication with global audiences. One of the most impactful applications is in accessibility technology. Screen readers powered by TTS assist visually impaired users in consuming digital content in their preferred languages. However, the effectiveness of these tools depends on the availability of high-quality TTS voices for less commonly supported languages. Organizations like the Mozilla Common Voice project are addressing this gap by crowdsourcing speech datasets for underrepresented languages, fostering inclusivity in voice technology. Moreover, preserving endangered languages is another critical application of TTS. Many indigenous languages face extinction due to declining native speakers. By developing TTS systems for these languages, researchers and communities can document and revitalize linguistic heritage, ensuring that future generations have access to spoken forms of these languages.

5.2.4 Challenges and Ethical Considerations

Despite the progress in multilingual TTS, several challenges remain. One major issue is bias in speech synthesis systems, where certain accents or dialects may be underrepresented or mispronounced. For example, a TTS model trained primarily on American English may struggle with Indian or Scottish accents, leading to miscommunication or exclusion. Ensuring diversity in training data is essential to mitigate such biases.

Another concern is the misuse of TTS technology, such as deepfake voice cloning for fraudulent purposes. As TTS systems become more realistic, the risk of impersonation and misinformation increases. Developing robust authentication mechanisms and watermarking synthesized speech are potential solutions to prevent misuse.

Additionally, the computational cost of training multilingual TTS models can be prohibitive, particularly for organizations with limited resources. Optimizing model efficiency and exploring lightweight architectures are ongoing research areas to make TTS technology more accessible.

5.3 MULTILINGUAL VOICE ASSISTANTS AND VIRTUAL AGENTS

Multilingual voice assistants and virtual agents represent a significant advancement in human-computer interaction, enabling users to communicate naturally and efficiently in their native languages. The technology behind these systems, including automatic speech recognition, natural language understanding, and text-to-speech synthesis, continues to evolve, driven by innovations in artificial intelligence and machine learning. Applications in smart homes, customer service, healthcare, and education demonstrate the versatility and impact of multilingual voice assistants in various domains.

Despite the challenges, such as data scarcity for low-resource languages and cultural contextual understanding, ongoing research and development efforts are addressing these issues. Future trends, including emotion recognition, real-time translation, edge computing, and voice commerce, promise to further enhance the capabilities and accessibility of multilingual voice assistants. As these technologies continue to advance, they will play an increasingly vital role in bridging linguistic and cultural gaps, making digital interactions more inclusive and user-friendly for people worldwide. The future of multilingual voice assistants is likely to be shaped by several emerging trends. One significant development is the integration of emotion recognition and affective computing, enabling voice assistants to detect and respond to the user's emotional state. This capability can enhance user experience by allowing the assistant to adjust its tone and responses based on the user's mood, making interactions more natural and empathetic.

Another trend is the advancement of real-time translation and interpretation, allowing voice assistants to facilitate seamless communication between speakers of different languages. This feature is particularly useful in international business, travel, and customer service, where language barriers can hinder effective communication. Improved neural machine translation models will enable more accurate and contextually appropriate translations, further enhancing the utility of voice assistants.

The rise of edge computing is also expected to impact the development of multilingual voice assistants. By processing data locally on devices rather than relying on cloud-based servers, voice assistants can operate faster and with greater privacy. This shift reduces latency and improves responsiveness, making voice interactions smoother and more efficient. Edge computing also addresses privacy concerns by minimizing the transmission of sensitive voice data to external servers.

Furthermore, the increasing adoption of voice commerce and voice-enabled transactions will drive the evolution of multilingual voice assistants. Users will be able to make purchases, conduct banking transactions, and access financial services using voice commands in their preferred language. This trend will require voice assistants to integrate securely with payment systems and financial institutions, ensuring that transactions are both convenient and secure.

5.3.1 Technology behind Multilingual Voice Assistants

The functionality of multilingual voice assistants depends on several key technologies, including automatic speech recognition (ASR), natural language understanding (NLU), and text-to-speech (TTS) synthesis. ASR systems convert spoken language into text, enabling the assistant to process user input. Modern ASR models leverage deep learning techniques, such as recurrent neural networks (RNNs) and transformers, to achieve high accuracy across different languages and accents.

Natural language understanding plays a critical role in interpreting the user's intent and extracting meaningful information from spoken or written input. Multilingual NLU models are trained on diverse datasets to recognize linguistic nuances, idiomatic expressions, and contextual variations. These models must handle language-specific challenges, such as grammatical differences, word order variations, and cultural references, to provide accurate responses. Text-to-speech synthesis is another essential component, allowing voice assistants to generate human-like speech in multiple languages. Advanced TTS systems use neural networks to produce natural-sounding voices with appropriate intonation and pronunciation.

Multilingual TTS models are trained on extensive audio datasets, ensuring that the generated speech is clear and culturally appropriate for different linguistic groups. Additionally, machine translation and cross-lingual transfer learning enable voice assistants to operate seamlessly across languages. Techniques such as zero-shot learning and multitask learning allow models to generalize knowledge from high-resource languages to low-resource ones, improving performance in less commonly spoken languages. These technological advancements collectively contribute to the effectiveness of multilingual voice assistants in real-world applications.

5.3.2 Applications of Multilingual Voice Assistants

Multilingual voice assistants have found applications in various domains, including smart home automation, customer service, healthcare, and education. In smart homes, voice assistants like Amazon Alexa and Google Assistant allow users to control devices, set reminders, and access information using voice commands in their preferred language.

This functionality enhances convenience and accessibility, particularly for users who may not be proficient in the dominant language of their region. In customer service, virtual agents equipped with multilingual capabilities improve user engagement by providing support in multiple languages. Businesses can deploy AI-driven chatbots and voice assistants to handle customer inquiries, process orders, and offer personalized recommendations. This not only reduces operational costs but also ensures that customers receive assistance in their native language, leading to higher satisfaction and loyalty.

The healthcare sector benefits from multilingual voice assistants by enabling better patient-doctor communication and providing medical information in various languages. Patients who speak different languages can interact with voice-enabled health applications to schedule appointments, receive medication reminders, and access health-related resources. This capability is particularly valuable in multicultural societies where language barriers can hinder effective healthcare delivery. Education is another field where multilingual voice assistants play a significant role. Language learning applications use voice recognition and speech synthesis to help users practice pronunciation, vocabulary, and grammar in different languages. Additionally, virtual tutors can provide personalized learning experiences by adapting to the linguistic needs of students, making education more inclusive and accessible.

5.3.3 Challenges in Developing Multilingual Voice Assistants

Despite the advancements in multilingual voice assistant technology, several challenges persist. One of the primary difficulties is the lack of high-quality training data for low-resource languages. Many languages, particularly those with fewer speakers, do not have sufficient annotated datasets for training accurate ASR and NLU models. This limitation affects the performance of voice assistants in these languages, leading to lower accuracy and user frustration.

Another challenge is handling dialects and regional variations within a single language. For example, Spanish spoken in Spain differs significantly from Spanish spoken in Latin America, both in vocabulary and pronunciation. Voice assistants must be trained to recognize and adapt to these variations to provide consistent performance across different regions. This requires extensive data collection and model fine-tuning, which can be resource-intensive.

Cultural and contextual understanding also poses a challenge for multilingual voice assistants. Language is deeply tied to culture, and certain phrases or expressions may carry different meanings in different cultural contexts. Misinterpretations can lead to incorrect responses, affecting user trust and satisfaction. Developers must incorporate cultural knowledge into their models to ensure that interactions are contextually appropriate.

Privacy and security concerns are additional challenges in the deployment of multilingual voice assistants. Voice interactions often involve sensitive personal information, and users must trust that their data is handled securely. Companies must implement robust encryption and data protection measures to prevent unauthorized access and misuse of voice data. Transparency in data usage and compliance with privacy regulations are essential to maintaining user confidence.

5.4 CROSS-LANGUAGE SPEAKER IDENTIFICATION AND DIARIZATION

Cross-language speaker identification and diarization represent an important evolution of traditional speaker processing techniques to meet the demands of an increasingly multilingual world. By overcoming challenges such as feature mismatch, language-induced variability, and limited multilingual data, these systems can enable reliable recognition and segmentation of speakers across languages.

Through the use of language-invariant features, multilingual training, transfer learning, and advanced deep learning methods, significant progress has been made toward achieving robust cross-language performance. Continued research in this field will not only improve accuracy and efficiency but also expand the applicability of speaker identification and diarization in real-world multilingual scenarios, from security and media indexing to customer service and international communications. The future of cross-language speaker identification and diarization lies in increasingly sophisticated machine learning architectures and larger, more diverse training datasets. Advances in self-supervised learning promise to reduce the dependence on annotated multilingual data by enabling models to learn universal speech representations from raw audio. Incorporating prosodic, phonotactic, and articulatory features alongside spectral features may further enhance language robustness.

Another emerging direction is the integration of multimodal information, such as video-based lip movement analysis, to support speaker identification when language-related acoustic variability is high. Cloud-based deployment of multilingual speaker processing systems will make these capabilities widely accessible, but it will also raise new challenges in terms of privacy, security, and ethical considerations.

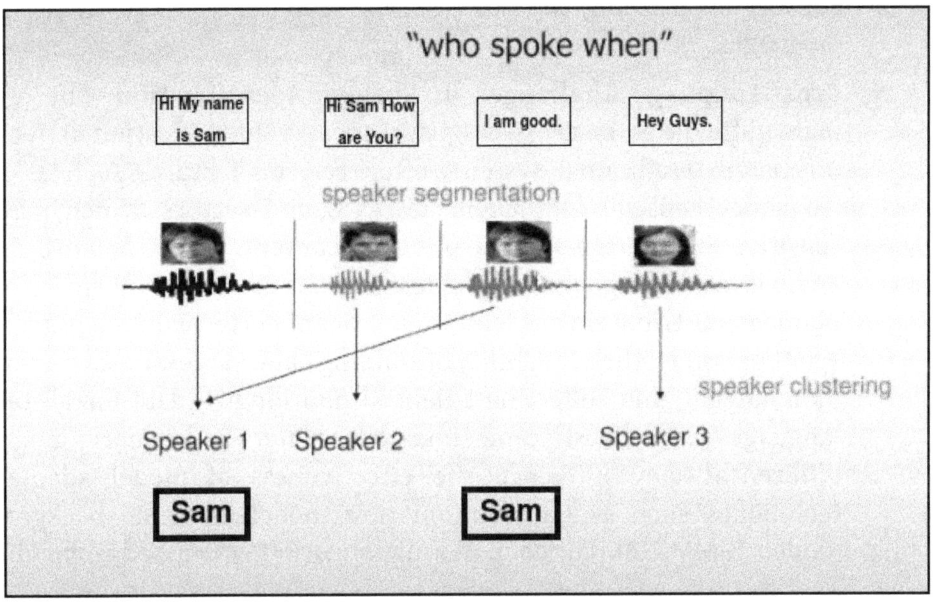

Fig: Speaker Diarization (Problem Formulation)

- **Fundamentals of Speaker Identification:** Speaker identification involves extracting features from speech that are unique to an individual's voice, often referred to as a voiceprint. These features are based on both physiological characteristics of the vocal tract and behavioral patterns in speech production. In a cross-language context, the primary challenge is that language affects the acoustic and prosodic characteristics of speech, which may influence the extracted features. For instance, vowel distributions, consonant articulation, and intonation patterns vary between languages, potentially reducing the similarity between samples from the same speaker if they are in different languages. Therefore, effective cross-language identification requires methods that capture speaker-specific traits independent of language-specific variations.

- **Fundamentals of Speaker Diarization:** Speaker diarization is often described as the "who spoke when" problem. It aims to partition an audio recording into segments corresponding to each speaker present. This involves multiple steps such as speech activity detection, segmentation, feature extraction, clustering, and labeling. In cross-language settings, diarization must cope with the fact that language switching can occur within a single speaker's turn or even mid-sentence. This can affect the stability of clustering algorithms that rely on language-sensitive features. Robust diarization systems must therefore integrate features that remain consistent despite linguistic changes, as well as models capable of handling the acoustic variability introduced by multiple languages.
- **Cross-Language Challenges in Speaker Identification:** One of the main difficulties in cross-language speaker identification is feature mismatch. Traditional systems often rely on features such as Mel-frequency cepstral coefficients (MFCCs) or i-vectors, which may be sensitive to language-specific phonetic content. When the enrollment audio is in one language and the test audio is in another, mismatches in phoneme distribution can lead to significant performance degradation. Another issue is the availability of training data. Large datasets are often monolingual, and collecting balanced multilingual data for all target languages can be costly and time-consuming. Furthermore, language differences may influence the effectiveness of model adaptation techniques such as Gaussian mixture model–universal background models (GMM-UBM) or deep neural network (DNN)-based embeddings.
- **Cross-Language Challenges in Speaker Diarization:** In diarization, the main challenge in a cross-language environment is maintaining speaker cluster consistency despite language switching. Language shifts can cause sudden changes in spectral features, which may lead a clustering algorithm to mistakenly split one speaker into multiple clusters. In broadcast or meeting scenarios where code-switching is common, this results in reduced diarization accuracy. Another problem is the interaction between language identification and speaker clustering. Some diarization pipelines integrate language identification as a preliminary step, which may help guide speaker segmentation but can also propagate errors if the language identification is incorrect.

Additionally, in multilingual audio streams, overlapping speech from multiple speakers in different languages further complicates the segmentation and labeling process.

- **Techniques for Cross-Language Robustness:** To achieve effective cross-language speaker identification and diarization, researchers have explored several approaches. Language-invariant feature extraction is one strategy, focusing on identifying aspects of the speech signal that are minimally affected by language differences. For example, features derived from the speaker's vocal tract characteristics, pitch patterns, and glottal waveform properties may exhibit greater language independence. Another strategy is using phonetic-aware models that normalize language-dependent phoneme variations, enabling better matching of cross-language speech. Deep learning methods, particularly speaker embeddings from models like x-vectors or ECAPA-TDNN, have shown promise when trained on diverse multilingual datasets, as they can learn to generalize across language boundaries.
- **Multilingual Training and Transfer Learning:** One effective method for improving cross-language performance is multilingual training, where the model is trained on data from multiple languages simultaneously. This exposure allows the model to learn shared representations of speaker characteristics that are not tied to a single language. Transfer learning is another promising approach, in which a model pre-trained on a large multilingual corpus is fine-tuned using smaller amounts of target language data. By leveraging knowledge from related languages, the system can adapt to new linguistic conditions more efficiently. For diarization, multilingual training of clustering and segmentation models can help maintain robustness when language switching occurs during speech segments.
- **Role of Language Identification in Cross-Language Systems:** Language identification plays a dual role in cross-language speaker identification and diarization systems. On one hand, it can assist by providing context to adapt speaker models to specific language characteristics or to adjust feature extraction parameters. On the other hand, over-reliance on language identification can lead to error propagation if the language detection is incorrect. In some hybrid systems, language identification is performed alongside speaker identification in a joint learning framework, enabling mutual reinforcement of both tasks. This integrated approach allows the system to exploit correlations between speaker traits and language cues while mitigating the negative effects of incorrect language classification.

- **Applications in Real-World Scenarios:** Cross-language speaker identification and diarization have critical applications in many fields. In security and forensics, these systems can identify persons of interest from multilingual surveillance recordings. In international call centers, diarization helps monitor and analyze customer service interactions across different languages for quality control. In the media industry, they enable accurate indexing and retrieval of multilingual audio archives, facilitating content search and personalization. In political or diplomatic contexts, they support transcription and analysis of multilingual meetings, ensuring accurate attribution of statements to specific speakers.

5.5 SPEECH TRANSLATION MODELS (E.G., WHISPER, TRANSLATOTRON)

Speech translation models like Whisper and Translatotron represent a transformative development in artificial intelligence, enabling seamless cross-lingual communication through advanced neural networks. These models have revolutionized how individuals and businesses interact across language barriers, offering applications in international business, healthcare, education, and entertainment. While challenges such as data scarcity, dialect variations, and privacy concerns persist, ongoing research and technological advancements are addressing these issues.

The future of speech translation models holds exciting possibilities, with innovations in real-time processing, edge computing, and transfer learning poised to enhance their capabilities further. As these models continue to evolve, they will play an increasingly vital role in fostering global connectivity and accessibility, making communication more inclusive and efficient for people worldwide. The progress in this field underscores the potential of AI to bridge linguistic divides and create a more interconnected world.

5.5.1 Whisper: A Multilingual Speech Recognition and Translation Model

Whisper, developed by OpenAI, is a state-of-the-art speech recognition and translation model that has garnered significant attention for its ability to process and translate speech across multiple languages. Unlike traditional models that rely on separate ASR and MT components, Whisper employs an end-to-end approach, where a single model performs both transcription and translation. This integration enhances efficiency and reduces the potential for errors that can arise from cascaded systems. One of the standout features of Whisper is its multilingual capability, supporting a wide range of languages and dialects. The model is trained on a vast and diverse dataset, enabling it to recognize and translate speech with high accuracy, even in low-resource languages. This makes Whisper particularly useful in scenarios where traditional translation models struggle due to limited training data. Additionally, Whisper's architecture is designed to handle noisy audio inputs, making it robust in real-world environments where background noise or varying speech patterns may be present.

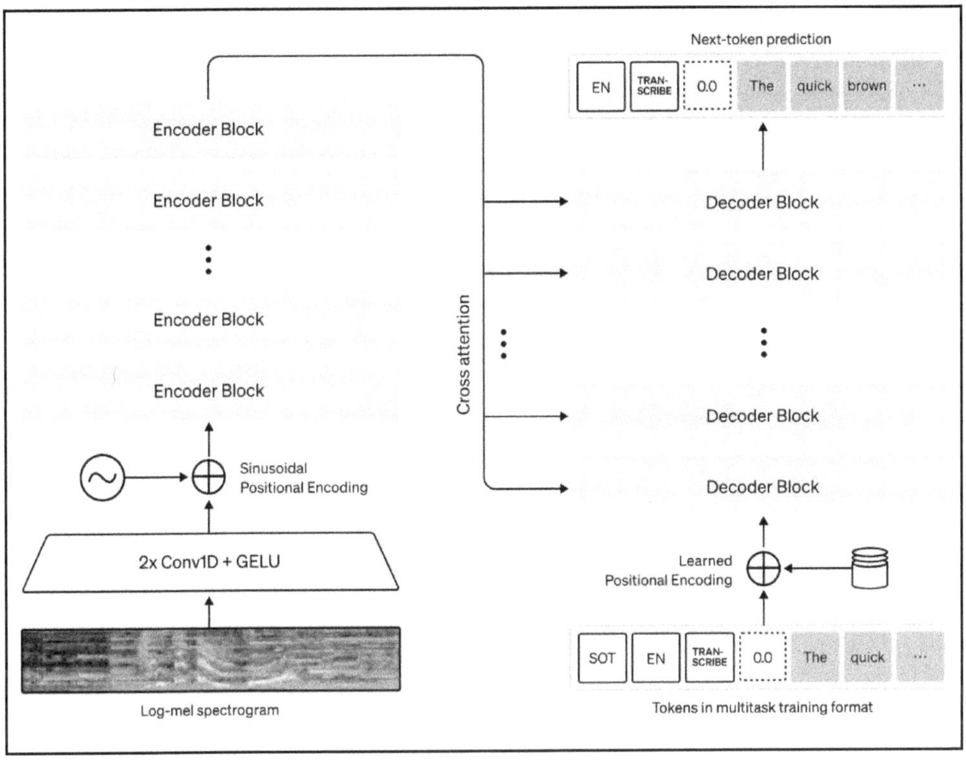

Whisper's performance is further enhanced by its use of transformer-based neural networks, which allow the model to capture long-range dependencies in speech and generate coherent translations. The model's ability to produce timestamps for transcribed and translated text also adds to its utility, enabling applications in subtitling, transcription services, and real-time translation.

OpenAI's decision to release Whisper as an open-source model has facilitated widespread adoption and further research, contributing to the advancement of speech translation technology. Despite its strengths, Whisper faces challenges, particularly in handling highly specialized or technical vocabulary, where domain-specific training may be required. Additionally, while the model performs well in many languages, its accuracy can vary depending on the availability of training data. Ongoing research aims to address these limitations by incorporating more diverse datasets and refining the model's architecture to improve performance in niche applications.

5.5.2 Translatotron: Direct Speech-to-Speech Translation

Translatotron, developed by Google Research, represents another significant advancement in speech translation by introducing a direct speech-to-speech translation model. Unlike traditional systems that convert speech to text and then translate the text, Translatotron translates speech directly into speech in another language, preserving the speaker's voice characteristics. This approach eliminates the intermediate text conversion step, reducing latency and potential errors associated with cascaded models.

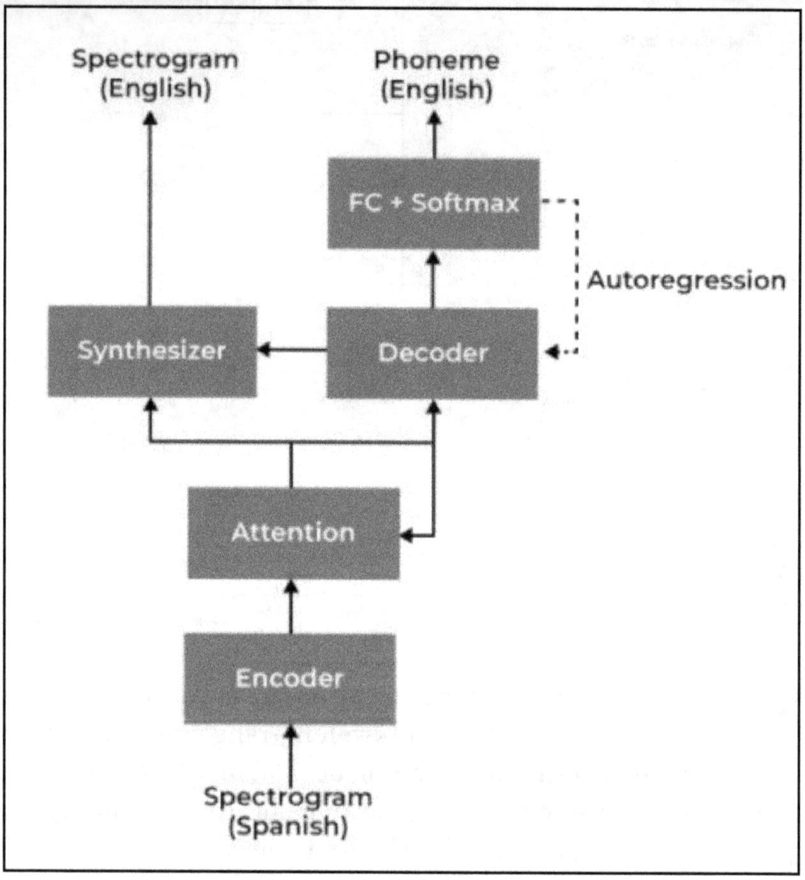

Fig: Translatotron 2 Architecture

The key innovation of Translatotron lies in its ability to retain the original speaker's voice, including tone, pitch, and emotional nuances, in the translated output. This feature is particularly valuable in applications where maintaining the speaker's identity and emotional context is important, such as in media dubbing or personalized virtual assistants. The model achieves this by using a sequence-to-sequence architecture that maps the source speech spectrogram directly to the target speech spectrogram, bypassing the need for text transcription. Translatotron's architecture incorporates attention mechanisms and convolutional neural networks to process audio signals effectively. The model is trained on parallel speech datasets, where aligned audio samples in different languages are used to learn the mapping between source and target speech. This training approach enables the model to generalize well across different languages and accents, although its performance is still influenced by the quality and diversity of the training data.

One of the challenges associated with Translatotron is the requirement for high-quality parallel speech data, which can be difficult to obtain for many language pairs. Additionally, while the model excels in preserving voice characteristics, it may struggle with languages that have significant phonetic differences from the source language. Researchers are exploring techniques such as data augmentation and transfer learning to mitigate these issues and improve the model's robustness in low-resource scenarios.

5.5.3 Applications of Speech Translation Models

Speech translation models like Whisper and Translatotron have a wide range of applications across various industries, enhancing communication and accessibility. In international business, these models facilitate real-time translation during meetings, conferences, and negotiations, enabling participants to communicate effectively regardless of their native languages. This capability is particularly valuable in multinational corporations, where teams from different linguistic backgrounds collaborate on projects. In the healthcare sector, speech translation models assist medical professionals in communicating with patients who speak different languages. This application is crucial in emergency situations, where clear and immediate communication can impact patient outcomes. Additionally, these models can be integrated into telemedicine platforms, allowing doctors to provide remote consultations to patients in different regions without language barriers.

Education is another field where speech translation models are making a significant impact. Language learning applications use these models to provide real-time translation and pronunciation feedback, helping students practice and improve their language skills. Furthermore, educational institutions can use speech translation to offer multilingual support in classrooms, ensuring that students from diverse linguistic backgrounds have equal access to learning materials. The entertainment industry also benefits from speech translation models, particularly in media localization. Translatotron's ability to preserve the original speaker's voice makes it ideal for dubbing movies, TV shows, and video games, providing a more natural and immersive experience for audiences. This technology reduces the need for traditional dubbing processes, which can be time-consuming and costly, while maintaining high-quality audio output.

5.5.4 Challenges and Future Directions

Despite the advancements in speech translation models, several challenges remain that need to be addressed to enhance their performance and applicability. One of the primary challenges is the lack of high-quality training data for many languages, particularly low-resource languages with limited digital presence. This scarcity affects the accuracy and robustness of translation models, making it difficult to achieve consistent performance across all languages.

Another challenge is handling dialects, accents, and regional variations within a single language. Speech translation models must be trained to recognize and adapt to these variations to provide accurate translations. This requires extensive data collection and model fine-tuning, which can be resource-intensive. Additionally, cultural and contextual nuances pose difficulties, as certain phrases or expressions may carry different meanings in different cultural settings.

Privacy and security concerns are also critical considerations in the deployment of speech translation models. Voice data often contains sensitive information, and users must trust that their data is handled securely. Companies developing these models must implement robust encryption and data protection measures to prevent unauthorized access and misuse. Transparency in data usage and compliance with privacy regulations are essential to maintaining user confidence.

Looking ahead, future research in speech translation models is likely to focus on improving real-time processing capabilities, reducing latency, and enhancing accuracy in low-resource languages. Techniques such as transfer learning, where models leverage knowledge from high-resource languages to improve performance in low-resource ones, show promise in addressing data scarcity issues. Additionally, advancements in edge computing could enable speech translation models to operate locally on devices, improving speed and privacy.

CHAPTER

5

Cross-Lingual NLP Applications

6.1 SENTIMENT ANALYSIS ACROSS LANGUAGES

Cross-lingual sentiment analysis empowers global-scale understanding of opinions and emotions, bridging language divides and amplifying the reach of NLP. While machine translation, cross-lingual embeddings, and multilingual pre-trained models have made remarkable progress, challenges persist—especially around nuance, domain adaptation, code-switching, and evaluation. Continued advancements in multilingual representation learning, adaptive training methods, and inclusive data resources will further unlock the potential of sentiment analysis across languages. In an increasingly interconnected world, robust, culturally intelligent models will help ensure voices in all languages are heard and understood.

6.1.1 Background: Why Cross-Lingual Sentiment Analysis Matters

- **Global Communication:** With millions of users expressing opinions online in diverse languages, businesses and researchers need tools capable of analyzing sentiment at scale, across regions—from social media monitoring to customer feedback, political opinions, public health concerns, and more.
- **Resource Disparity:** Although English benefits from abundant annotated datasets, robust lexicons, and pre-trained models, most world languages—including Hindi, Swahili, Arabic dialects—lack comparable resources. Cross-lingual methods aim to bridge this gap by transferring sentiment knowledge from one language to another.
- **Cost-Efficiency:** Building sentiment resources from scratch for each language is resource-intensive. Cross-lingual approaches (e.g., translation, multi-lingual models) offer cost-effective alternatives while retaining reasonable performance.

6.1.2 Approaches to Cross-Lingual Sentiment Analysis

Machine Translation (MT)–Based Approach

One straightforward method is translating texts from a target language into a source language (typically English), then applying a well-trained sentiment classifier.

Alternatively, translating labeled data from English into the target language allows training target-language classifiers.

- **Pros:**
  - Leverages high-performance translation engines.
  - Allows re-use of mature monolingual models.
- **Cons:**
  - Translation errors can distort sentiment nuances, especially for idioms, sarcasm, or emotionally colored phrases.
  - MT systems may not support low-resource languages.

Cross-Lingual Word Embeddings

By embedding words from different languages into a shared vector space (aligned via bilingual dictionaries or parallel corpora), these models allow models trained in one language to process inputs from another. Examples include:

- **Mapping-Based Methods**: Learn a linear mapping between monolingual embedding spaces.
- **Joint Training Methods**: Create embeddings for multiple languages simultaneously using parallel corpora.
- These embeddings feed into standard classifiers trained on, say, English data, and applied directly to target-language text.

Multilingual Pre-trained Language Models (PLMs)

Models like multilingual BERT (mBERT), XLM, XLM-R, and mT5 are pre-trained on massive multilingual corpora. Fine-tuning them on labeled sentiment data in one language enables them to generalize sentiment understanding to other languages—often with impressive zero- or few-shot capabilities.

Pivot-Based and Unsupervised Techniques

Some approaches use sentiment "pivots"—words or features that have reliable sentiment across languages—to bridge monolingual models. Unsupervised or weakly supervised methods, such as utilizing hashtags or emoticons as noisy labels on social media, can also generate sentiment signals in multiple languages with minimal annotation.

Hybrid Techniques

Hybrid systems combine the strengths of the above—e.g., using machine translation for some parts, cross-lingual embeddings for others, and PLMs as a backbone—tailoring the approach to language pairs, resource availability, and application domains.

6.1.3 Challenges and Limitations

- **Semantic and Cultural Nuance:** Sentiment isn't purely lexical; cultural context shapes emotional tone. For example, certain words may express irony or positivity in one culture but not in another. Direct transfer of sentiment models risks misinterpretation.
- **Scarcity of Evaluation Data:** Benchmark datasets for low-resource languages are rare, which complicates evaluation. This limitation makes it hard to measure progress or compare methods rigorously across languages.
- **Domain and Register Shift:** User-generated content—tweets, reviews, forum posts—varies greatly in style and domain. Sentiment models may overfit English review data and underperform on, say, informal or code-mixed target-language posts.
- **Code-Switching:** In multilingual regions, code-switching (mixing languages within a sentence) complicates both tokenization and sentiment modeling. Traditional pipelines often break under such fluid text.

6.1.4 Applications

- **Customer Feedback and Market Research:** Multinational companies leverage CLSA to understand product sentiment across markets—e.g., sentiment on a new smartphone launch in Hindi, Arabic, or Portuguese—including social media reactions, app store reviews, and support tickets.
- **Social Media Monitoring:** Governments and NGOs monitor sentiments related to elections, public policy, or crisis response. Tools that work across languages (e.g., English, Spanish, Hindi, Swahili) help detect emerging public moods and misinformation.
- **Cross-Cultural Studies and Journalism:** Researchers and journalists can compare emotional responses across language communities to global events—sports, disasters, awards, or cultural phenomena—without requiring manual translation or multiple pipelines.
- **Chatbots and Customer Support:** Multilingual chatbots rely on sentiment detection to route conversations—e.g., positive sentiment may trigger upsell; negative sentiment may direct to human agents. Cross-lingual models enable better service across diverse user bases.
- **Public Health and Social Causes:** During pandemics, sentiment analysis in multiple languages helps gauge public fear, misinformation, and compliance with health guidance—crucial for targeted outreach and policy-making.

6.1.5 Future Directions

- **Improved Multilingual Pre-Training:** As PLMs scale further—covering more languages and dialects with better tokenization and balanced data—cross-lingual sentiment transfer will likely improve, especially for underrepresented languages.
- **Better Cultural Sensitivity:** Future models may incorporate cultural embeddings or adapt sentiment lexicons dynamically based on locale and context—enhancing understanding of idiomatic or culturally-specific sentiment.
- **Active Learning and Few-Shot Adaptation:** Leveraging small amounts of target-language data via active learning, few-shot prompts, or human-in-the-loop adaptation can significantly boost performance without full annotation efforts.
- **Handling Code-Switching and Mixed Registers:** Advancements in tokenization, language ID, and code-switch aware architectures will better handle real-world multilingual text, where languages mix mid-sentence.
- **Benchmarking and Open Datasets:** The creation of standardized, multilingual sentiment datasets and benchmarks, particularly in low-resource or code-switched settings, will accelerate research and facilitate meaningful comparisons.

6.2 NAMED ENTITY RECOGNITION AND PART-OF-SPEECH TAGGING

Named Entity Recognition and Part-of-Speech Tagging are foundational NLP tasks that become even more powerful when applied cross-lingually. Advances in multilingual models like mBERT and XLM-R have enabled robust applications in translation, search, and information extraction. However, challenges like morphological complexity and data scarcity remain. Future research should focus on improving low-resource language support and reducing biases in multilingual NLP systems. As global communication grows, Cross-Lingual NLP will continue to bridge language barriers, making technology more accessible worldwide.

6.2.1 Understanding Named Entity Recognition (NER)

Named Entity Recognition (NER) is an NLP task that identifies and classifies named entities in text into predefined categories such as:

- **Person names** (e.g., "Albert Einstein").
- **Organizations** (e.g., "United Nations").
- **Locations** (e.g., "Paris").

- **Dates & Times** (e.g., "January 2025").
- **Numerical values** (e.g., "$1 million").

How NER Works

NER systems use:

- **Rule-based approaches** (handcrafted patterns).
- **Machine Learning models** (CRF, BiLSTM).
- **Deep Learning & Transformers** (BERT, GPT).
- For example, in the sentence:
  - *"Apple Inc. was founded by Steve Jobs in Cupertino."*
  - NER would tag:
- **Apple Inc.** → Organization
- **Steve Jobs** → Person
- **Cupertino** → Location

6.2.2 Part-of-Speech (POS) Tagging

POS tagging assigns grammatical categories (tags) to words in a sentence, such as:

- **Noun (NN)** – "book".
- **Verb (VB)** – "run".
- **Adjective (JJ)** – "beautiful".
- **Adverb (RB)** – "quickly".
- **Approaches to POS Tagging:**
  - **Rule-based tagging** (using linguistic rules).
  - **Stochastic (Probabilistic) tagging** (HMMs).
  - **Neural Network-based tagging** (LSTMs, Transformers).

6.2.3 Cross-Lingual NLP: Extending NER and POS Tagging to Multiple Languages

Cross-Lingual NLP aims to apply NLP techniques across different languages without language-specific training for each.

- **Challenges in Cross-Lingual NER & POS Tagging:**
  - **Morphological Variations** (e.g., German compounds vs. English).
  - **Language-Specific Syntax** (e.g., Subject-Object-Verb in Japanese).
  - **Limited Labeled Data** for low-resource languages.
  - **Entity Ambiguity** (e.g., "Paris" as a city or a person's name).

- **Solutions for Cross-Lingual Adaptation:**
  - **Multilingual Pretrained Models** (mBERT, XLM-R).
  - **Transfer Learning** (fine-tuning on target language).
  - **Translation-Based Approaches** (translate then tag).
  - **Adversarial Training** (aligning embeddings across languages).

6.2.4 Applications of Cross-Lingual NER and POS Tagging

Machine Translation Enhancement:

- POS tags help in reordering words (e.g., English SVO → Japanese SOV).
- NER ensures proper translation of names (e.g., "Washington" as a person or place).
- **Multilingual Information Extraction:** Extracting entities from news in multiple languages (e.g., tracking global events).
- **Cross-Lingual Search Engines:** Improving search results by recognizing entities in different languages.
- **Sentiment Analysis Across Languages:** POS helps identify sentiment-bearing words (adjectives, adverbs).
- **Chatbots & Virtual Assistants:** Understanding user queries in multiple languages (e.g., Siri, Google Assistant).

6.2.5 Case Studies & Real-World Implementations

- **Case Study 1: Google Translate's NER Integration:** Google Translate uses NER to detect and properly translate names (e.g., "Beijing" instead of "Peking" in Chinese).
- **Case Study 2: Facebook's Multilingual POS Tagger:** Facebook's NLP pipeline uses XLM-R for POS tagging across 100+ languages to improve content moderation.
- **Case Study 3: Biomedical NER in Multiple Languages:** Researchers use cross-lingual NER to extract drug and disease names from medical texts in Spanish, French, and German.

6.3 CROSS-LINGUAL QUESTION ANSWERING AND INFORMATION RETRIEVAL

Cross-lingual question answering and information retrieval systems represent transformative advancements in natural language processing, offering solutions that bridge linguistic divides and facilitate global communication. These applications have revolutionized how we access and interact with information, enabling seamless understanding and retrieval across language boundaries. As the field continues to evolve, the development of more sophisticated models and evaluation frameworks promises to enhance the capabilities of these systems, supporting more accurate and culturally aware language technologies.

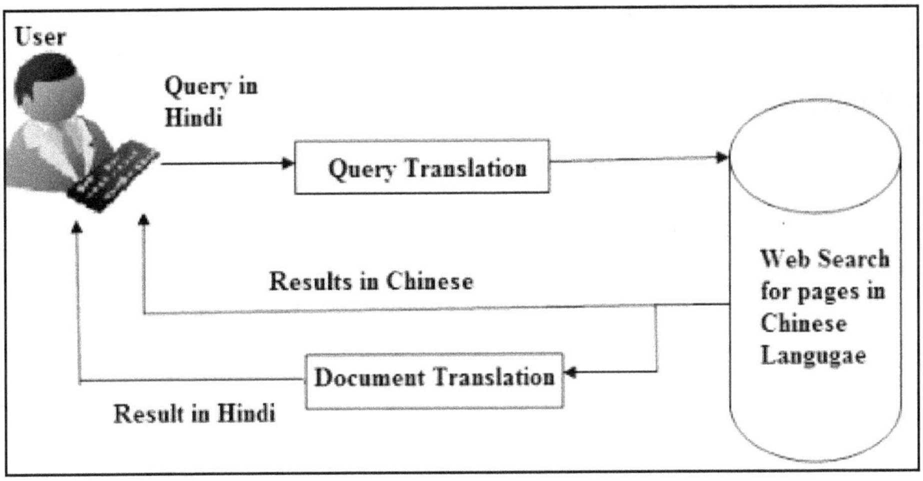

Fig: Cross Language Information Retrieval System

The future of cross-lingual NLP is marked by opportunities for innovation and collaboration, with the potential to further transform global communication and information access. Through continued research and development, these systems will play an increasingly central role in connecting global communities, supporting cross-cultural understanding, and enabling more inclusive language technologies. The evolution of cross-lingual applications reflects the growing recognition of linguistic diversity and the importance of developing technologies that can accommodate the rich spectrum of human communication.

The future of cross-lingual question answering and information retrieval is marked by exciting opportunities for further advancement and innovation. The integration of multimodal approaches that combine language with visual or auditory information presents new possibilities for comprehensive understanding and retrieval. The development of more sophisticated architectures that can capture complex cross-lingual relationships will enhance the ability to process and generate information across diverse linguistic inputs.

Advances in few-shot and zero-shot learning will enable models to adapt more effectively to new languages or domains with limited training data. The development of techniques for continual learning and adaptation will support systems that can update and improve over time, accommodating evolving language use and new linguistic patterns. Research into more efficient architectures that reduce computational requirements while maintaining performance will facilitate deployment in resource-constrained environments, expanding the accessibility of these technologies. The creation of more diverse and representative training datasets will support continued improvement in cross-lingual applications. Collaborative efforts to collect and annotate data from underrepresented languages will enhance the inclusivity and effectiveness of these systems. The development of ethical guidelines and best practices will ensure the responsible advancement of these technologies, supporting global communication and cultural exchange.

6.3.1 Evolution

The development of cross-lingual natural language processing applications has followed a trajectory marked by increasing sophistication and capability. Early approaches to multilingual processing relied on simple translation pipelines, where text would be translated into a single language before processing. While functional, these methods often struggled with the nuances of language and the preservation of meaning across translations. The limitations of these approaches became particularly apparent in complex tasks such as question answering, where contextual understanding and semantic relationships are crucial.

Modern cross-lingual systems have evolved to incorporate more sophisticated architectures that can process multiple languages simultaneously within a unified framework. These advancements reflect a paradigm shift from translation-based approaches to models that develop shared representations across languages. The development of transformer-based architectures has been particularly transformative, enabling systems to capture complex linguistic patterns and relationships that span multiple languages. This evolution has paved the way for more accurate and contextually aware cross-lingual applications that can handle the rich diversity of human communication.

6.3.2 Architectural Foundations of Cross-Lingual Systems

The architectural foundations of modern cross-lingual question answering and information retrieval systems build upon the successes of transformer-based models while incorporating innovations specific to multilingual processing. These systems typically employ large language models pre-trained on diverse multilingual corpora, enabling them to develop representations that capture linguistic patterns across different languages. The transformer architecture's self-attention mechanism is particularly well-suited to cross-lingual tasks, as it can identify and relate concepts regardless of their language of expression.

A key innovation in these architectures is the development of shared representation spaces where languages with similar characteristics are positioned in proximity. This approach allows the model to leverage knowledge from high-resource languages to improve performance on languages with limited training data. The models employ sophisticated tokenization strategies that can handle diverse linguistic structures, including languages with different scripts or complex morphological systems.

These architectural innovations enable cross-lingual systems to process and understand information across language boundaries while maintaining contextual coherence and semantic relationships.

6.3.3 Cross-Lingual Question Answering: Bridging Language Barriers

Cross-lingual question answering represents one of the most challenging and valuable applications of multilingual natural language processing. These systems enable users to pose questions in one language and receive answers from documents written in another, effectively bridging linguistic divides in information access.

The development of effective cross-lingual QA systems requires sophisticated models that can understand the semantic content of questions and match them to relevant information regardless of language differences. The architecture of these systems typically involves several key components working in concert. A multilingual encoder processes the input question and potential answer passages, developing representations that capture their semantic content.

A cross-lingual matching component then identifies relevant information by comparing these representations across languages. Finally, a generation or extraction module produces the final answer in the desired language. This pipeline enables the system to handle the complexity of cross-lingual information retrieval while maintaining accuracy and contextual understanding.

6.3.4 Information Retrieval across Languages

Cross-lingual information retrieval systems have transformed how users access and interact with multilingual content. These applications enable search queries in one language to retrieve relevant documents written in other languages, significantly expanding the scope of accessible information. The development of effective cross-lingual IR systems requires models that can understand and match semantic content across linguistic boundaries, identifying relevant documents regardless of their language of origin.

The architecture of these systems typically employs dense retrieval methods that represent both queries and documents in a shared semantic space. This approach allows for efficient comparison of content across languages, identifying documents that contain relevant information regardless of linguistic differences.

The models incorporate sophisticated ranking algorithms that consider both semantic similarity and cross-lingual relevance, ensuring that retrieved documents are not only linguistically compatible but also contextually appropriate. These systems have revolutionized global information access, enabling users to find relevant content regardless of language barriers.

6.3.5 Challenges in Cross-Lingual NLP Applications

Despite significant advancements, cross-lingual question answering and information retrieval systems still face considerable challenges that reflect the complexity of multilingual processing. One persistent issue is the imbalance in available training data across different languages, which can lead to performance disparities between high-resource and low-resource languages. The models often struggle with languages that have limited digital representation or those with complex linguistic structures that differ significantly from well-represented languages.

Another significant challenge is the preservation of meaning and context across languages, particularly when dealing with culturally specific concepts or idiomatic expressions. The models must capture not only the literal translation of content but also the nuanced semantic relationships that exist within and between languages. This requirement for deep cross-lingual understanding presents a considerable computational challenge, as it demands sophisticated representations that can accommodate diverse linguistic patterns while maintaining semantic coherence.

6.3.6 Evaluation Metrics and Benchmarks

The evaluation of cross-lingual question answering and information retrieval systems requires specialized metrics and benchmarks that account for the unique challenges of multilingual processing. Traditional evaluation methods often focus on monolingual performance, which may not adequately capture the complexities of cross-lingual tasks. The development of comprehensive benchmarks that include diverse language pairs and assess both linguistic compatibility and semantic relevance is crucial for advancing these applications.

Recent efforts have produced several valuable benchmarks for evaluating cross-lingual systems. These include datasets that pair questions and documents in different languages, enabling assessment of the models' ability to retrieve and understand information across linguistic boundaries. The evaluation metrics for these benchmarks typically consider both the accuracy of retrieved information and the quality of generated answers, providing a comprehensive assessment of system performance. The continued development of these evaluation frameworks is essential for guiding research and improvement in cross-lingual NLP applications.

6.4 TEXT SUMMARIZATION AND CONTENT GENERATION

Text summarization and content generation are two pivotal tasks in Natural Language Processing (NLP) that have gained prominence in an increasingly interconnected digital ecosystem. Text summarization condenses large volumes of information into concise, coherent overviews, while content generation creates new text that is coherent, contextually relevant, and stylistically consistent. With the proliferation of digital communication in hundreds of languages, the need for cross-lingual applications—systems capable of working across multiple languages—has become more pressing than ever. Cross-lingual NLP seeks to bridge linguistic divides, allowing summarization and generation systems to function seamlessly between languages, even when resources are unevenly distributed.

Text summarization and content generation are essential NLP capabilities that are increasingly being extended to cross-lingual contexts. These applications not only enhance the accessibility of information across linguistic boundaries but also empower industries, governments, and individuals to communicate more effectively in a multilingual world. The progress achieved through translation-based methods, multilingual pre-trained models, and direct cross-lingual techniques has been impressive, yet challenges related to meaning preservation, data scarcity, and evaluation persist. As research continues, the focus will shift toward culturally aware, context-sensitive, and adaptable models that can produce high-quality summaries and content in any language. In a future where linguistic diversity is respected and supported by advanced NLP systems, cross-lingual summarization and content generation will be central to fostering global understanding and cooperation.

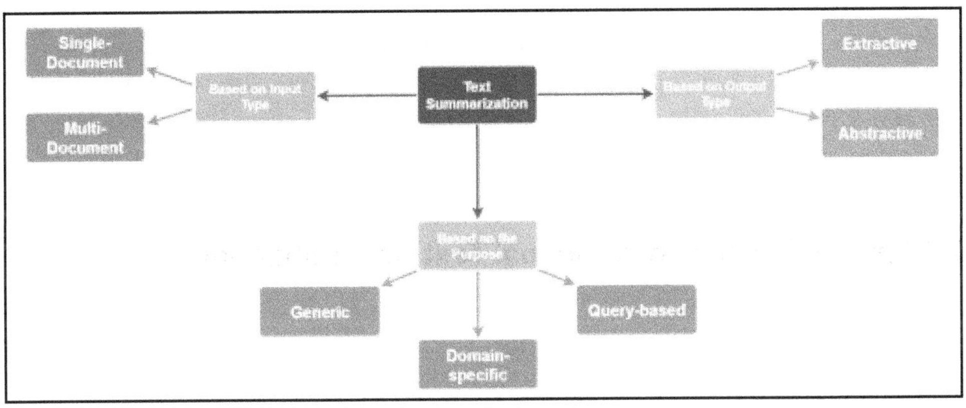

Fig: Text Summarization

Recent advances in multilingual pre-trained models have significantly improved the quality of cross-lingual summarization and generation. Models such as mT5, BLOOM, and GPT-style multilingual architectures are pushing the boundaries of zero-shot and few-shot learning, enabling systems to handle languages for which little or no training data exists. Transfer learning, combined with fine-tuning on even small amounts of in-domain data, can yield substantial performance gains. Future research is likely to focus on improving cultural and contextual sensitivity. This may involve integrating knowledge graphs, cultural embeddings, or adaptive style transfer mechanisms into multilingual models. The ability to dynamically adjust tone, formality, and stylistic features according to the target language's norms will be crucial for high-quality generation. Additionally, more robust evaluation frameworks that combine automated metrics with semantic similarity measures and cultural appropriateness checks will be developed to better assess cross-lingual output.

Another important direction is enhancing the handling of code-switching and mixed-language texts, which are common in social media and informal communication. Developing models that can seamlessly summarize or generate content from such inputs without forcing a monolingual representation will be a key step toward real-world applicability.

6.4.1 Importance of Cross-Lingual Capabilities

In a monolingual setting, text summarization and content generation have reached impressive levels of fluency, coherence, and relevance. However, much of this progress has been concentrated in English and a handful of high-resource languages. The majority of the world's languages lack the extensive annotated datasets, linguistic resources, and computational investment required to train sophisticated NLP systems. Cross-lingual techniques address this disparity by transferring knowledge from resource-rich to resource-poor languages, enabling summarization and generation even when direct training data is scarce. This transfer can be accomplished through approaches such as multilingual pre-trained models, parallel corpora, or translation pipelines. The result is a powerful set of tools that not only facilitate multilingual communication but also make information more inclusive by ensuring that linguistic barriers do not limit access to knowledge.

6.4.2 Approaches to Cross-Lingual Text Summarization

Cross-lingual text summarization (CLTS) refers to the process of generating a summary in a target language from a source document written in another language. One common method is the translate-then-summarize approach, where the source text is first translated into the target language, and then a monolingual summarizer produces the final output. This method benefits from mature machine translation systems but risks introducing translation artifacts that can distort meaning. Another approach is summarize-then-translate, in which the source text is summarized first, followed by translation of the shorter summary. This reduces translation costs and potential errors but requires accurate summarization in the source language, which may not always be available for low-resource languages.

A more advanced approach involves direct cross-lingual summarization, where models are trained or fine-tuned to produce summaries in a target language directly from a source-language input without an intermediate translation step. Recent multilingual pre-trained transformers, such as mBART, mT5, and XLM-R, have shown promise in enabling this capability. These models can be fine-tuned with parallel summarization datasets, even if limited in size, and leverage transfer learning to generalize across languages. Direct cross-lingual summarization has the advantage of preserving nuanced meaning and producing more fluent outputs, but it remains a challenging task due to linguistic and cultural variations.

6.4.3 Cross-Lingual Content Generation

While summarization condenses existing information, content generation creates new text that may be factual, creative, instructional, or persuasive. Cross-lingual content generation expands this ability to produce coherent, contextually appropriate content in one language based on prompts or source material in another language. This is particularly valuable in fields such as journalism, marketing, education, and entertainment, where localized content is needed for different linguistic markets.

One prominent example is multilingual storytelling, where a narrative written in one language is adapted and creatively rephrased into another while retaining its emotional tone, cultural resonance, and stylistic features. Similarly, in e-commerce, product descriptions can be generated in multiple languages from a single master template, ensuring that global audiences receive consistent yet culturally adapted information. Multilingual dialogue systems and chatbots also rely on cross-lingual content generation to deliver helpful, context-aware responses in the user's preferred language, even if the original data or logic is maintained in another.

The technical backbone of such systems often includes multilingual language models trained on diverse corpora, along with fine-tuning on domain-specific content. For instance, a model might be fine-tuned on marketing copy in English but be capable of generating persuasive text in French, Arabic, or Hindi without separate training in each. However, ensuring that the generated content is culturally appropriate, grammatically accurate, and semantically faithful to the original intent remains a significant challenge.

6.4.4 Challenges in Cross-Lingual Summarization and Generation

Cross-lingual applications face numerous hurdles that go beyond the difficulties of their monolingual counterparts. A major challenge is the preservation of meaning across languages that differ significantly in structure, syntax, and semantics. Idiomatic expressions, humor, and cultural references are particularly prone to distortion during translation or cross-lingual processing. For summarization, the risk lies in omitting crucial context or altering the tone, while for content generation, the challenge is to maintain stylistic fidelity and intended impact.

Another difficulty is the scarcity of aligned training data for many language pairs. High-quality parallel corpora for summarization or generation are rare, particularly for languages outside the top ten in terms of internet content. Without such data, models must rely heavily on transfer learning or synthetic data generation, which may introduce biases or inaccuracies. Moreover, low-resource languages often have less standardized orthography and greater dialectal variation, further complicating cross-lingual processing.

Finally, evaluation of cross-lingual summarization and generation is not straightforward. Automatic metrics such as ROUGE or BLEU can measure lexical overlap but often fail to capture semantic adequacy or cultural appropriateness. Human evaluation is more reliable but costly and difficult to scale. Developing robust, multilingual evaluation frameworks remains an ongoing research priority.

6.4.5 Applications across Domains

The real-world applications of cross-lingual summarization and content generation span multiple industries and sectors. In news media, journalists can use CLTS to provide multilingual coverage of global events, ensuring that audiences in different linguistic communities have access to accurate and timely summaries. This not only promotes inclusivity but also helps counter misinformation by providing reliable summaries across languages.

In education, cross-lingual content generation can create instructional materials in multiple languages from a single source. For example, an educational platform might generate science lesson summaries in Spanish, Swahili, and Mandarin from English-language content, expanding access to quality education for non-English-speaking learners. Similarly, in international organizations, cross-lingual summarization allows for efficient dissemination of policy briefs, research findings, and meeting minutes to stakeholders in multiple regions without requiring manual translation for each document.

In the corporate world, marketing teams can use cross-lingual content generation to produce localized advertising campaigns, product descriptions, and press releases. This ensures consistent branding while adapting to local cultural norms and linguistic preferences. For global customer support, multilingual chatbots equipped with cross-lingual summarization capabilities can condense customer queries from one language and generate helpful responses in another, enhancing service efficiency.

6.5 MULTILINGUAL CHATBOTS AND CONVERSATIONAL AI

Multilingual chatbots and conversational AI represent a significant leap forward in Cross-Lingual NLP, enabling seamless communication across linguistic boundaries. From customer service to healthcare and education, these systems are transforming how businesses and institutions interact with global audiences. However, challenges such as language ambiguity, data scarcity, and cultural nuances must be addressed to achieve truly universal conversational AI. Future advancements in adaptive learning, emotion recognition, and speech technologies will further enhance the capabilities of multilingual chatbots, making them more intuitive and inclusive. As AI continues to evolve, the vision of a world where language is no longer a barrier to communication is becoming increasingly attainable. By investing in research and development, we can ensure that conversational AI serves as a bridge, connecting people across languages and cultures effortlessly.

Fig: Multilanguage Chatbot

The future of multilingual chatbots lies in overcoming current limitations through advanced AI research and innovative solutions. One promising direction is the development of more inclusive language models that better represent low-resource languages. Initiatives like Meta's No Language Left Behind (NLLB) aim to improve machine translation for underrepresented languages, which will enhance chatbot capabilities globally. Another area of innovation is real-time adaptive learning, where chatbots dynamically improve their language understanding based on user interactions. By incorporating few-shot and zero-shot learning techniques, these systems can quickly adapt to new languages without extensive retraining.

Emotion and tone recognition will also play a crucial role in future chatbots, enabling them to respond appropriately to user sentiments across different cultures. For instance, while direct communication may be appreciated in some cultures, others may prefer more polite or indirect responses. Enhancing cultural awareness in chatbots will make interactions more natural and user-friendly.

Furthermore, the integration of speech recognition and synthesis will expand multilingual chatbots beyond text-based interactions, allowing voice-enabled assistants like Siri and Alexa to support more languages seamlessly. Advances in neural voice cloning could enable chatbots to speak in region-specific accents, improving user engagement.

6.5.1 Architecture

Multilingual chatbots rely on sophisticated NLP architectures that enable them to process and generate responses in multiple languages. At the core of these systems are pretrained multilingual language models such as mBERT (Multilingual BERT), XLM-R (Cross-lingual Language Model RoBERTa), and GPT-3.5/4. These models are trained on vast datasets encompassing numerous languages, allowing them to capture linguistic patterns and semantic relationships across different tongues.

A typical multilingual chatbot pipeline involves several key components. First, the system detects the user's input language using language identification algorithms. Once the language is identified, the text is processed through tokenization and embedding layers, where words or subwords are converted into numerical representations. Next, intent recognition and entity extraction modules determine the user's request and extract relevant information. Finally, the system generates a response in the same language or translates it into the user's preferred language using neural machine translation (NMT).

One of the critical advantages of modern multilingual chatbots is their ability to perform zero-shot or few-shot learning, meaning they can handle languages they were not explicitly trained on by leveraging similarities between languages. This is particularly useful for low-resource languages where training data is scarce. Additionally, contextual embeddings ensure that the chatbot maintains coherence in conversations, even when users switch between languages mid-dialogue.

6.5.2 Applications

The applications of multilingual chatbots span various industries, enhancing accessibility and efficiency in global interactions. In customer support, companies deploy chatbots that can assist users in their native languages, reducing the need for human translators and minimizing response times. For instance, airlines use multilingual chatbots to handle booking inquiries, flight updates, and cancellations across different regions.

In e-commerce, chatbots facilitate seamless shopping experiences by providing product recommendations, processing orders, and resolving customer issues in multiple languages. Platforms like Amazon and Alibaba employ conversational AI to engage with a global customer base, ensuring that language differences do not hinder sales. Similarly, banking and finance sectors utilize multilingual chatbots for account inquiries, fraud detection, and transaction support, making financial services more inclusive.

The healthcare industry benefits from multilingual chatbots by offering medical advice, appointment scheduling, and symptom checking in various languages. This is particularly valuable in regions with diverse linguistic populations where access to healthcare information may be limited. Educational institutions also leverage these systems to provide language learning assistance, student support, and automated tutoring in multiple languages.

Another emerging application is in government and public services, where chatbots assist immigrants and tourists with visa applications, public transport information, and emergency services in their preferred languages. By integrating multilingual conversational AI, governments can improve communication efficiency and public satisfaction.

6.5.3 Challenges

Despite their advantages, developing robust multilingual chatbots presents several challenges. One major issue is language ambiguity, where words or phrases have different meanings across languages. For example, the word "gift" means "poison" in German, which can lead to misunderstandings if not handled correctly. Additionally, idiomatic expressions and cultural references often do not translate directly, requiring the chatbot to understand context beyond literal translations.

Another challenge is the lack of high-quality training data for low-resource languages. While models like mBERT and XLM-R perform well for widely spoken languages such as English, Spanish, and Mandarin, they may struggle with languages like Swahili or Bengali due to insufficient datasets. This imbalance can lead to biased performance, where the chatbot excels in some languages but fails in others.

Code-switching, where users mix multiple languages in a single sentence, further complicates chatbot interactions. For instance, a user might say, "Can I reservar a table for tomorrow?" blending English and Spanish. Handling such inputs requires advanced NLP techniques that can recognize and process hybrid language structures.

Additionally, dialectal variations within the same language can affect chatbot performance. For example, Spanish spoken in Spain differs significantly from Latin American Spanish in vocabulary and pronunciation. A chatbot trained on one dialect may misinterpret queries from users of another dialect, leading to errors in responses.

CHAPTER

Data in Multilingual AI

7

7.1 MULTILINGUAL CORPORA: PARALLEL, COMPARABLE, AND MONOLINGUAL

Multilingual corpora—parallel, comparable, and monolingual—form the essential data backbone for multilingual AI, each contributing unique strengths to the development of cross-lingual capabilities. Parallel corpora provide precise alignment for supervised learning, comparable corpora expand coverage where direct translations are lacking, and monolingual corpora build strong foundations for individual languages. The integration of these resources, along with advances in AI modeling techniques, is driving rapid improvements in multilingual applications, from translation and sentiment analysis to cross-lingual information retrieval. As the demand for global communication grows, the thoughtful creation, curation, and ethical use of multilingual corpora will remain central to the future of AI.

The future of multilingual corpora lies in expanding coverage, improving quality, and integrating multimodal data such as images, audio, and video alongside text. Advances in self-supervised and unsupervised learning are expected to reduce dependence on large-scale parallel corpora, allowing AI systems to learn cross-lingual patterns from less structured data.

Collaborative initiatives between governments, academic institutions, and private organizations are also playing a role in building open-access multilingual corpora, particularly for underrepresented languages. Crowdsourcing and community-driven projects are enabling the collection of culturally relevant and linguistically diverse datasets, which can be crucial for building inclusive AI systems.

7.1.1 Parallel Corpora: The Foundation of Cross-Lingual Learning

Parallel corpora are collections of texts in two or more languages where each sentence or segment in one language has a direct translation in the other. This alignment makes parallel corpora the most valuable type of data for training supervised machine translation models. Examples include the Canadian Hansard corpus, which contains parliamentary debates in English and French, and the

Europarl corpus, consisting of proceedings from the European Parliament in multiple languages.

The advantage of parallel corpora lies in their precision. Since the sentences are aligned at a granular level, they allow AI systems to learn exact word correspondences, syntactic structures, and context-based translations. This makes them ideal for neural machine translation (NMT) systems, which require large volumes of high-quality paired data to achieve fluency and accuracy. Parallel corpora also aid in creating bilingual dictionaries, improving alignment algorithms, and training multilingual embeddings that map words from different languages into a shared semantic space.

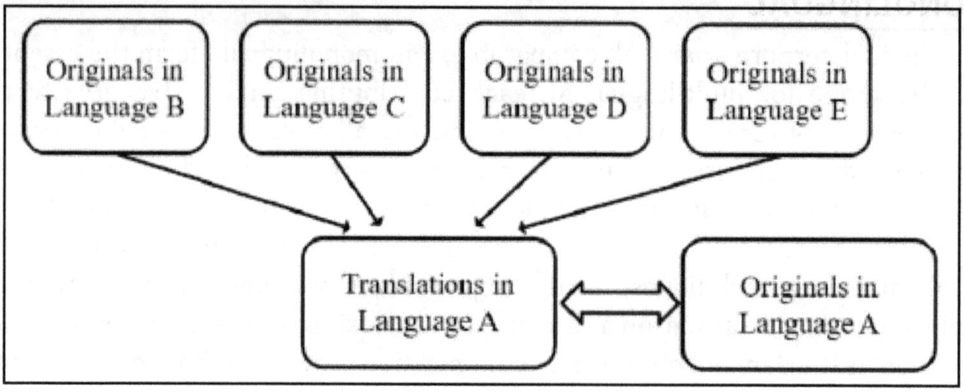

Fig: The Monolingual-Comparable-Cum-Parallel Corpus Design

However, building parallel corpora is resource-intensive. It requires professional translations, careful alignment, and significant editorial oversight. Moreover, parallel corpora are often limited to specific language pairs, domains, or topics, which can lead to coverage gaps when dealing with less-resourced languages or specialized subject matter. These limitations have motivated researchers to explore alternative data sources, such as comparable corpora, to fill in the gaps.

7.1.2 Comparable Corpora: Bridging the Gap in Resource Scarcity

Comparable corpora consist of texts in different languages that are not direct translations of each other but share similar topics, genres, or domains. For instance, news articles covering the same international event in multiple languages may have overlapping content, even though the wording and structure differ. Wikipedia articles on the same topic in various languages also form a valuable source of comparable corpora. These corpora are especially useful for low-resource languages, where parallel data is scarce or nonexistent. By analyzing thematic similarities, AI models can learn cross-lingual mappings and concepts without requiring exact sentence-to-sentence translations. Comparable corpora play a crucial role in tasks such as cross-lingual information retrieval, multilingual topic modeling, and semantic similarity analysis. A major advantage of comparable corpora is their availability. Large amounts of multilingual content—news, scientific publications, and user-generated data—exist in the digital sphere, making it easier to collect such corpora automatically. Furthermore, they allow AI systems to generalize across domains by exposing them to varied linguistic expressions of the same concepts.

However, comparable corpora also present challenges. Since there is no direct alignment, extracting meaningful cross-lingual relationships requires sophisticated statistical and embedding-based techniques. Noise in data, differences in writing styles, and cultural variations in reporting the same event can reduce alignment accuracy. Despite these hurdles, comparable corpora remain a valuable asset in building robust multilingual AI systems.

7.1.3 Monolingual Corpora: Strengthening Language-Specific Foundations

Monolingual corpora contain text or speech in only one language and serve as the foundation for training strong language models before integrating them into multilingual systems. They are essential for understanding the grammar, syntax, semantics, and idiomatic expressions unique to a language. Monolingual data ranges from books, articles, and social media posts to transcribed speeches and conversational dialogues. While monolingual corpora do not directly facilitate cross-lingual learning, they are crucial in multilingual AI for pretraining large language models. For instance, transformer-based architectures such as multilingual BERT and XLM-R leverage monolingual data in multiple languages to learn contextual word embeddings. This pretraining enables models to capture language-specific nuances, which can later be aligned across languages using parallel or comparable corpora.

One of the major strengths of monolingual corpora is their abundance. Many languages have vast digital footprints, especially dominant global languages like English, Spanish, and Chinese. However, for less widely spoken languages, building sizable monolingual datasets remains challenging. Techniques such as web scraping, OCR digitization of printed texts, and community-based data collection are often employed to overcome this limitation.

7.1.4 Integration of Corpora Types in Multilingual AI

In practice, multilingual AI systems rarely rely on a single type of corpus. Instead, they combine parallel, comparable, and monolingual corpora to maximize linguistic coverage and improve model performance. For example, in neural machine translation pipelines, parallel corpora provide supervised learning data, comparable corpora augment vocabulary and concept coverage, and monolingual corpora contribute to language model pretraining and back-translation techniques.

Back-translation is a widely used method where a model trained on parallel data is used to translate monolingual data into another language, effectively generating synthetic parallel corpora. This method helps expand the training dataset for low-resource language pairs. Similarly, comparable corpora can be mined to extract high-confidence sentence pairs, gradually increasing the size of parallel datasets.

The integration process also benefits from multilingual embeddings, which create a shared semantic space for words across languages. These embeddings can be trained using a combination of corpora types, enabling zero-shot transfer learning, where a model trained on one language pair can perform well on another without direct parallel training data.

7.1.5 Applications of Multilingual Corpora in AI

Multilingual corpora underpin a wide range of AI applications beyond machine translation. In multilingual sentiment analysis, corpora enable models to understand emotional tone across languages, even when direct translations are unavailable. In information retrieval, comparable corpora support cross-lingual search, where a user can query in one language and retrieve relevant results in another. Speech recognition and synthesis also rely heavily on multilingual corpora, especially when integrating linguistic and acoustic data. For example, training a multilingual speech-to-text model requires large amounts of transcribed audio in each target language, often aligned with text in other languages for translation purposes.

Furthermore, in domains such as healthcare, law, and education, multilingual corpora facilitate the development of AI tools that break down language barriers, enabling better access to information and services for non-native speakers.

7.1.6 Challenges and Ethical Considerations

Despite their importance, multilingual corpora come with challenges related to quality, bias, and representativeness. Data collected from certain domains may overrepresent specific linguistic styles or cultural viewpoints, leading to biased AI outputs. Low-resource languages often lack sufficient data, creating performance disparities between languages in multilingual models.

Ethical concerns also arise when collecting corpora from the internet, especially regarding copyright, privacy, and the use of personal communications. Ensuring transparency in data sources and obtaining appropriate permissions are critical steps in ethical corpus development. Additionally, there is a growing emphasis on including underrepresented languages to promote linguistic diversity and prevent the dominance of only a few major languages in AI systems.

7.2 LANGUAGE COVERAGE AND RESOURCE IMBALANCE

Language coverage and resource imbalance in AI present a pressing challenge that affects millions of people worldwide. While high-resource languages enjoy advanced AI support, many others remain neglected, reinforcing global inequalities. Addressing this issue requires concerted efforts in data collection, model development, policy-making, and community engagement. By fostering equitable language representation in AI, we can build more inclusive technologies that empower all linguistic communities, preserving cultural heritage and enabling fair access to the digital future. The path toward truly multilingual AI is complex, but with sustained commitment, a more balanced and just linguistic landscape in technology is achievable.

To address language coverage and resource imbalance, a multi-stakeholder approach is necessary. Tech companies should invest in underrepresented languages, not just for ethical reasons but also to tap into new markets. Collaborative efforts between governments, academia, and local communities can accelerate data collection and model development for low-resource languages.

Additionally, AI researchers should explore innovative techniques such as unsupervised learning, where models can learn from minimal data, and federated learning, which allows decentralized data training while preserving privacy. Encouraging open-source contributions and sharing pre-trained models can also democratize access to multilingual AI tools. Raising awareness about linguistic diversity in AI is crucial. Advocacy campaigns, public funding initiatives, and educational programs can highlight the importance of preserving and digitizing minority languages. By prioritizing inclusivity, the AI community can ensure that technological progress benefits all languages and cultures, not just the most dominant ones.

7.2.1 Current State of Language Coverage in AI

Modern AI models, particularly large language models (LLMs), rely on vast amounts of textual data for training. Languages like English dominate the digital landscape, with an abundance of books, articles, websites, and social media content available for machine learning. As a result, AI systems perform exceptionally well in English but struggle with languages that have limited digital footprints. For instance, OpenAI's GPT-4 and Google's Gemini exhibit strong proficiency in high-resource languages but often underperform in languages like Swahili, Bengali, or Quechua.

The disparity in language coverage is evident in datasets used for training AI. Common multilingual datasets, such as Wikipedia, Common Crawl, and OSCAR, are heavily skewed toward a few dominant languages. While English Wikipedia contains over six million articles, many African and Indigenous languages have only a few hundred or even fewer entries. This data scarcity makes it difficult to develop robust NLP tools for underrepresented languages, perpetuating a cycle of exclusion where speakers of these languages are left behind in the AI revolution.

7.2.2 Causes of Resource Imbalance in Multilingual AI

Several factors contribute to the uneven distribution of language resources in AI. Historical and socioeconomic influences play a significant role, as colonial legacies and economic power have shaped which languages are prioritized in education, media, and technology. English, for example, has become the lingua franca of the internet, research, and global business, leading to disproportionate investment in English-centric AI tools.

Another key factor is the digital divide. Many low-resource languages are spoken in regions with limited internet access, reducing the amount of digitally available text. Even when speakers of these languages go online, they often use dominant languages for communication, further diminishing the digital presence of their native tongues. Additionally, the lack of standardized orthography for some languages complicates data collection and processing, making it harder to develop AI models for these languages. Finally, commercial incentives influence AI development. Tech companies prioritize languages with large user bases to maximize profitability, neglecting languages spoken by smaller populations. This market-driven approach exacerbates resource imbalances, leaving many languages without adequate AI support.

7.2.3 Consequences of Language Resource Imbalance

The consequences of unequal language coverage in AI are far-reaching. Linguistic bias in AI systems can marginalize entire communities, limiting their access to information, education, and economic opportunities. For example, machine translation tools like Google Translate perform well for high-resource languages but produce poor or nonsensical translations for many African and Indigenous languages. This creates barriers in healthcare, legal services, and education, where accurate communication is crucial.

Moreover, the lack of representation in AI entrenches cultural erasure. Language is deeply tied to identity, and when AI systems fail to support certain languages, the associated cultures and knowledge systems are further marginalized. Indigenous languages, which often carry unique ecological and historical knowledge, risk disappearing if they are not integrated into digital platforms.

From a technological standpoint, the over-reliance on high-resource languages limits the generalizability of AI models. A truly multilingual AI should perform well across diverse linguistic contexts, but current systems struggle with code-switching, dialectal variations, and low-resource language processing. This undermines the potential of AI to serve as a universal communication tool.

7.2.4 Efforts to Address Language Imbalance in AI

Recognizing the urgency of this issue, researchers and organizations are taking steps to improve language coverage in AI. One approach is the creation of specialized datasets for underrepresented languages. Projects like Masakhane, a community-driven initiative, focus on building NLP resources for African languages by engaging local speakers in data collection and model development. Similarly, the National Language Processing Consortium in India works on enhancing AI support for regional Indian languages.

Another strategy involves transfer learning and multilingual pre-training. Models like mBERT (multilingual BERT) and XLM-R are trained on multiple languages simultaneously, allowing knowledge from high-resource languages to improve performance on low-resource ones. While not a perfect solution, these methods help bridge the gap for languages with limited data. Governments and international bodies also play a role in promoting linguistic diversity in AI. Policies that mandate digital inclusion, funding for minority language projects, and partnerships with local communities can help expand language resources. The European Union, for instance, supports language technology projects through its Digital Single Market strategy, ensuring that smaller European languages are not left behind.

7.2.5 Challenges in Achieving Equitable Language Coverage

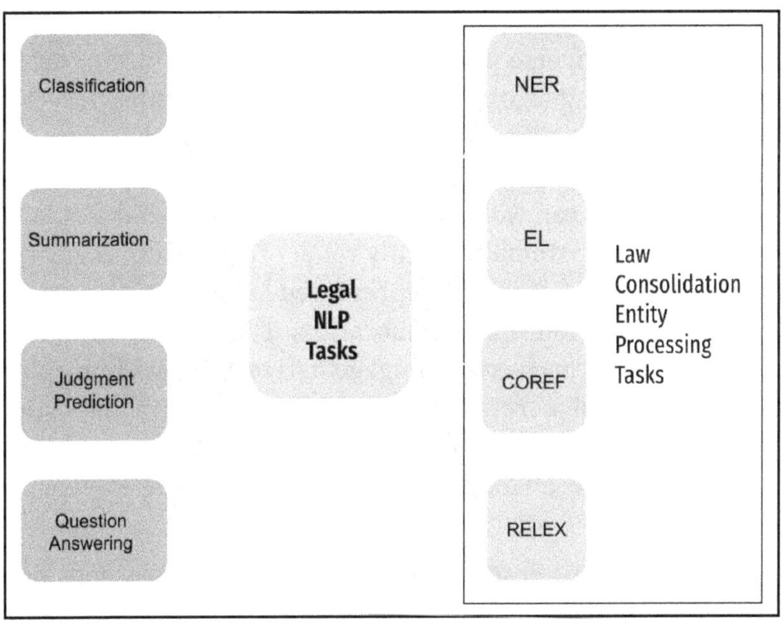

Fig: Challenges and Advances in Natural Language Processing

Despite these efforts, significant challenges remain in achieving balanced language representation in AI. Data scarcity is a persistent issue, as many languages lack sufficient digital content for training reliable models. Even when data exists, it may be fragmented across different dialects or writing systems, complicating NLP development. Another challenge is the lack of linguistic expertise in AI research. Many low-resource languages require native speakers and linguists to annotate data and validate models, but such collaborations are often underfunded. Without community involvement, AI systems may misinterpret cultural nuances or produce inaccurate outputs. Computational constraints also pose a barrier. Training multilingual models requires substantial computational power, which is expensive and environmentally taxing. Smaller organizations and researchers from low-income regions may lack the resources to develop competitive AI solutions for their languages, reinforcing dependency on Western tech giants.

7.3 DATA COLLECTION FOR UNDERREPRESENTED LANGUAGES

The collection of linguistic data for underrepresented languages represents a crucial challenge in the development of inclusive natural language processing technologies. Community-centered approaches, crowdsourcing methods, and technological innovations have created new opportunities for gathering the resources needed to build effective multilingual AI systems. The ethical considerations and quality control mechanisms essential to these efforts ensure that data collection practices are responsible and beneficial to language communities.

As research in this area continues to advance, the creation of more comprehensive and representative linguistic datasets will support the development of technologies that serve diverse global populations. The future of data collection for underrepresented languages is marked by opportunities for collaboration and innovation that will enhance our ability to build language technologies accommodating the rich diversity of human communication. Through continued efforts in this domain, we can work toward bridging the digital divide in language technology and creating systems that truly reflect the world's linguistic diversity. The future of data collection for underrepresented languages is marked by exciting opportunities for innovation and collaboration. The continued development of community-centered approaches that engage native speakers in meaningful ways will support the creation of more authentic and representative linguistic resources. Advances in mobile and web technologies will facilitate more distributed and accessible data collection, enabling contributions from diverse populations of language users.

The integration of linguistic research with computational methods presents new possibilities for developing sophisticated data collection strategies. The application of techniques from fields such as computational sociolinguistics can enhance our understanding of language variation and use patterns. As natural language processing technologies continue to evolve, the development of more efficient and effective data collection methods will support the creation of language technologies that serve diverse global communities. The combination of technological innovations with community engagement strategies promises to further advance our ability to build inclusive language technologies that accommodate the rich diversity of human communication.

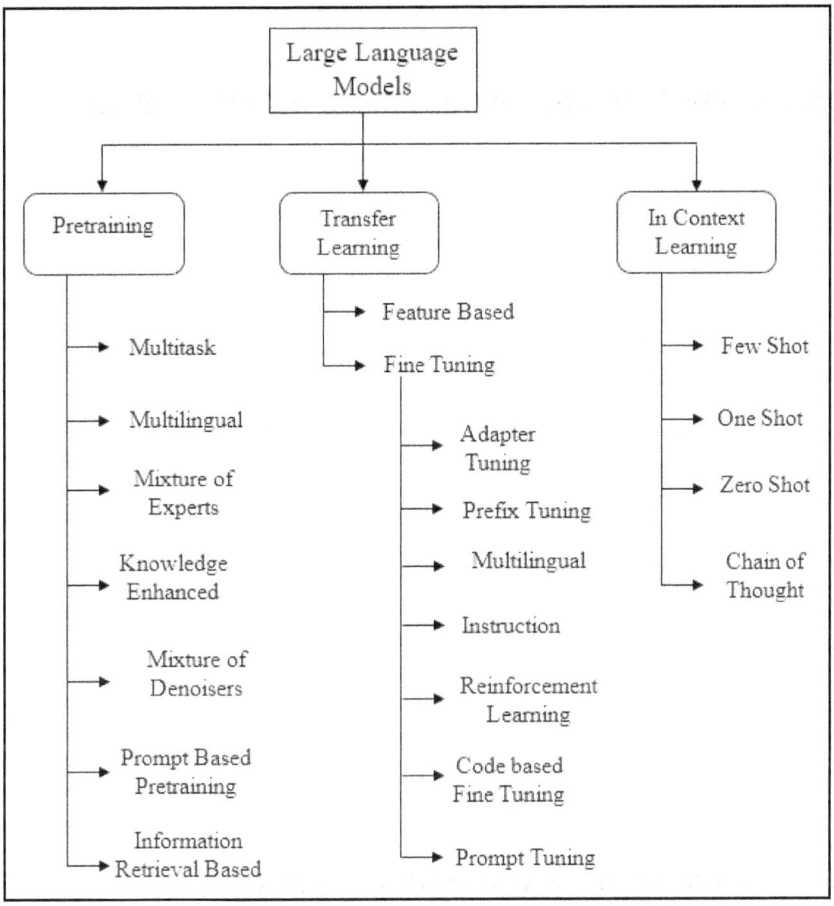

Fig: Current Trends, Techniques, and Challenges in Large Language Models

7.3.1 Digital Divide in Language Technology

The disparity in available digital resources between high-resource and low-resource languages represents one of the most significant challenges in modern computational linguistics. While languages like English, Chinese, and Spanish benefit from vast amounts of annotated text data, many of the world's languages lack sufficient digital documentation to support the development of effective natural language processing systems. This digital divide reflects broader issues of representation and access in technology development, where certain linguistic communities remain underserved by the latest advancements in artificial intelligence. The consequences of this imbalance extend beyond mere technological limitations to encompass cultural and social dimensions. When language technologies primarily support a small subset of the world's linguistic diversity, they risk marginalizing communities whose languages lack digital representation. This situation creates barriers to information access, educational opportunities, and participation in the digital economy. Addressing this challenge requires concerted efforts to collect and curate linguistic data from underrepresented languages, creating the foundational resources needed to develop more inclusive AI systems.

7.3.2 Community-Centered Approaches to Data Collection

Effective data collection for underrepresented languages necessitates approaches that center the knowledge and participation of native speaker communities. These methods recognize that linguistic data carries cultural significance and must be gathered in ways that respect community values and priorities. Community-centered approaches involve collaborating with language speakers to determine what data should be collected, how it should be gathered, and what purposes it might serve. This participatory model ensures that the resulting datasets reflect authentic language use while empowering communities to shape the development of technologies that affect them.

The implementation of community-centered data collection requires building trust and establishing meaningful relationships with language communities. Researchers must engage with community members as equal partners in the process, recognizing their expertise and cultural knowledge. This approach often involves training community members in data collection techniques while adapting methods to accommodate local contexts and linguistic characteristics. The resulting datasets tend to be more representative of actual language use patterns and cultural contexts, providing better foundations for developing culturally appropriate AI systems.

7.3.3 Crowdsourcing and Participatory Platforms

Crowdsourcing has emerged as a valuable method for collecting linguistic data from geographically dispersed communities of speakers. When implemented with careful consideration of ethical principles and community engagement, these approaches can efficiently gather large volumes of text, speech, and annotated data. Participatory platforms that enable community members to contribute language samples through mobile applications or web interfaces have shown particular promise for underrepresented languages. These systems can be designed to accommodate various input methods, including speech recording, text entry, and collaborative annotation.

The success of crowdsourcing initiatives depends on several key factors that ensure quality and engagement. Clear instructions and examples help contributors understand what types of data are needed and how to provide them effectively.

Feedback mechanisms allow for continuous improvement of the collection process while recognizing valuable contributions. Incentive structures should be designed to appropriately compensate participants for their time and expertise. Gamification elements can enhance engagement by making the contribution process more interactive and rewarding. When properly implemented, these approaches can create substantial datasets that reflect diverse language use patterns across different contexts.

7.3.4 Ethical Considerations in Linguistic Data Collection

The collection of linguistic data from underrepresented languages raises important ethical considerations that must be carefully addressed to ensure responsible research practices. Issues of informed consent are particularly significant, as contributors should fully understand how their language samples will be used and what potential applications might emerge from the collected data. The protection of privacy becomes especially crucial when dealing with languages that may contain culturally sensitive information or personal narratives. Researchers must implement robust data protection measures and establish clear guidelines for data usage and sharing.

Cultural sensitivity represents another critical ethical consideration in linguistic data collection. Language carries deep cultural significance, and its documentation must respect community values and traditions. Researchers should engage with cultural experts and community leaders to ensure that collection methods and potential applications align with local norms. The development of ethical guidelines that address issues of representation, ownership, and potential commercialization of linguistic data is essential for conducting responsible research. These considerations help ensure that data collection efforts benefit language communities while respecting their rights and cultural heritage.

7.3.5 Annotation Challenges and Quality Control

The annotation of linguistic data from underrepresented languages presents particular challenges that require specialized approaches. Many of these languages lack standardized orthographies or established annotation guidelines, necessitating the development of language-specific protocols. The creation of these annotation schemes should involve collaboration with native speakers who can provide insights into the linguistic and cultural nuances that affect how data should be labeled. This participatory approach helps ensure that the resulting annotations accurately reflect the language's structure and usage patterns.

Quality control mechanisms are crucial for maintaining the reliability of annotated data. These may include multiple rounds of review by different annotators, consistency checks that verify labeling accuracy, and validation procedures that assess inter-annotator agreement. The training of annotators who are native speakers of the target language can significantly improve annotation quality, as they bring essential linguistic and cultural knowledge to the process. The development of annotation tools that support the specific scripts and linguistic features of underrepresented languages is also important for facilitating accurate labeling. These quality assurance measures help create datasets that can effectively support the development of natural language processing technologies.

7.3.6 Leveraging Existing Linguistic Resources

While many underrepresented languages lack extensive digital resources, there are often existing materials that can support data collection efforts. Historical texts, literary works, and media content in the target language can provide valuable sources of linguistic data when properly digitized and processed. Existing linguistic research and documentation may contain important information about grammatical structures, vocabulary, and language use patterns that can inform data collection strategies. The adaptation of these resources requires careful consideration of copyright and cultural sensitivity issues but can provide foundational corpora for developing language technologies.

The transfer of knowledge from related languages can also support data collection efforts. Languages that belong to the same family or share geographical proximity often exhibit similar linguistic characteristics that can be leveraged to bootstrap NLP development. Techniques such as transfer learning can help overcome the initial scarcity of data by applying knowledge from high-resource to low-resource languages. These approaches require careful adaptation to account for linguistic differences but can provide valuable starting points for developing language technologies. The combination of existing resources with new data collection efforts creates more comprehensive datasets that better represent underrepresented languages.

7.3.7 Technological Innovations Supporting Data Collection

Recent technological advancements have created new opportunities for collecting linguistic data from underrepresented languages. Mobile applications and web platforms can facilitate distributed data collection, enabling contributors to submit language samples from various locations. These technologies can incorporate speech recognition, text input, and annotation tools that accommodate the specific characteristics of different languages. The development of user-friendly interfaces that support multiple scripts and input methods is essential for engaging diverse contributors and gathering comprehensive datasets.

Automated transcription and translation tools can support data collection efforts by providing initial processing of speech or text samples. While these tools may not be perfectly accurate for underrepresented languages, they can offer a starting point for human review and correction. The integration of active learning techniques can help prioritize which samples should be collected or annotated next, optimizing the data collection process. These technological approaches can significantly enhance the efficiency and effectiveness of linguistic data collection, particularly when combined with community engagement strategies.

7.4 ANNOTATION AND LABELING CHALLENGES

Annotation and labeling challenges in multilingual AI reflect the broader complexities of language diversity, cultural context, and technological limitations. Accurate labeling requires more than simple linguistic competence; it demands deep cultural awareness, consistency across annotators, and the ability to work with diverse scripts and orthographies. Technical constraints in annotation tools, scarcity of qualified annotators for low-resource languages, and ethical considerations further complicate the process.

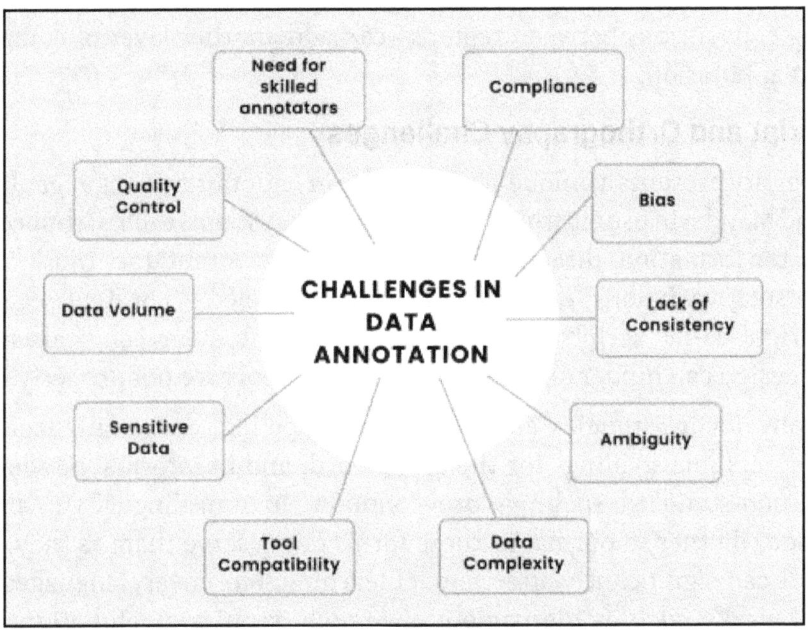

Fig: Data Annotation and Labeling

As multilingual AI continues to advance, overcoming these challenges will require a combination of technological innovation, improved training for annotators, and stronger cross-lingual collaboration. Building inclusive and representative datasets is essential not only for enhancing AI performance but also for ensuring that multilingual systems serve global communities fairly and effectively. By addressing the difficulties of annotation and labeling head-on, researchers and practitioners can create more robust, equitable, and culturally sensitive AI systems that bridge language barriers worldwide.

7.4.1 Complexity of Linguistic Diversity

One of the primary challenges in annotating multilingual data is the inherent diversity of languages. Each language possesses unique grammatical structures, syntactic rules, idiomatic expressions, and semantic frameworks. What may be a straightforward annotation task in English could require entirely different rules in a morphologically rich language such as Finnish or Turkish. For example, labeling part-of-speech tags becomes more complicated when a single word in one language may carry multiple morphemes that express tense, number, and case. Additionally, some languages rely heavily on word order to convey meaning, while others use inflection, making alignment and labeling inconsistent across datasets.

The diversity is further amplified when dealing with multilingual corpora containing both resource-rich and low-resource languages. In low-resource languages, the scarcity of linguistic expertise often means that annotators may have to work with limited guidelines or develop them from scratch, increasing the likelihood of errors. Furthermore, orthographic variations—such as differences in spelling conventions between regions—can add another layer of complexity to consistent annotation.

7.4.2 Script and Orthography Challenges

Script diversity presents a unique set of hurdles in annotation. Languages like Hindi, Arabic, and Mandarin use entirely different writing systems, each with specific rules for character formation, directionality, and spacing. Annotators must be trained to handle such variations, ensuring that text is labeled accurately regardless of script. In right-to-left scripts such as Arabic or Hebrew, even technical aspects like interface design can hinder annotation if software tools are not properly localized.

Orthography inconsistencies also complicate labeling. Some languages permit multiple acceptable spellings for the same word, and in informal or social media contexts, non-standard spellings are common. In multilingual AI, annotators must decide whether to normalize these forms or preserve them as they appear, a choice that can significantly affect model learning. Moreover, languages that use diacritical marks, such as Vietnamese or French, require careful attention since omitting or misplacing such marks can change meanings entirely.

7.4.3 Cultural and Contextual Ambiguity

A significant challenge in multilingual annotation arises from cultural and contextual ambiguity. Words and phrases often carry meanings deeply rooted in cultural contexts, and a direct translation or literal annotation may fail to capture their true significance. Sentiment analysis offers a clear example: certain expressions that indicate irony, sarcasm, or politeness in one culture may not translate neatly into another language. Annotators must therefore understand not only the language but also the sociocultural norms governing its usage.

In multilingual AI, domain-specific contexts add further complexity. Legal terminology, medical jargon, or technical language often require specialized knowledge. Annotators working in one language may have difficulty finding exact equivalents in another, leading to inconsistent labels. For instance, a medical term in English may have multiple possible translations in another language, each varying in precision or regional acceptance. This variability can result in models that underperform when applied in cross-lingual settings.

7.4.4 Inconsistency among Annotators

Human annotation inevitably involves subjective judgment, and this subjectivity can lead to inconsistencies—especially in multilingual projects where multiple annotators are involved. Even with detailed annotation guidelines, different annotators may interpret instructions differently depending on their linguistic background and personal understanding of the task. This issue is exacerbated in multilingual contexts where guidelines must be adapted for different languages without losing their intended meaning. For example, in labeling named entities such as organizations or locations, some annotators may choose to translate names into the target language, while others may leave them in their original form. Such inconsistencies can produce noisy datasets that hinder the learning process for AI models. The problem becomes more pronounced when annotators come from different regions where the same language is spoken but with distinct dialects, spelling preferences, or word usage patterns.

7.4.5 Tool Limitations in Multilingual Annotation

The tools used for annotation often present limitations when handling multilingual data. Many annotation platforms are optimized for Latin-script languages, making it difficult to work with non-Latin scripts without encountering technical glitches. Poor font rendering, lack of support for bidirectional text, and absence of script-specific input methods can slow down annotation work and introduce errors. Additionally, automated pre-annotation systems, which are commonly used to speed up manual labeling, may not perform equally well across all languages. Models trained primarily on English or other dominant languages may produce inaccurate predictions for low-resource languages, forcing annotators to spend more time correcting mistakes. This can negate the efficiency gains such tools are meant to provide.

7.4.6 Quality Control and Evaluation Difficulties

Ensuring high-quality annotation in multilingual AI requires robust quality control measures, which themselves are challenging to implement across multiple languages. Gold standard datasets, often used for evaluation, may be available only for a few languages, making it difficult to assess annotation accuracy in low-resource settings. Even when gold standards exist, variations in cultural interpretation and linguistic norms can make them less universally applicable.

Inter-annotator agreement, a common metric for quality control, becomes harder to maintain in multilingual environments. Differences in training, cultural background, and language expertise among annotators can result in lower agreement scores, even when annotators are equally skilled. To address this, project managers often need to invest more in training and calibration sessions, which increases project costs and timelines.

7.4.7 Resource Constraints for Low-Resource Languages

Low-resource languages face unique annotation and labeling challenges due to a shortage of linguistic experts, reference materials, and pre-existing corpora. Annotators for such languages are often bilingual speakers with varying levels of formal training in linguistics, leading to inconsistencies in their work. In some cases, there may be so few qualified annotators that the workload becomes overwhelming, increasing the risk of fatigue-related errors. The scarcity of resources also limits the ability to create comprehensive annotation guidelines. Without clear rules, annotators may rely on personal judgment, which can cause significant variation in labeling. Additionally, the cost of recruiting and training annotators for rare languages can be prohibitive, making it difficult for research projects to scale multilingual efforts equitably.

7.4.8 Ethical and Privacy Considerations

Ethical concerns play a central role in annotation for multilingual AI. Annotators often work with sensitive data such as personal communications, legal documents, or medical records. In multilingual contexts, these concerns are amplified because privacy laws and cultural attitudes toward data usage differ from country to country. Annotators must be trained to recognize sensitive content and adhere to relevant privacy regulations while performing their tasks. There is also the issue of bias in labeled data. If annotators' cultural or linguistic perspectives influence labeling decisions, the resulting models may perpetuate stereotypes or produce discriminatory outputs. For example, sentiment labels in one cultural context may inadvertently reinforce negative associations when applied cross-culturally. Ethical annotation requires not only technical accuracy but also cultural sensitivity and inclusivity.

7.4.9 Emerging Solutions and Best Practices

Despite the many challenges, several strategies are being developed to improve annotation and labeling in multilingual AI. Advances in cross-lingual transfer learning reduce the need for extensive labeled data in every language, allowing models trained on one language to be adapted for others. Annotation guidelines are increasingly being designed with multilingual adaptability in mind, incorporating examples from multiple languages to reduce ambiguity.

Crowdsourcing platforms are also becoming more effective for multilingual annotation, as they allow diverse contributors to participate from different regions. While crowdsourcing can introduce variability, robust quality control mechanisms and training modules can help mitigate these risks. Additionally, integrating human-in-the-loop approaches ensures that annotators work alongside AI systems, correcting errors and refining datasets iteratively.

7.5 ETHICAL DATA SOURCING AND COMMUNITY PARTICIPATION

The development of multilingual AI must be guided by principles of ethical data sourcing and meaningful community participation. Without these considerations, AI risks replicating historical injustices, where dominant languages and cultures overshadow those with less power. By adopting transparent, consent-based data collection methods and actively involving language communities in AI development, researchers and companies can create more equitable and effective technologies. The future of AI should not be one of extraction and exclusion but of collaboration and empowerment, where all languages and their speakers have a voice in shaping the digital world. Ethical multilingual AI is not just a technical challenge—it is a moral imperative.

As AI continues to advance, the demand for diverse language data will only grow. Without ethical safeguards, this demand could lead to further exploitation of marginalized communities. However, if ethical data sourcing and community participation become standard practices, AI can become a force for linguistic empowerment rather than erasure.

Governments and regulatory bodies can play a role by establishing guidelines for ethical AI data collection, similar to the General Data Protection Regulation (GDPR) for personal data. International organizations like UNESCO could advocate for linguistic rights in AI, ensuring that minority languages are protected and promoted in digital spaces.

At the same time, AI developers must recognize that ethical practices are not just a moral obligation but also a strategic advantage. Models built with community involvement are more likely to be accurate, culturally relevant, and widely adopted. Companies that prioritize ethical sourcing will also build trust with users, avoiding the backlash that comes with exploitative data practices.

7.5.1 Importance of Ethical Data Sourcing in AI

Ethical data sourcing refers to the responsible collection, use, and distribution of linguistic data in ways that respect the rights and dignity of the people who generate it. In the context of multilingual AI, this means ensuring that datasets are gathered transparently, with informed consent, and in a manner that benefits the communities involved. Many widely used AI models are trained on data scraped from the internet without explicit permission from content creators, raising concerns about privacy, intellectual property, and cultural appropriation.

For example, large language models such as GPT-4 and BERT rely on massive datasets compiled from books, websites, and social media posts, often without the knowledge of the original authors. This practice is particularly problematic for Indigenous and minority languages, where data is scarce and often tied to cultural heritage. When AI companies extract this data without consultation, they risk exploiting communities that have historically been marginalized in technological development. Ethical sourcing requires a shift toward more accountable practices, where data contributors are recognized, compensated, or at least informed about how their language is being used.

7.5.2 Challenges in Ethical Data Collection for Multilingual AI

One of the primary challenges in ethical data sourcing is the lack of standardized frameworks for obtaining and using linguistic data. Unlike medical or financial data, which are often protected by strict regulations, language data exists in a legal gray area. Many AI developers assume that publicly available text can be freely used for training models, but this ignores the ethical implications of commodifying language without consent. Additionally, low-resource languages often lack formal documentation, making it difficult to ensure that datasets are accurate, representative, and culturally appropriate.

Another challenge is the power imbalance between AI developers and language communities. Large tech corporations and research institutions typically control the resources needed to build AI systems, while the speakers of minority languages have little influence over how their data is used. This dynamic can lead to situations where AI models are trained on data without community input, resulting in misrepresentations, stereotypes, or harmful biases. For instance, machine translation systems may produce offensive or incorrect outputs for certain languages if the training data is not carefully curated with native speakers' input.

Furthermore, the economic incentives of AI development often prioritize speed and scalability over ethical considerations. Companies racing to deploy multilingual AI solutions may cut corners in data collection, bypassing community engagement to save time and costs. This approach not only undermines trust but also risks producing AI systems that fail to meet the real needs of the languages they claim to serve.

7.5.3 Role of Community Participation in AI Development

Community participation is a crucial component of ethical AI development, ensuring that the people whose languages are being modeled have a say in how their data is used. Engaging native speakers, linguists, and cultural experts in the data collection and model training process can lead to more accurate, culturally sensitive, and inclusive AI systems. When communities are actively involved, they can help identify biases, correct errors, and ensure that their linguistic and cultural contexts are properly represented.

Several initiatives have demonstrated the value of community-driven AI projects. For example, Masakhane, a grassroots organization, works with African linguists and researchers to build natural language processing (NLP) tools for Indigenous African languages. By involving local speakers in dataset creation and model evaluation, the project ensures that AI solutions are tailored to the needs of the communities they serve.

Similarly, the First Nations Information Governance Centre in Canada advocates for Indigenous data sovereignty, emphasizing that Indigenous communities should control how their languages and knowledge are used in technology. Community participation also fosters long-term sustainability in AI development. When local stakeholders are empowered to contribute to and maintain language datasets, they can continuously improve AI models rather than relying on external entities that may lose interest over time. This approach not only enhances model performance but also strengthens linguistic preservation efforts, helping endangered languages thrive in the digital age.

7.5.4 Best Practices for Ethical Data Sourcing and Community Engagement

To address the ethical challenges in multilingual AI, developers and researchers should adopt best practices that prioritize fairness, transparency, and collaboration. One key principle is obtaining informed consent from data contributors. Rather than scraping text indiscriminately, AI teams should seek permission from authors, speakers, and cultural custodians before using their language data. This could involve partnerships with universities, cultural organizations, or local governments that act as intermediaries between AI developers and language communities.

Another important practice is compensating contributors fairly. Many low-resource language speakers come from economically disadvantaged backgrounds, and their labor in data annotation, transcription, or translation should be valued appropriately. Projects like the Latin American Alliance for Civic Technology have experimented with micro-payments and revenue-sharing models to ensure that data contributors benefit from the AI systems built using their input.

Transparency in data usage is also critical. AI developers should clearly document the origins of their datasets, the methods used for collection, and any potential biases or limitations. Open-access repositories with detailed metadata can help researchers and community members audit datasets, ensuring accountability in AI development. Additionally, AI models should be regularly evaluated with input from native speakers to detect and correct harmful biases or inaccuracies.

Finally, fostering long-term partnerships with language communities is essential. Rather than treating data collection as a one-time extraction process, AI developers should engage in ongoing dialogue with speakers, educators, and cultural leaders. This collaborative approach ensures that AI tools evolve in ways that align with community needs and values.

CHAPTER 8

Low-Resource and Endangered Languages

8.1 APPROACHES TO LOW-RESOURCE LANGUAGE MODELING

Approaches to low-resource language modeling require a careful balance of technological innovation, linguistic expertise, and community engagement. Transfer learning, data augmentation, multilingual modeling, and unsupervised methods offer powerful tools for overcoming data scarcity. However, the success of these methods depends heavily on the quality of the data, the availability of linguistic resources, and the cultural context in which the language is used.

For endangered languages, the stakes are especially high. AI technologies hold the potential not only to bridge communication gaps but also to preserve and revitalize languages at risk of extinction. Achieving this potential requires ethical collaboration with language communities, ensuring that they are active partners in the process. By combining advanced modeling techniques with respect for linguistic diversity, the AI community can contribute to a future where every language, no matter how small its speaker base, has a place in the digital world.

Ethical responsibility is central to work on low-resource and endangered languages. The process of collecting and modeling language data must respect community consent, cultural sensitivities, and intellectual property rights. Outsider-led projects that fail to engage with the language community risk exploitation, misrepresentation, and cultural harm.

Furthermore, the deployment of AI models for these languages should benefit the speakers themselves. This means prioritizing applications that address community needs, such as educational tools or communication aids, rather than focusing solely on commercial or academic goals. Ethical AI development also involves ensuring that technologies do not inadvertently accelerate language shift toward dominant languages by replacing rather than complementing local languages.

8.1.1 Low-Resource and Endangered Languages

Low-resource languages are characterized by a scarcity of digitized content, lack of comprehensive lexicons, and minimal availability of annotated corpora. These limitations hinder the application of data-intensive machine learning methods.

Endangered languages, while often low-resource, face the added urgency of being at risk of disappearing altogether. Many such languages are primarily spoken rather than written, which further complicates data collection. Additionally, they may exist in multilingual communities where dominant languages overshadow their use in education, media, and official contexts.

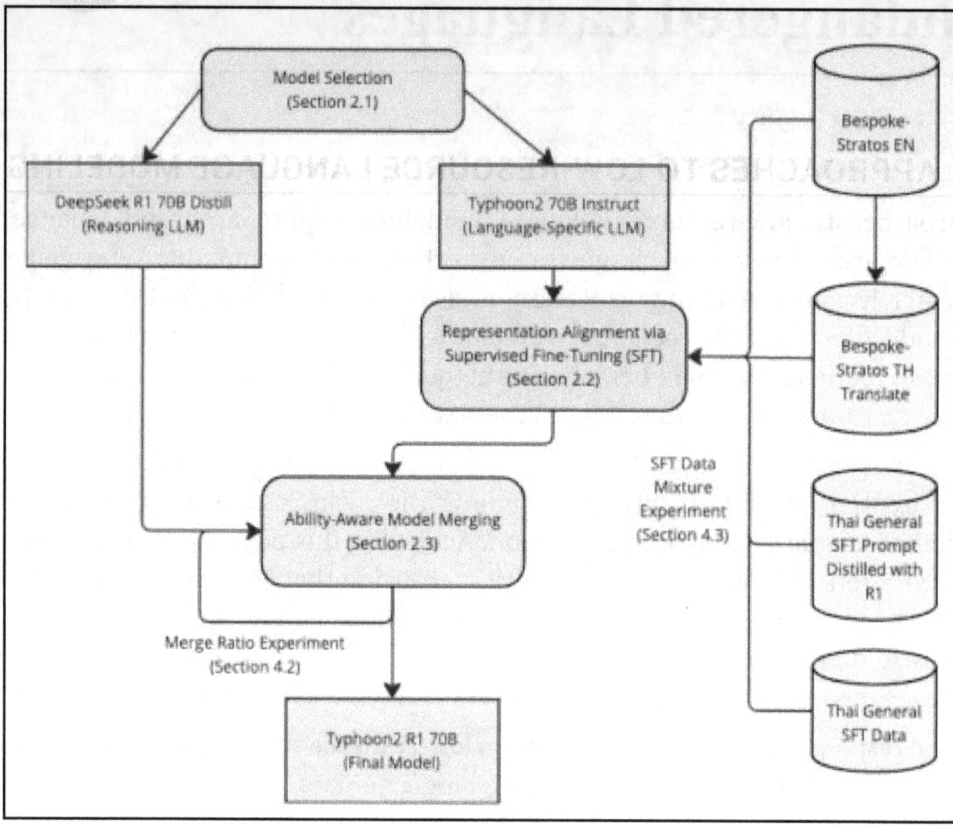

Fig: Approaches to Low-Resource Language Modeling

The challenges in modeling low-resource languages arise from their diversity in grammar, syntax, and phonetics. Some may use unique scripts that have little technological support, while others may be unwritten and rely solely on oral traditions. The variability of dialects, regional pronunciation differences, and limited standardization can further complicate the creation of robust AI systems for these languages.

8.1.2 Role of Transfer Learning in Low-Resource Language Modeling

Transfer learning has emerged as one of the most promising approaches for low-resource language modeling. In this method, models trained on high-resource languages are adapted for low-resource ones. The rationale is that many linguistic features are shared across languages, especially those from the same language family. Pretrained models such as multilingual BERT, XLM-R, and mT5 capture these shared patterns by training on multiple languages simultaneously. Once trained, they can be fine-tuned with a small amount of data in a target low-resource language. Transfer learning is particularly effective when the source and target languages share similar syntactic structures or vocabulary. For example, models trained on Spanish can often transfer knowledge to Catalan or Galician with relatively high accuracy. However, the approach is less effective when there are major typological differences, such as between English and Navajo. In such cases, additional techniques like cross-lingual embedding alignment are often necessary to bridge the gap.

8.1.3 Data Augmentation for Low-Resource Languages

Data augmentation strategies aim to artificially expand the available training data for low-resource languages. One widely used method is back-translation, where monolingual text in the low-resource language is translated into a high-resource language and then translated back, creating synthetic parallel corpora. This process increases the size of the dataset without requiring extensive human translation.

Another approach involves generating new training examples through paraphrasing, synonym replacement, or morphological variations, especially for morphologically rich languages. In speech processing tasks, augmentation can include speed perturbation, pitch modification, or background noise addition to diversify the training data. These techniques help improve the robustness of models, allowing them to generalize better to unseen data.

However, data augmentation has its limits. If the original dataset contains biases or errors, augmentation may amplify them. Careful quality control is essential to ensure that synthetic data maintains linguistic accuracy and cultural appropriateness.

8.1.4 Cross-Lingual and Multilingual Modeling Approaches

Cross-lingual models are designed to handle multiple languages within a single architecture, enabling knowledge sharing between them. By training a model on multiple languages simultaneously, low-resource languages can benefit from the richer data of high-resource ones. This approach is particularly useful in cases where languages share structural or lexical similarities.

Multilingual neural machine translation systems, for instance, can be trained on many languages at once, using a shared encoder-decoder framework. Such systems can perform zero-shot translation, where a model translates between two languages without having seen direct translation pairs during training. Cross-lingual embeddings also enable semantic representations of words from different languages to occupy a shared vector space, allowing for tasks like cross-lingual information retrieval and sentiment analysis.

While these models are powerful, they are not without drawbacks. When the number of languages grows, capacity constraints can lead to reduced performance for some languages. Balancing representation between high-resource and low-resource languages in the same model remains a challenge.

8.1.5 Community Involvement in Data Collection

One of the most effective strategies for building resources for low-resource and endangered languages is active collaboration with the language community itself. Native speakers are invaluable in collecting, verifying, and annotating data that accurately reflects the linguistic and cultural nuances of their language. This participation ensures that the data is representative and avoids the pitfalls of outsider-only interpretations.

Community-based projects often involve the development of dictionaries, transcription of oral histories, and recording of everyday conversations. In many cases, mobile applications are created to allow speakers to contribute content directly. Crowdsourcing platforms can facilitate this process, enabling distributed data collection from geographically dispersed communities.

Engaging with communities also promotes a sense of ownership over the preservation and technological development of their language. It aligns technological innovation with cultural preservation, ensuring that AI systems serve the people who use the language rather than replacing or marginalizing it.

8.1.6 Importance of Linguistic Resources and Standardization

For low-resource languages, developing standardized orthographies, dictionaries, and grammars is an essential preliminary step to effective language modeling. Standardization enables the consistent representation of words, phrases, and syntactic structures across datasets. Without this foundation, models may struggle to learn meaningful patterns.

Creating linguistic resources often involves collaboration between linguists, educators, and community leaders. In cases where multiple dialects exist, decisions about standardization must be made carefully to avoid excluding certain speaker groups. Digital tools such as keyboard layouts for unique scripts, optical character recognition systems, and spell checkers can also be developed alongside linguistic resources, supporting both human and machine processing of the language.

8.1.7 Leveraging Unsupervised and Semi-Supervised Learning

In scenarios where annotated data is extremely limited, unsupervised and semi-supervised learning methods can be powerful. Unsupervised learning enables models to discover patterns and structures in raw text or speech without labeled examples. For example, unsupervised machine translation systems learn to translate between languages by aligning their latent representations, even without parallel corpora. Semi-supervised learning combines a small set of labeled data with a much larger pool of unlabeled data, using the labeled examples to guide the learning process. Pseudo-labeling, where the model assigns labels to unlabeled data and then retrains on the expanded dataset, is one such technique. These methods can significantly reduce the reliance on costly manual annotation while still improving model performance.

8.1.8 Preservation of Endangered Languages through AI

Beyond enabling technological applications, low-resource language modeling plays a vital role in preserving endangered languages. AI-powered tools can help document these languages before they vanish, creating digital archives of text, speech, and cultural narratives. Machine learning systems can assist linguists in transcribing and analyzing recorded materials, speeding up the process of creating comprehensive language resources.

Moreover, educational applications built on AI models can support language revitalization efforts. These tools can provide interactive learning experiences, translation aids, and speech synthesis in endangered languages, encouraging younger generations to learn and use their heritage language. By integrating technology into everyday communication, the risk of language loss can be reduced.

8.2 TRANSFER LEARNING AND MULTILINGUAL PRETRAINING

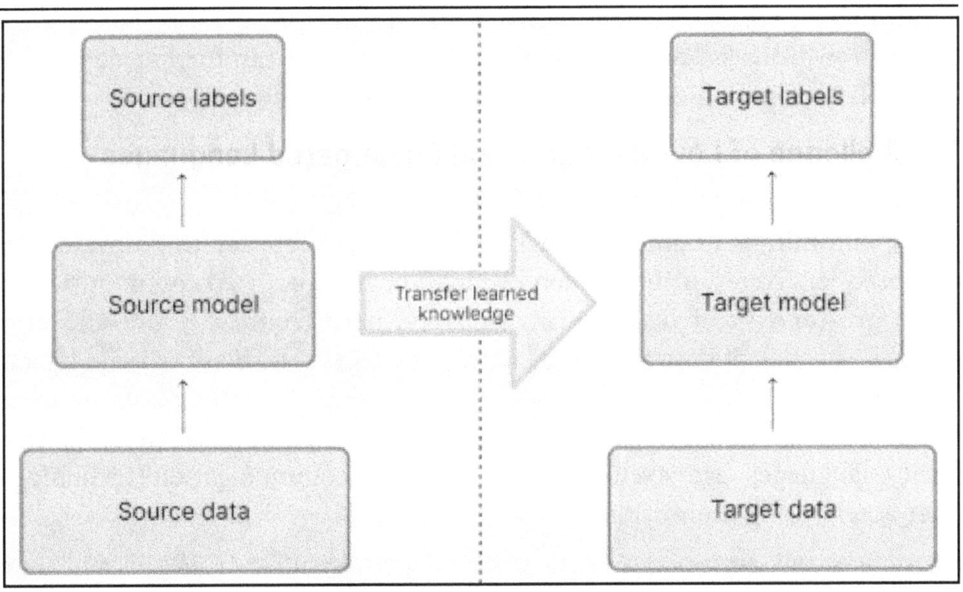

Fig: Transfer Learning

Transfer learning and multilingual pretraining represent powerful tools for addressing the challenges faced by low-resource and endangered languages in AI development. By leveraging knowledge from high-resource languages and fostering cross-lingual generalization, these techniques can help build more inclusive and effective NLP systems. However, technical solutions alone are insufficient—ethical data practices, community engagement, and sustainable development frameworks are equally crucial to ensuring that linguistic diversity thrives in the digital era.

The preservation of endangered languages is not just a technological challenge but a moral imperative. As AI continues to shape global communication, it must do so in a way that empowers rather than erases the world's linguistic heritage. Through collaborative innovation, we can harness the potential of transfer learning to create a future where no language is left behind. The future of transfer learning and multilingual pretraining lies in refining these techniques to better serve linguistic diversity. One promising direction is the use of unsupervised and self-supervised learning methods, which reduce reliance on annotated data by allowing models to learn from raw text or speech. Advances in few-shot and meta-learning could also enable models to adapt to new languages with even fewer examples.

Another critical area is the development of specialized models for language families or regional groups. Instead of training one massive model for hundreds of languages, researchers could create smaller, more efficient models tailored to specific linguistic clusters, improving performance and reducing computational costs. Interdisciplinary collaboration between AI researchers, linguists, anthropologists, and community advocates will be essential to ensure that technological advancements align with cultural preservation goals. Digital archives, crowdsourced datasets, and open-source tools can further democratize access to NLP technologies for endangered languages.

8.2.1 Challenge of Low-Resource and Endangered Languages

Low-resource languages are those with limited digital text corpora, few annotated datasets, and minimal computational resources available for NLP development. Endangered languages, often spoken by small or marginalized communities, face an even greater risk of disappearing entirely, both from daily use and digital platforms. The lack of data for these languages makes it difficult to train effective AI models using traditional methods, which rely on large amounts of labeled examples. Without intervention, this data scarcity perpetuates a cycle where minority languages are excluded from modern communication technologies, further accelerating their decline.

Many Indigenous, regional, and minority languages suffer from this imbalance. For instance, while languages like English have billions of words available in digital form, many African, Indigenous American, and Pacific Islander languages have only a few thousand—or even fewer—digitized texts. This disparity limits the development of essential NLP tools such as machine translation, speech recognition, and text-to-speech systems for these languages, reinforcing digital inequities.

8.2.2 Transfer Learning: Leveraging Knowledge across Languages

Transfer learning is a machine learning technique where a model trained on one task or dataset is adapted for use on another related task. In NLP, this often involves pretraining a model on a large corpus of high-resource language data and then fine-tuning it for a low-resource language. The underlying assumption is that linguistic patterns, such as syntax, semantics, and grammar, share universal features that can be transferred across languages.

One of the most successful applications of transfer learning in NLP is the use of pretrained language models like BERT (Bidirectional Encoder Representations from Transformers) and GPT (Generative Pretrained Transformer). These models are first trained on vast amounts of multilingual or monolingual text, learning general language representations. They can then be fine-tuned on smaller datasets specific to a low-resource language, significantly reducing the amount of task-specific data required. For example, a BERT model pretrained on a mix of Spanish, French, and English can be adapted to perform well in Quechua or Nahuatl with only a fraction of the data that would normally be needed.

8.2.3 Multilingual Pretraining: A Unified Approach for Multiple Languages

Multilingual pretraining takes transfer learning a step further by training a single model on data from multiple languages simultaneously. The idea is that the model will learn shared linguistic features that generalize across languages, allowing it to perform well even on those with limited individual data. Models like mBERT (multilingual BERT), XLM-R (Cross-lingual Language Model-RoBERTa), and mT5 (multilingual T5) have demonstrated strong cross-lingual capabilities, enabling tasks such as translation, text classification, and named entity recognition in low-resource settings.

A key advantage of multilingual pretraining is its ability to perform zero-shot or few-shot learning, where a model can handle a language it was not explicitly fine-tuned on by leveraging similarities with related languages. For instance, a model trained on several Bantu languages might generalize reasonably well to a new, under-resourced Bantu language with minimal additional training. This is particularly valuable for endangered languages, where even small gains in model performance can make a meaningful difference in digital preservation efforts.

8.2.4 Case Studies: Successes and Limitations

Several projects have demonstrated the potential of transfer learning and multilingual pretraining for low-resource languages. Google's Universal Speech Model (USM), for example, uses self-supervised learning on massive multilingual datasets to improve automatic speech recognition (ASR) for languages with little transcribed audio. Similarly, Meta's No Language Left Behind (NLLB) initiative employs advanced transfer learning techniques to enhance machine translation for over 200 languages, including many with scarce resources.

However, these approaches are not without limitations. One challenge is the risk of bias transfer, where models trained predominantly on high-resource languages may inherit structural or cultural biases that do not apply to the target language. For instance, a multilingual model might default to Western sentence structures when generating text in an Indigenous language with a different grammatical order. Additionally, languages with extremely limited data or significant dialectal variations may still struggle to achieve high accuracy, even with transfer learning.

8.2.5 Community Involvement and Ethical Considerations

While transfer learning and multilingual pretraining offer technical solutions to data scarcity, their success depends heavily on collaboration with the communities that speak low-resource and endangered languages. Ethical considerations must guide how data is collected, used, and shared to avoid exploitation or misrepresentation. Many Indigenous and minority language communities have expressed concerns about outside researchers or corporations extracting linguistic data without consent or proper acknowledgment.

Participatory approaches, where native speakers and local linguists are actively involved in dataset creation and model evaluation, can help ensure that AI tools are culturally appropriate and accurate. Initiatives like Masakhane in Africa and the Indigenous AI Consortium in North America emphasize community-led development, where technology serves the needs of language speakers rather than imposing external frameworks.

Moreover, long-term sustainability requires that these communities have the tools and knowledge to maintain and adapt AI models independently. Capacity-building programs that train local researchers in NLP techniques can empower communities to take ownership of their linguistic digital futures.

8.3 LEVERAGING HUMAN-IN-THE-LOOP SYSTEMS

Human-in-the-loop systems represent powerful tools for addressing the challenges of preserving low-resource and endangered languages. By combining computational efficiency with human expertise, these approaches create more effective solutions for language documentation, processing, and revitalization. The ethical implementation of these systems, through meaningful community engagement and cultural sensitivity, ensures that they support rather than undermine preservation efforts. As technology continues to advance, human-in-the-loop systems will play an increasingly important role in language preservation. The future of these technologies is marked by opportunities for innovation and collaboration that will enhance our ability to document and revitalize the world's linguistic diversity. Through continued development and responsible implementation, these systems promise to support the preservation of cultural knowledge and traditional practices embedded in endangered languages, helping to maintain the rich tapestry of global linguistic heritage for future generations.

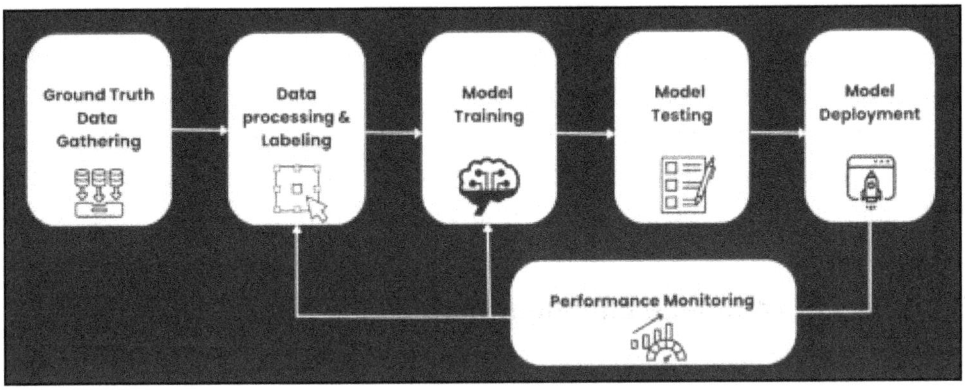

Fig: Human-in-the-Loop (HITL)

The development and implementation of human-in-the-loop systems for language preservation raise important ethical considerations that must be carefully addressed. Issues of cultural sensitivity and representation are particularly significant, as these technologies interact with languages that carry deep cultural meaning. The involvement of community members in the development process helps ensure that these systems respect cultural values and serve the needs of language communities.

The establishment of meaningful partnerships with language communities is essential for creating effective human-in-the-loop systems. These collaborations should be based on principles of mutual respect and shared benefits, where community members participate as equal partners in the development process. The implementation of clear guidelines for data usage and sharing helps protect cultural knowledge and intellectual property rights. The creation of technologies that empower rather than exploit language communities ensures that these systems support rather than undermine preservation efforts.

The future of human-in-the-loop systems for language preservation is marked by exciting opportunities for innovation and advancement. The continued development of more sophisticated computational models that can better leverage human expertise promises to enhance the effectiveness of these systems. The integration of multimodal approaches that combine language with visual or auditory information presents new possibilities for comprehensive documentation and processing. Advances in active learning techniques that can more efficiently incorporate human feedback will improve the performance of these systems while reducing the required human effort. The development of more accessible interfaces that accommodate users with varying technical expertise will expand the potential applications of these technologies. The creation of community-driven platforms that enable language speakers to contribute to and benefit from these systems will support more sustainable preservation efforts.

The ongoing collaboration between linguists, computer scientists, and language communities will be essential for advancing human-in-the-loop systems. The establishment of shared resources and best practices will support more effective development and implementation of these technologies. As these systems continue to evolve, they promise to play an increasingly central role in language preservation efforts, supporting the documentation and revitalization of the world's diverse linguistic heritage.

8.3.1 Crisis of Language Endangerment

The current state of global linguistic diversity reveals a troubling trend of language loss, with many of the world's languages facing imminent extinction. UNESCO estimates that nearly half of the approximately 7,000 languages spoken today are at risk of disappearing by the end of this century. This crisis of language endangerment stems from multiple factors including globalization, cultural assimilation, and the dominance of major languages in education and media. The consequences of language loss extend far beyond mere communication, encompassing the erosion of cultural knowledge, traditional practices, and unique worldviews embedded in these linguistic systems.

The documentation and preservation of endangered languages have become urgent priorities for linguists, anthropologists, and cultural preservationists. Traditional methods of language documentation, while valuable, often struggle to capture the full complexity of linguistic systems and their cultural contexts. The development of digital technologies offers new possibilities for comprehensive language preservation, but these approaches must be carefully designed to accommodate the specific characteristics of diverse linguistic structures. Human-in-the-loop systems present particularly promising solutions by combining computational efficiency with human expertise to create more effective documentation and processing tools.

8.3.2 Role of Human-in-the-Loop Systems

Human-in-the-loop systems represent a paradigm shift in language technology development by integrating human knowledge and judgment into computational processes. These approaches recognize that while artificial intelligence can process vast amounts of data efficiently, human expertise remains essential for understanding complex linguistic structures and cultural contexts. In the domain of language preservation, human-in-the-loop systems enable the creation of more accurate documentation by leveraging both computational power and human linguistic knowledge.

The implementation of these systems typically involves several key components working in concert. Computational models process initial language data, identifying patterns and generating preliminary analyses. Human experts then review and refine these outputs, providing corrections and additional context that improve the system's performance. This iterative process creates a feedback loop where the system continuously improves through human guidance. The result is a more sophisticated and culturally aware language technology that can better support preservation efforts.

8.3.3 Documentation and Corpus Development

One of the most critical applications of human-in-the-loop systems in language preservation is the development of comprehensive linguistic documentation and corpora. These resources serve as foundational elements for language revitalization efforts, providing materials for education, research, and cultural preservation. The creation of high-quality documentation requires sophisticated methods that can capture the full complexity of linguistic structures while accommodating cultural contexts.

Human-in-the-loop approaches to corpus development involve several stages of collaborative work between computational systems and human experts. Initial automated processing can identify basic linguistic patterns and generate preliminary transcriptions or translations. Human reviewers then refine these outputs, correcting errors and adding cultural context that enhances the documentation's accuracy and value. This collaborative process results in more comprehensive and reliable linguistic resources that can support various preservation efforts.

The development of these corpora must consider several important factors to ensure their effectiveness and cultural appropriateness. The inclusion of diverse language samples that represent different dialects, registers, and use contexts helps create more comprehensive documentation. The incorporation of metadata that captures cultural and situational information enhances the value of these resources for preservation purposes. The creation of accessible formats that can be used by community members and researchers alike ensures that these materials can effectively support language revitalization efforts.

8.3.4 Speech Recognition and Processing

Speech recognition technologies adapted for low-resource and endangered languages present significant challenges that human-in-the-loop systems can effectively address. The development of accurate automatic speech recognition (ASR) systems for these languages requires sophisticated methods that can handle unique phonological characteristics and limited training data. Human-in-the-loop approaches combine computational processing with human expertise to create more effective speech technologies.

The implementation of these systems typically involves initial automated processing of speech samples to generate preliminary transcriptions. Human experts then review and correct these outputs, providing valuable feedback that improves the system's accuracy. This iterative process allows the ASR system to learn from human corrections, gradually improving its performance on the specific language. The incorporation of linguistic knowledge about phonological patterns and cultural contexts enhances the system's ability to handle the unique characteristics of endangered languages.

The development of these speech technologies must consider several important factors to ensure their effectiveness. The collection of diverse speech samples that represent different speakers, dialects, and use contexts helps create more robust systems. The incorporation of prosodic and paralinguistic information that captures cultural nuances enhances the technology's ability to process natural speech. The creation of user-friendly interfaces that accommodate community members with varying technical expertise ensures that these technologies can effectively support language preservation efforts.

8.3.5 Machine Translation and Text Processing

Machine translation systems for low-resource and endangered languages face particular challenges that human-in-the-loop approaches can effectively address. The development of accurate translation technologies for these languages requires methods that can handle complex grammatical structures and limited parallel corpora. Human-in-the-loop systems combine computational processing with human linguistic expertise to create more effective translation solutions. The implementation of these systems typically involves initial automated translation of text samples followed by human review and correction. This process allows the system to learn from human feedback, gradually improving its performance on the specific language pair. The incorporation of cultural and contextual knowledge enhances the translation system's ability to produce more natural and appropriate outputs. This iterative approach results in more accurate and culturally sensitive translation technologies that can support language preservation efforts. The development of these machine translation systems must consider several important factors to ensure their effectiveness. The collection of diverse text samples that represent different genres, registers, and use contexts helps create more comprehensive systems. The incorporation of domain-specific knowledge that captures cultural nuances enhances the technology's ability to produce appropriate translations. The creation of accessible interfaces that accommodate community members with varying technical expertise ensures that these technologies can effectively support language revitalization efforts.

8.4 COMMUNITY-LED LANGUAGE TECHNOLOGY INITIATIVES

Community-led language technology initiatives represent a transformative approach to addressing the challenges of preserving low-resource and endangered languages. By placing native speakers at the center of technological development, these approaches create more culturally appropriate and sustainable solutions for language documentation and revitalization. The participatory nature of these initiatives ensures that technology serves the actual needs of language communities while respecting traditional knowledge systems and cultural values.

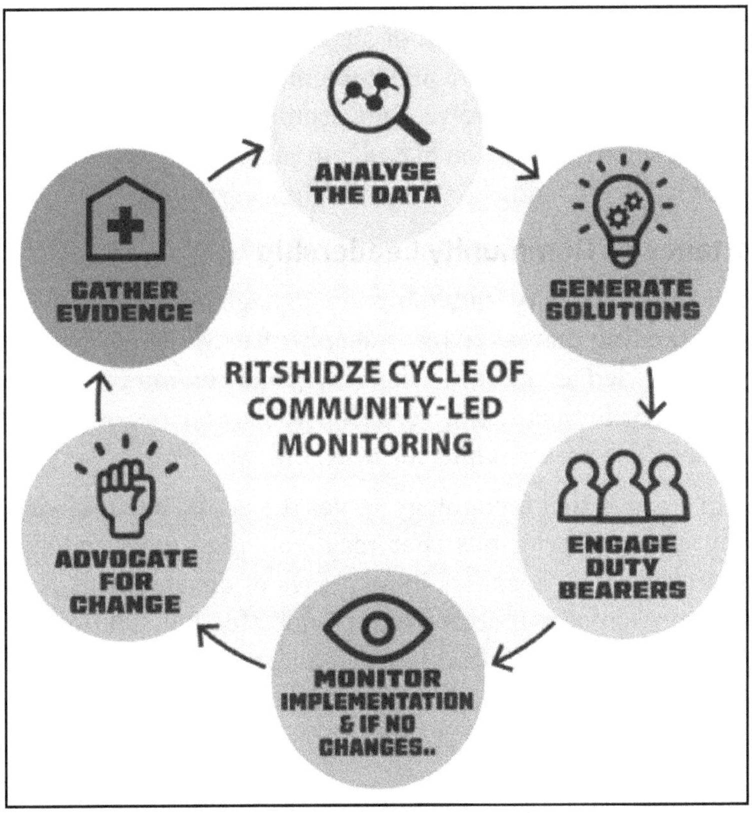

Fig: The Model for Community-Led Monitoring

As these community-led approaches continue to develop, they offer promising pathways for supporting the preservation of the world's linguistic diversity. The future of these initiatives is marked by opportunities for innovation and collaboration that will enhance our ability to develop language technologies accommodating the rich spectrum of human communication. Through continued efforts in this domain, we can work toward creating more inclusive technological solutions that support the revitalization of endangered languages and the preservation of cultural knowledge for future generations.

The future of community-led language technology initiatives is marked by exciting opportunities for innovation and collaboration. The continued development of participatory approaches that engage language communities in meaningful ways will support more effective and culturally appropriate solutions. Advances in mobile and web technologies will facilitate more accessible and distributed participation in language preservation efforts. The integration of traditional knowledge systems with computational methods presents new possibilities for developing sophisticated language technologies that respect cultural values.

The establishment of long-term partnerships between language communities, researchers, and technology developers will foster more sustainable language preservation initiatives. The creation of shared resources and best practices will support more effective development and implementation of language technologies. As these initiatives continue to evolve, they promise to play an increasingly central role in supporting the revitalization of endangered languages and the preservation of cultural knowledge embedded in these linguistic systems.

8.4.1 Importance of Community Leadership

The central role of community leadership in language technology initiatives stems from the understanding that language is deeply intertwined with cultural identity and traditional knowledge systems. When language communities take ownership of technological development, the resulting tools and resources better reflect authentic language use patterns and cultural contexts.

This leadership ensures that technology serves the actual needs of speakers rather than imposing external priorities that may not align with community values. The involvement of native speakers in all stages of development—from planning to implementation—creates more relevant and effective solutions for language preservation. Community-led initiatives also address historical power imbalances in language documentation, where external researchers often controlled the process and outcomes of linguistic studies.

By centering community knowledge and priorities, these approaches help redress these inequities while building local capacity for language preservation. The empowerment of language communities through technology initiatives fosters self-determination in cultural preservation efforts, supporting more sustainable and meaningful outcomes. This shift in approach represents a fundamental change in how language technology is developed and deployed.

8.4.2 Participatory Design in Language Technology

Participatory design methodologies have become essential components of community-led language technology initiatives. These approaches involve language community members as equal partners in the development process, from initial conceptualization through implementation and evaluation. The collaborative nature of participatory design ensures that technological solutions address actual community needs while respecting cultural values and traditional knowledge systems. This methodology typically involves iterative cycles of development where community feedback continuously shapes the evolving technology.

The implementation of participatory design in language technology initiatives requires careful attention to several key factors. Researchers must establish trust and build meaningful relationships with language communities, recognizing their expertise and cultural knowledge. The design process should accommodate diverse participation methods that consider varying levels of technical familiarity among community members. Clear communication about the purposes and potential applications of the technology helps ensure informed participation. These approaches often incorporate cultural protocols and traditional knowledge systems into the development process, creating more culturally appropriate solutions.

8.4.3 Community-Based Data Collection and Annotation

Data collection and annotation represent critical components of language technology development where community leadership proves particularly valuable. Language communities possess unique knowledge about authentic language use patterns, cultural contexts, and appropriate documentation methods that external researchers may overlook. Community-based approaches to data collection involve native speakers in gathering linguistic samples that reflect actual communication patterns across different contexts. This participatory process results in more comprehensive and culturally relevant datasets that better support language preservation efforts.

The annotation of linguistic data benefits significantly from community involvement, as native speakers can provide insights into the cultural and contextual nuances that affect how language should be documented. Community members can identify appropriate labels for linguistic features, determine relevant cultural metadata, and establish protocols for handling sensitive information. The training of community annotators helps build local capacity for language documentation while ensuring high-quality outputs. These collaborative approaches to data collection and annotation create more accurate and culturally appropriate resources for developing language technologies.

8.4.4 Localization and Adaptation of Language Tools

The localization and adaptation of language technology tools to specific cultural contexts represents another crucial area where community leadership proves essential. Generic language processing tools often fail to accommodate the unique linguistic structures, cultural references, and use patterns of specific communities. Community-led initiatives focus on adapting these technologies to local contexts, ensuring that they support authentic language use and traditional knowledge systems. This localization process typically involves modifying interfaces, adjusting processing algorithms, and incorporating cultural protocols that make the tools more relevant and effective.

The adaptation of language tools requires careful consideration of several important factors. Community members can identify which features and functionalities would be most valuable for local language preservation efforts. The incorporation of traditional knowledge systems and cultural references enhances the tools' ability to process language in culturally appropriate ways. The development of user interfaces that accommodate local scripts, input methods, and interaction patterns makes the technologies more accessible to community members. These localized tools better support language documentation, education, and revitalization efforts by aligning with actual community needs and use contexts.

8.4.5 Education and Capacity Building

Education and capacity building initiatives represent fundamental components of community-led language technology programs. These efforts focus on developing local expertise in language documentation, technology development, and preservation strategies. By building community capacity, these initiatives create more sustainable language preservation efforts that can continue beyond the duration of specific projects. The training programs typically involve multiple components that address both technical skills and cultural knowledge relevant to language preservation.

The implementation of education initiatives requires careful attention to several key considerations. The development of culturally appropriate curricula that incorporate traditional knowledge systems helps ensure that training aligns with community values. The use of participatory teaching methods that engage learners in meaningful ways enhances the effectiveness of these programs. The provision of ongoing support and mentorship helps participants apply their new skills to actual language preservation efforts. These capacity building initiatives create local expertise that can lead future technology development and language revitalization projects, fostering more sustainable outcomes.

8.4.6 Ethical Considerations and Cultural Protocols

The development and implementation of community-led language technology initiatives raise important ethical considerations that must be carefully addressed. Issues of cultural sensitivity and representation are particularly significant, as these technologies interact with languages that carry deep cultural meaning. The establishment of clear protocols that respect traditional knowledge systems and cultural values helps ensure that technology development aligns with community priorities. The protection of intellectual property rights and sensitive cultural information requires robust data management practices that consider local norms and values.

The creation of ethical guidelines that govern technology development and use helps prevent potential misuse or exploitation of cultural knowledge. These guidelines should be developed in collaboration with language communities to ensure they reflect local values and priorities. The implementation of informed consent procedures that clearly communicate the purposes and potential applications of the technology supports responsible participation. The establishment of ongoing relationships between researchers and communities fosters mutual understanding and helps maintain ethical standards throughout the development process.

8.4.7 Technological Innovations Supporting Community Initiatives

Recent technological innovations have created new opportunities for supporting community-led language technology initiatives. Mobile applications and web platforms can facilitate distributed participation in language documentation and technology development efforts. These tools can be adapted to accommodate local scripts, input methods, and interaction patterns that make them more accessible to community members. The development of user-friendly interfaces that support diverse technical expertise levels helps ensure broad participation in these initiatives.

Automated processing tools can assist with initial language documentation tasks while still incorporating human review and correction. These technologies can help manage large volumes of data while allowing community members to focus on the cultural and contextual aspects of annotation. The integration of machine learning techniques that can adapt to local language patterns enhances the effectiveness of these tools. The combination of technological innovations with community knowledge creates more powerful solutions for language preservation that better serve the needs of native speakers.

8.5 PRESERVATION OF INDIGENOUS AND ENDANGERED LANGUAGES WITH AI

The preservation of Indigenous and endangered languages is a race against time, but AI offers powerful tools to document, revitalize, and sustain them for future generations. However, technology alone is not enough—success depends on centering Indigenous voices, respecting data sovereignty, and fostering long-term collaborations that empower communities as active partners rather than passive beneficiaries.

AI's role should be that of an enabler, helping to amplify human efforts in language preservation rather than replacing them. By combining cutting-edge technology with deep cultural understanding, we can create a future where no language is left to silence, and every community has the means to keep its linguistic heritage alive in the digital age. The loss of any language diminishes humanity's collective wisdom; with ethical and innovative AI applications, we can help ensure that this wisdom endures.

8.5.1 Crisis of Language Endangerment and Its Implications

Language extinction is not merely the loss of words but the erosion of cultural identity, traditional knowledge, and historical memory. Indigenous languages encode unique worldviews, ecological wisdom, and oral traditions that are irreplaceable. When a language disappears, so does a community's connection to its ancestors, land, and collective identity. The decline of these languages is often accelerated by socioeconomic pressures, forced assimilation policies, and the dominance of global lingua francas such as English, Spanish, and Mandarin in education and media.

Many endangered languages also suffer from a severe lack of digital resources, making them invisible in the modern technological landscape. Without written corpora, speech datasets, or machine-readable dictionaries, these languages are excluded from natural language processing (NLP) advancements. This digital exclusion exacerbates their marginalization, as speakers are unable to access technology in their native tongues, further pushing them toward dominant languages. AI can help reverse this trend by creating tools that not only document but also actively support language use in digital and everyday contexts.

8.5.2 AI Technologies for Language Documentation and Preservation

One of the most immediate applications of AI in language preservation is automated speech recognition (ASR), which can transcribe spoken language into text. For languages with no or limited writing systems, ASR can help create the first written records, enabling literacy development and textual preservation. Projects like Google's Project Relate and Mozilla's Common Voice are pioneering community-driven efforts to collect speech data for underrepresented languages, empowering native speakers to contribute to their language's digital footprint.

Machine translation is another critical tool, allowing endangered languages to be accessible in more widely spoken languages and vice versa. While high-quality translation typically requires large parallel datasets, recent advances in low-resource machine translation, such as unsupervised and few-shot learning, are making it possible to develop usable systems with minimal data. For example, Meta's No Language Left Behind initiative has demonstrated promising results in translating between hundreds of languages, including those with scarce resources.

Text generation and conversational AI also offer innovative ways to keep languages alive. Chatbots and virtual assistants built for endangered languages can provide interactive learning tools for new speakers, while AI-generated stories or dialogues can supplement traditional oral storytelling. These technologies can be particularly impactful for younger generations, who may be more engaged with digital platforms than traditional language-learning methods.

8.5.3 Challenges in Applying AI to Low-Resource Languages

Despite its potential, AI-driven language preservation faces significant hurdles. The most pressing issue is data scarcity—many endangered languages lack sufficient audio recordings, transcribed texts, or annotated linguistic resources to train AI models effectively. In some cases, the only available data may be decades-old ethnographic recordings or handwritten notes from linguists, which are difficult to process algorithmically.

Another challenge is the diversity of linguistic structures. Indigenous languages often have complex morphological, phonetic, or syntactic features that differ drastically from high-resource languages. For instance, polysynthetic languages, which form entire sentences within single words, pose unique difficulties for NLP models trained on analytic languages like English. Without specialized adaptation, AI tools may produce inaccurate or nonsensical outputs, undermining their usefulness for preservation efforts.

Additionally, there are ethical concerns around data ownership and consent. Many Indigenous communities have historically been exploited by researchers who extract linguistic knowledge without providing long-term benefits. AI projects must avoid replicating these harms by ensuring that data collection and usage are governed by the communities themselves, with clear agreements on how the technology will serve their needs.

8.5.4 Community-Led AI: The Key to Ethical and Effective Preservation

The most successful AI preservation projects are those that prioritize community involvement at every stage, from data gathering to model deployment. Rather than imposing external solutions, researchers must collaborate with native speakers, elders, and local educators to co-develop tools that align with cultural values and practical needs. Participatory approaches ensure that AI systems are not only linguistically accurate but also contextually relevant.

Organizations like the Living Tongues Institute and the Endangered Languages Project have demonstrated the power of community-driven documentation, combining AI tools with grassroots activism. In Australia, the Barngarla language, once considered dormant, is being revitalized through a combination of AI-assisted dictionary development and community-led teaching programs. Similarly, the Cherokee Nation has integrated AI-powered speech recognition into language-learning apps, helping new learners practice pronunciation and fluency.

These initiatives highlight the importance of capacity building—training community members in AI and NLP techniques so they can maintain and expand language technologies independently. By equipping Indigenous groups with technical skills, preservation efforts become sustainable, allowing languages to evolve alongside digital innovation rather than being static artifacts of the past.

8.5.5 Innovations and Future Directions in AI for Language Preservation

Emerging AI methodologies are opening new possibilities for low-resource language preservation. Self-supervised learning, where models learn from raw data without extensive human annotation, is particularly promising for languages with limited labeled datasets. Projects like OpenAI's Whisper, which transcribes speech in multiple languages with minimal supervision, could be adapted to endangered languages with small amounts of recorded speech.

Another frontier is the use of AI for predictive language reconstruction. For languages with fragmentary records, neural networks can hypothesize missing vocabulary or grammatical structures by analyzing related languages. While not a replacement for native speaker knowledge, such tools can provide valuable starting points for reconstruction efforts. Gamification and immersive technologies also offer engaging ways to promote language use. AI-powered virtual reality (VR) environments, where learners interact with digital elders or practice conversations in simulated cultural settings, could make language acquisition more dynamic and culturally resonant.

CHAPTER 9

Ethics, Bias, and Responsible AI

9.1 LANGUAGE BIAS AND REPRESENTATION IN AI

Language bias and representation in AI highlight the intersection of technology, culture, and society. While AI systems offer unprecedented opportunities for global communication and knowledge access, they also risk reinforcing existing inequalities if biases in language processing go unaddressed. From gender and racial stereotypes in embeddings to the underrepresentation of low-resource languages, the consequences of bias are far-reaching.

Overcoming these challenges requires a comprehensive approach that combines technical innovations with ethical responsibility and cultural sensitivity. Inclusive data practices, community collaboration, and transparency in AI development are essential to creating systems that represent humanity in its full diversity. Ultimately, addressing language bias is not only about improving AI performance but also about ensuring that digital technologies serve as tools for equity, representation, and cultural preservation in a multilingual world.

The question of language bias in AI extends beyond fairness in technical performance to broader ethical and social dimensions. Who gets represented in language models, and whose voices are excluded, shapes how societies experience digital technologies. If AI continues to reproduce stereotypes or exclude minority languages, it risks reinforcing existing inequalities and marginalization. Conversely, inclusive representation in AI can empower communities, preserve linguistic diversity, and foster cross-cultural understanding.

There is also the issue of consent and ownership in data collection. Communities whose languages are digitized for AI systems should have agency over how their linguistic resources are used. Without such agency, there is a risk of data extraction that benefits corporations or researchers while offering little in return to the communities whose language is being modeled. Ethical AI development must therefore respect the rights of language communities and ensure that technological progress benefits them directly. Looking forward, the challenge of language bias requires sustained efforts across research, industry, and policy. Technological innovations such as unsupervised learning and multilingual pretraining hold promise for reducing dependence on large annotated datasets, potentially narrowing the gap between high-resource and low-resource languages. However, technology alone cannot solve the problem. Policies that prioritize linguistic diversity and inclusivity, combined with educational initiatives to raise awareness about bias in AI, are equally important.

Collaborative global initiatives can also play a transformative role. Partnerships between governments, academic institutions, and local communities can help build open-access datasets for underrepresented languages, ensuring broader participation in AI development. Such initiatives not only reduce language bias but also contribute to preserving endangered languages in the digital sphere.

9.1.1 Sources of Language Bias in AI

Bias in language-based AI systems originates from several sources, the most significant being training data. Machine learning models are trained on large corpora, much of which is scraped from the internet. Since online platforms contain uneven distributions of linguistic styles, cultural perspectives, and social demographics, models trained on such data may overrepresent dominant groups while underrepresenting marginalized communities. For example, English-language content vastly outweighs material in less widely spoken languages, leading to systems that perform well for English but poorly for others.

Algorithmic design choices also contribute to bias. Word embeddings, for instance, capture statistical associations between words in a corpus. If the training data associates certain professions primarily with men and caregiving roles with women, the embedding space will encode these stereotypes, which then propagate into downstream applications. Additionally, evaluation benchmarks, which are often created in high-resource languages and specific cultural contexts, may not account for the full diversity of human language, reinforcing biased performance assessments.

9.1.2 Representation and Power Dynamics in Language Data

Language is not only a means of communication but also a reflection of power dynamics in society. In AI, the overrepresentation of certain languages, dialects, and cultural expressions reinforces existing inequalities. For example, global AI systems often privilege standard forms of major world languages such as English, French, or Mandarin, while dialects, creoles, and indigenous languages remain underrepresented. This lack of representation can marginalize speakers of these languages by excluding them from accessing AI-driven technologies.

The dominance of Western cultural norms in training datasets also leads to skewed representations of values, idioms, and worldviews. When AI systems interpret or generate text, they may present these perspectives as universal, inadvertently silencing alternative cultural narratives. In multilingual AI systems, this imbalance becomes particularly pronounced, as the voices of smaller linguistic communities are drowned out by those of larger, more influential groups. Thus, language bias in AI is not merely a technical issue but also a question of cultural equity and representation.

9.1.3 Gender, Racial, and Cultural Bias in Language Models

One of the most visible forms of language bias in AI is the reinforcement of gender and racial stereotypes. Studies have shown that large language models trained on internet data often associate women with domestic roles and men with professional roles. Similarly, certain racial or ethnic groups are disproportionately linked with negative attributes in generated text. These associations arise because the models learn from the statistical regularities in their training data without distinguishing between neutral information and harmful stereotypes.

Cultural bias also manifests when AI systems fail to recognize or appropriately handle expressions from specific cultural contexts. Humor, irony, or idioms often lose their meaning when processed by AI that is not trained on diverse cultural corpora. In customer service chatbots or translation systems, such failures can lead to miscommunication and frustration, further alienating users who do not conform to the dominant cultural norms encoded in the system. The persistence of these biases raises important ethical questions about fairness and inclusivity in AI applications.

9.1.4 Multilingual Inequities and Low-Resource Languages

Language bias is particularly evident in the disparity between high-resource and low-resource languages. High-resource languages benefit from large amounts of digitized text and extensive linguistic research, enabling AI models to achieve high accuracy in tasks such as translation, summarization, and sentiment analysis. In contrast, low-resource languages often lack sufficient training data, annotated corpora, or technological infrastructure. As a result, AI systems tend to perform poorly for these languages, perpetuating digital exclusion for their speakers.

Endangered and indigenous languages face even greater risks. Without deliberate efforts to collect and model these languages, they may remain invisible in AI systems, reinforcing broader trends of linguistic marginalization. This inequity limits access to digital services for entire communities and reduces the chances of preserving linguistic diversity in the digital age. Efforts to incorporate low-resource languages into AI systems must therefore go hand in hand with broader initiatives to address language bias and representation.

9.1.5 Consequences of Language Bias in AI Applications

The impact of language bias extends into numerous real-world applications. In machine translation, biased systems may mistranslate gendered pronouns or perpetuate stereotypes in translated text. In sentiment analysis, models trained predominantly on Western cultural expressions of emotion may misinterpret sentiment in non-Western languages. Speech recognition systems trained on standard dialects may fail to accurately transcribe regional or minority accents, creating barriers in accessibility technologies.

Bias also affects the credibility and trustworthiness of AI systems. Users who experience consistent misrepresentation of their language, culture, or identity may lose trust in AI tools, limiting their adoption. In high-stakes domains such as healthcare, legal systems, or education, biased language technologies can have particularly harmful consequences by misclassifying critical information or excluding vulnerable populations from equitable access.

9.1.6 Strategies for Mitigating Language Bias

Addressing language bias in AI requires a combination of technical, cultural, and ethical strategies. On the technical front, diversifying training data is essential. This means deliberately including data from underrepresented languages, dialects, and cultural contexts. Balanced corpora can help reduce the dominance of majority voices in AI systems. Another approach involves debiasing algorithms, which adjust embeddings or model weights to reduce harmful associations while preserving semantic accuracy.

Beyond technical solutions, collaboration with diverse communities is critical. Engaging native speakers, cultural experts, and marginalized groups in data collection and evaluation processes ensures that AI systems reflect a broader spectrum of human experience. Transparency in how datasets are constructed and how biases are mitigated also builds accountability. Ethical frameworks must guide developers in prioritizing fairness and inclusivity, ensuring that AI systems serve not only the majority but also those on the margins.

9.2 CULTURAL SENSITIVITY IN MULTILINGUAL MODELS

Cultural sensitivity in multilingual AI is not a luxury but a necessity. As these technologies become ubiquitous, their ability to navigate cultural complexities will determine whether they unite or divide global communities. Achieving this goal requires a commitment to diversity, collaboration, and continuous learning—from diversifying datasets to engaging with cultural experts and prioritizing transparency.

The path forward is clear: AI must be designed with cultural humility, recognizing that no model can fully capture the richness of human experience but striving to do better with each iteration. By centering cultural sensitivity in AI development, we can create systems that not only communicate across languages but also bridge cultural divides, fostering understanding and respect in an increasingly interconnected world. The future of AI should be one where every language and culture is not just represented but truly seen and valued.

9.2.1 Importance of Cultural Context in Language AI

Language does not exist in a vacuum; it is shaped by history, traditions, and societal values. A word or phrase that is neutral in one culture may carry strong connotations in another. For example, idiomatic expressions, honorifics, and even humor vary widely across languages, and AI models that lack cultural awareness can misinterpret or misrepresent them. When machine translation systems convert text without considering these subtleties, the results can range from awkward to outright harmful. A well-known example is Google Translate's historical tendency to default to masculine pronouns in gender-neutral languages, reinforcing stereotypes and erasing non-binary identities.

Cultural sensitivity also extends to how AI handles topics such as religion, politics, and social hierarchies. In some cultures, certain names, gestures, or historical references may be deeply significant or taboo, and an AI that fails to recognize these sensitivities risks causing offense or spreading misinformation. For instance, an AI chatbot trained primarily on Western data might struggle to respond appropriately to queries about Indigenous land rights or traditional ceremonies, inadvertently trivializing or misrepresenting them. Addressing these challenges requires more than just larger datasets—it demands intentional design that prioritizes cultural competence alongside linguistic accuracy.

9.2.2 Challenges in Building Culturally Sensitive AI Models

One of the biggest obstacles to cultural sensitivity in AI is the inherent bias in training data. Most large-scale multilingual datasets are sourced from the internet, which disproportionately represents dominant languages and cultures. Low-resource languages, Indigenous languages, and dialects spoken by marginalized communities are often underrepresented or absent entirely. This imbalance means that AI models are more likely to reflect the perspectives of majority groups, further marginalizing minority voices. Additionally, datasets may contain outdated or stereotypical portrayals of certain cultures, which AI systems can inadvertently amplify.

Another challenge is the lack of standardized evaluation metrics for cultural sensitivity. While benchmarks like BLEU and ROUGE measure translation accuracy, they do not assess whether an AI's output respects cultural norms or avoids harmful stereotypes. Without clear guidelines, developers may prioritize fluency over appropriateness, leading to models that generate grammatically correct but culturally tone-deaf responses. Furthermore, cultural norms evolve over time, meaning that AI systems must be regularly updated to remain relevant and respectful. A third issue is the tension between generalization and localization. Multilingual models are often designed to handle many languages at once, which can lead to a "one-size-fits-all" approach that overlooks regional variations. For example, Spanish varies significantly between Spain, Mexico, and Argentina, not just in vocabulary but also in cultural references and social etiquette. An AI trained on a generic "Spanish" dataset may fail to capture these distinctions, resulting in outputs that feel foreign or inappropriate to local users.

9.2.3 Strategies for Improving Cultural Sensitivity in AI

To address these challenges, researchers and developers must adopt a multifaceted approach that prioritizes cultural awareness at every stage of AI development. One key strategy is diversifying training data to include more representative sources. This means actively seeking out texts, audio, and video from underrepresented communities, as well as collaborating with local speakers to annotate and validate datasets. Projects like Masakhane in Africa and the Indigenous AI Consortium demonstrate how community-driven data collection can lead to more culturally grounded models.

Another crucial step is incorporating cultural knowledge into model architectures. Techniques like cultural embeddings—where AI systems learn representations of cultural concepts alongside linguistic ones—can help models better understand context-specific meanings. For example, a model equipped with cultural embeddings might recognize that the word "thanks" carries different levels of formality in Japanese depending on the relationship between speakers. Similarly, fine-tuning models on culturally specific tasks, such as detecting and avoiding offensive language in particular regions, can improve their appropriateness.

Human-in-the-loop systems also play a vital role in ensuring cultural sensitivity. By involving native speakers and cultural experts in the training and evaluation process, developers can identify and correct biases before deployment. This might involve creating advisory boards of linguists and anthropologists or implementing real-time feedback mechanisms where users can flag culturally inappropriate outputs. For instance, Microsoft's Tay chatbot infamously adopted offensive language from users, highlighting the need for robust safeguards that align with cultural norms. Finally, transparency and accountability are essential. AI developers should document the cultural considerations behind their models, including data sources, potential biases, and limitations. Open-sourcing models and inviting community audits can help build trust and ensure that AI systems are held to high ethical standards. Companies should also establish clear protocols for addressing cultural missteps, such as issuing apologies or retraining models when errors occur.

9.2.4 Case Studies: Successes and Failures in Cultural Sensitivity

Several initiatives have shown promising progress in culturally sensitive AI. Google's Universal Speech Model (USM), for example, was trained on a diverse range of languages and dialects, enabling more accurate and context-aware speech recognition for underrepresented communities. Similarly, Meta's No Language Left Behind project incorporates cultural adaptation into its machine translation pipeline, ensuring that translations respect local idioms and customs.

On the other hand, there have been notable failures that underscore the consequences of neglecting cultural sensitivity. When Facebook auto-translated a Chinese user's name into an offensive term in Burmese, it sparked outrage and highlighted the dangers of language models that lack cultural context. Similarly, early versions of voice assistants like Siri and Alexa often misunderstood non-Western accents or failed to recognize culturally specific queries, alienating users from diverse backgrounds. These examples illustrate the real-world harm that can result from culturally insensitive AI and the urgent need for improvement.

9.2.5 Role of Policy and Industry Standards

Governments and regulatory bodies have a critical role to play in promoting cultural sensitivity in AI. Policies that mandate diverse representation in training data, require bias audits, and protect linguistic rights can help ensure that AI development aligns with societal values. The European Union's AI Act, for example, includes provisions for transparency and fairness that could be extended to cultural considerations. Similarly, UNESCO's guidelines on AI and ethics emphasize the importance of preserving cultural diversity in technology.

Industry-wide standards are also needed to establish best practices for culturally aware AI. Organizations like the Partnership on AI and the IEEE have begun developing frameworks for ethical NLP, but more work is required to create actionable guidelines for cultural sensitivity. Companies should adopt internal review processes that evaluate AI systems for cultural appropriateness, similar to how they assess privacy or security risks.

9.3 MISINFORMATION AND TOXICITY ACROSS LANGUAGES

The rapid advancement of artificial intelligence systems capable of processing multiple languages has transformed global communication, enabling unprecedented cross-lingual interactions and information exchange. However, this technological progress has also introduced complex challenges in identifying and mitigating misinformation and toxic content across diverse linguistic contexts. As AI systems become increasingly sophisticated in their multilingual capabilities, they face growing difficulties in accurately detecting harmful content that varies significantly across languages and cultures. The detection and prevention of misinformation and toxicity in multilingual environments present intricate technical and ethical challenges that demand innovative solutions combining computational methods with cultural and linguistic expertise.

The challenges of detecting and mitigating misinformation and toxicity in multilingual environments represent significant obstacles in the development of AI systems for global communication. The linguistic and cultural complexities of harmful content across diverse languages demand sophisticated solutions that combine computational methods with cultural and contextual understanding. As research in this area continues to advance, the development of more effective and culturally aware content moderation systems will support the creation of safer digital spaces that serve diverse global communities.

The future of multilingual content moderation is marked by opportunities for innovation and collaboration that will enhance our ability to build AI systems capable of addressing the complexities of global communication. Through continued efforts in this domain, we can work toward developing technologies that better understand and mitigate harmful content across the world's rich linguistic and cultural diversity. The evolution of these systems reflects the growing recognition of the need for culturally sensitive approaches to content moderation that respect and serve the diverse communities participating in digital discourse, ultimately supporting more inclusive and equitable global communication.

The development and deployment of AI systems for detecting and mitigating misinformation and toxicity in multilingual environments raise important ethical considerations that must be carefully addressed. Issues of bias and representation become particularly significant when dealing with diverse languages and cultures, as systems trained primarily on high-resource languages may not effectively serve all linguistic communities. The potential for misidentification of harmful content or the over-censorship of legitimate expression creates risks that must be carefully managed to avoid suppressing valid discourse or failing to detect actual harmful content. The cultural sensitivity of content moderation decisions demands careful consideration of how different communities perceive and are affected by harmful content, where what might be considered toxic in one culture could be acceptable in another.

The establishment of ethical guidelines for developing and deploying multilingual content moderation systems is essential for ensuring responsible AI development that serves diverse global communities. These guidelines should address issues of representation in training data to ensure all languages are adequately accounted for, the potential for cultural insensitivity in detection algorithms that might misinterpret certain expressions, and the transparency of moderation decisions to allow for review and correction. The involvement of diverse stakeholders including native speakers, cultural experts, and community representatives in the development process helps create systems that better understand and serve different linguistic communities. The implementation of accountability mechanisms that allow for the review and correction of moderation decisions supports more ethical and effective content management that respects the complexities of multilingual communication.

The future of AI systems for detecting and mitigating misinformation and toxicity across languages is marked by exciting opportunities for advancement and innovation. The development of more sophisticated architectures that can better capture cultural and contextual nuances will enhance the ability to identify harmful content in diverse linguistic environments. The integration of multimodal approaches that combine linguistic analysis with visual or auditory information presents new possibilities for comprehensive content understanding that goes beyond text-based analysis. Advances in few-shot and zero-shot learning will enable systems to adapt more effectively to new languages or cultural contexts with limited training data, making them more versatile and applicable across the world's linguistic diversity.

The creation of more diverse and representative training datasets will support continued improvement in multilingual content moderation, ensuring that systems can effectively serve all linguistic communities. Collaborative efforts to collect and annotate data from underrepresented languages will enhance the inclusivity and effectiveness of these systems, making them more capable of understanding and processing content from diverse cultural backgrounds. The development of evaluation frameworks that better assess cultural understanding alongside linguistic capabilities will support more accurate detection of harmful content, where the same words might have different meanings or implications in different languages. As these technologies continue to evolve, they promise to play an increasingly central role in creating safer digital communication environments that accommodate the world's rich linguistic and cultural diversity, supporting more inclusive and respectful global discourse.

9.4 TRANSPARENCY AND EXPLAINABILITY IN LANGUAGE MODELS

Transparency and explainability are central to the responsible development of language models in artificial intelligence. Transparency provides openness about design, data, and scope, while explainability ensures that users can understand and evaluate outputs. Together, they address the black box problem of modern AI, promoting accountability, fairness, and trust. Although challenges remain—ranging from technical complexity to commercial secrecy—progress in visualization, attribution methods, and regulatory frameworks shows that meaningful explainability is possible. More importantly, the ethical imperatives of fairness, inclusivity, and democratic accountability demand that transparency and explainability remain priorities in AI development. As language models continue to influence communication and decision-making globally, ensuring their transparency and explainability is not merely a technical necessity but a social responsibility that defines the future relationship between humans and intelligent machines.

The pursuit of transparency and explainability in language models is an ongoing journey. Future research is likely to focus on developing tools that make explanations more user-friendly and context-sensitive. Instead of technical visualizations alone, models may provide natural-language explanations tailored to the user's level of expertise. For instance, a medical AI system might explain its recommendations differently to a doctor than to a patient, ensuring clarity for both.

Another promising direction is participatory design, where communities and stakeholders are involved in shaping how transparency and explainability are implemented. By incorporating diverse perspectives, AI developers can ensure that explanations address the needs of different cultural and linguistic contexts. Advances in auditing and interpretability metrics will also strengthen the ability to evaluate AI systems objectively, making transparency more measurable and enforceable. Ultimately, the future of AI will depend not only on improving performance but also on building trust. Transparency and explainability are key to this trust, ensuring that AI systems function as reliable partners rather than opaque authorities.

9.4.1 Black Box Nature of Language Models

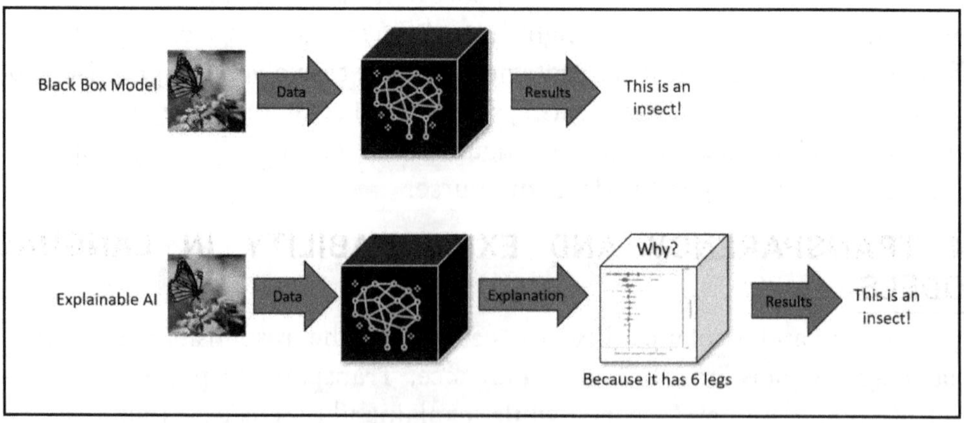

Fig: Box LLM APIs

One of the defining challenges of language models is their "black box" character. Modern models are based on deep neural networks with billions of parameters, making their decision-making processes complex and difficult to interpret. Unlike rule-based systems, where each output can be traced back to explicit instructions, neural networks rely on statistical associations learned from vast amounts of data. This makes it hard to pinpoint why a particular response was generated. For example, when a model translates a sentence or answers a question, the reasoning behind its choice of words is buried within layers of probability calculations.

This opacity raises concerns for users and developers alike. Users may question whether the output is trustworthy, while developers may struggle to identify errors, biases, or vulnerabilities in the model. The black box nature of language models thus highlights the urgent need for both transparency in design and explainability in practice.

9.4.2 Importance of Transparency in Language Models

Transparency in language models serves as the foundation for ethical and responsible AI. It involves clear disclosure of the datasets used, the methods applied in training, and the intended scope of application. Transparency helps users and stakeholders evaluate whether a system is suitable for their needs and whether its limitations have been properly accounted for. For example, if a language model is trained primarily on English-language news sources, it may not perform well in other languages or cultural contexts. Without transparency about training data, users may mistakenly assume broader reliability than actually exists.

Transparency also supports accountability. When organizations disclose their methods and datasets, external researchers can scrutinize the system for biases, inaccuracies, and ethical risks. This openness fosters trust and helps establish standards for safe AI deployment. In contrast, lack of transparency creates risks of misuse, misinterpretation, and diminished public confidence in AI technologies.

9.4.3 Explainability as a Bridge between Humans and AI

Explainability complements transparency by making the operations of language models interpretable to non-experts. While transparency emphasizes disclosure of system design, explainability provides insight into why a system produces specific outputs. For example, when a model classifies a text as positive in sentiment analysis, explainability techniques can highlight which words or phrases influenced this decision. Similarly, in translation tasks, explainability can reveal how the model mapped certain phrases from one language to another.

Explainability is essential for fostering human trust in AI. Without a clear understanding of how results are produced, users may be hesitant to rely on the system, particularly in sensitive domains such as healthcare, law, or finance. By providing accessible explanations, AI systems empower users to make informed decisions about when to trust the output and when to exercise caution.

9.4.4 Techniques for Explainability in Language Models

Various methods have been developed to improve explainability in language models. Attention visualization is one of the most widely used, as many transformer-based models rely on attention mechanisms to weigh the importance of different words in a sequence. By visualizing which words receive the most attention during processing, researchers can infer how the model prioritizes information.

Another technique is feature attribution, which identifies the contribution of individual tokens, phrases, or embeddings to the final prediction. Methods such as Layer-wise Relevance Propagation or SHAP values provide numerical insights into which elements of the input most strongly influenced the outcome. In text generation tasks, some approaches attempt to trace back generated words to the most relevant parts of the input data, offering users a sense of why the model "chose" specific phrases. These techniques, while helpful, are not without limitations. They provide approximations rather than definitive explanations, and they often require technical expertise to interpret. Nonetheless, they represent an important step toward making language models more interpretable and accountable.

9.4.5 Challenges to Achieving Transparency and Explainability

Despite growing efforts, transparency and explainability in language models face significant obstacles. One challenge lies in the sheer scale of these systems. With billions of parameters, it is practically impossible to fully explain every decision the model makes. This complexity raises the question of whether complete explainability is even achievable, or whether approximations must suffice.

Another challenge is balancing transparency with proprietary interests. Many organizations developing large language models view their training data and methods as trade secrets. Full disclosure could compromise competitive advantage, making companies reluctant to share information openly. This tension between commercial interests and societal demands for transparency remains unresolved.Furthermore, there is the risk of information overload. If developers provide exhaustive technical details, they may overwhelm users rather than enhance understanding. Effective transparency and explainability must therefore strike a balance between detail and accessibility, ensuring that explanations are comprehensible to both technical and non-technical audiences.

9.4.6 Ethical Dimensions of Transparency and Explainability

The ethical significance of transparency and explainability cannot be overstated. When AI systems influence decisions in critical areas such as healthcare, law, or hiring, lack of explainability can result in serious harm. Patients may not understand why an AI diagnostic tool recommends one treatment over another, or job applicants may be unfairly excluded by opaque selection algorithms. In such cases, transparency and explainability are necessary to safeguard fairness and accountability. Moreover, explainability has a role in combating bias and discrimination. By analyzing how language models arrive at certain outputs, researchers can identify and correct harmful stereotypes encoded in the system. Transparent reporting of model performance across demographic groups also helps prevent unequal treatment of users based on gender, race, or linguistic background.

Ethical responsibility extends to respecting the rights of users to understand and question the systems that affect them. In this sense, transparency and explainability are not only technical challenges but also fundamental principles of democratic accountability in the digital age.

9.4.7 Transparency and Explainability in Regulation and Policy

As concerns about opaque AI systems grow, policymakers are increasingly recognizing the need for regulation. Initiatives such as the European Union's AI Act emphasize transparency requirements, particularly for high-risk applications. These regulations aim to ensure that users are informed about the use of AI, have access to meaningful explanations of decisions, and can contest outcomes when necessary. Explainability is also linked to legal principles such as the right to explanation under data protection laws. For example, individuals affected by automated decisions may demand an understandable rationale for the outcome. Regulatory frameworks thus provide an important mechanism for enforcing transparency and ensuring that AI developers adhere to ethical standards.

However, the challenge lies in creating regulations that balance innovation with accountability. Overly rigid requirements may stifle technological progress, while insufficient oversight may leave users vulnerable to harm. Thoughtful policy design is therefore essential to achieving this balance.

9.5 FAIR ACCESS AND LANGUAGE JUSTICE

The pursuit of fair access and language justice in artificial intelligence represents a fundamental challenge and opportunity in the development of equitable language technologies. The digital language divide reflects broader issues of representation and equity in the technological era, demanding innovative solutions that address both technical and sociocultural dimensions. Community-led initiatives, culturally sensitive development processes, and thoughtful policy frameworks combine to create pathways toward more inclusive language technologies.

As research and development in this area continue to advance, the principles of language justice will play an increasingly central role in guiding technological progress. The future of AI development is marked by opportunities to create systems that better serve diverse linguistic communities while respecting and preserving their cultural heritage. Through continued efforts in this domain, we can work toward a digital landscape where all languages have equal opportunities to thrive in the technological age, maintaining the rich diversity of human communication for future generations.

The future of language justice in AI development is marked by exciting opportunities for innovation and progress. The continued advancement of computational methods that can better accommodate linguistic diversity will enhance the ability to serve underrepresented languages. The integration of cultural knowledge into technical development processes promises to create more appropriate and effective solutions. The expansion of community-led initiatives that empower language communities to guide technological development will support more sustainable and meaningful outcomes.

The development of more sophisticated evaluation frameworks that consider both technical performance and cultural impact will support better assessment of language technologies. The creation of funding models that prioritize underrepresented languages will help address existing resource disparities. The establishment of international collaborations that share knowledge and resources across linguistic communities will foster more comprehensive solutions. As these efforts continue to evolve, they promise to create a more equitable landscape for language technology development that serves diverse global communities while preserving the rich heritage embodied in the world's languages.

9.5.1 Digital Language Divide

The digital language divide represents one of the most pressing challenges in the development and deployment of artificial intelligence systems. While major languages like English, Mandarin, and Spanish benefit from extensive resources and sophisticated technological support, thousands of other languages receive minimal attention in AI development. This disparity creates significant barriers to digital participation for speakers of underrepresented languages, limiting their access to information, educational opportunities, and technological benefits. The consequences of this divide extend beyond mere inconvenience to encompass fundamental issues of equity and social justice in the digital era. The roots of this digital language divide are complex and multifaceted. Historical patterns of linguistic dominance have contributed to the prioritization of certain languages in technological development. Economic factors influence which languages receive attention from technology companies and researchers. The availability of digital resources and training data creates a feedback loop where well-resourced languages continue to receive more support. These factors combine to create a landscape where certain linguistic communities enjoy significant technological advantages while others struggle to maintain their languages in the digital sphere.

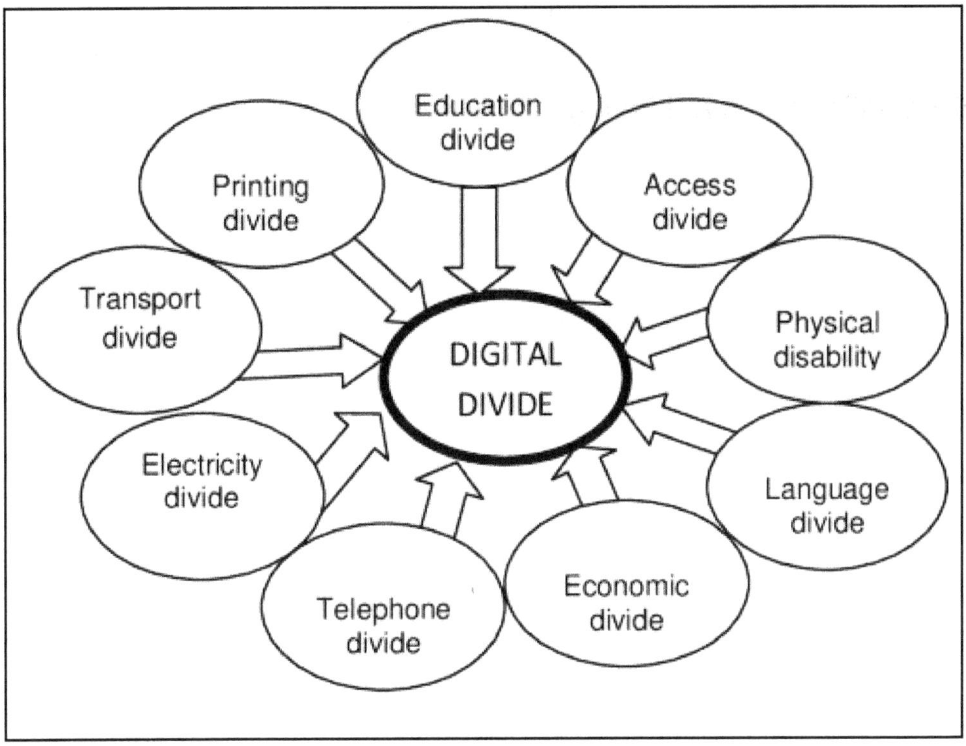

Fig: Dimensions of Digital Divide and Digital Opportunities

9.5.2 Principles of Language Justice

Language justice in the context of artificial intelligence encompasses several fundamental principles that guide the development and deployment of equitable language technologies. At its core, language justice demands that all linguistic communities have equal opportunities to participate in and benefit from digital technologies.

This principle extends to the representation of languages in AI systems, where each language should be afforded equal consideration in technological development. The preservation of linguistic diversity becomes an essential component of language justice, recognizing that each language embodies unique cultural knowledge and worldviews that deserve protection in the digital age. The implementation of language justice principles requires careful consideration of several key factors. The allocation of resources for language technology development must prioritize underrepresented languages to address existing disparities.

The involvement of native speaker communities in technological development ensures that solutions align with cultural values and actual language use patterns. The creation of evaluation frameworks that assess not only technical performance but also cultural appropriateness and social impact helps guide more equitable development. These principles form the foundation for building AI systems that serve diverse linguistic communities while respecting their cultural heritage.

9.5.3 Challenges in Achieving Fair Access

The realization of fair access to AI technologies across all languages faces significant challenges that reflect both technical and sociocultural complexities. The scarcity of digital resources for many languages creates fundamental obstacles to developing effective language technologies. The linguistic complexity of underrepresented languages, including their unique grammatical structures and cultural contexts, demands sophisticated approaches that current systems often struggle to accommodate. The economic realities of technological development frequently prioritize languages with larger speaker populations or greater commercial potential, leaving many linguistic communities underserved.

The technical challenges of developing AI systems for diverse languages are substantial. Current models often perform poorly on languages with limited training data or those that differ significantly from well-represented languages. The computational requirements for processing multiple languages simultaneously create practical limitations for deployment in resource-constrained environments.

The evaluation of language technologies across diverse linguistic contexts presents difficulties in assessing performance and cultural appropriateness. These challenges necessitate innovative solutions that can address the complexities of linguistic diversity while maintaining technical feasibility.

9.5.4 Strategies for Equitable Language Technology Development

The development of strategies for equitable language technology development requires multifaceted approaches that address both technical and sociocultural dimensions. Community-led initiatives that prioritize the knowledge and needs of native speakers have shown particular promise in creating more culturally appropriate solutions.

These approaches involve extensive collaboration between technologists, linguists, and language communities to ensure that AI systems align with actual language use patterns and cultural values. The creation of open-source resources and shared datasets helps level the playing field by providing all researchers with access to essential materials for developing language technologies.

The implementation of transfer learning techniques that can adapt models to new languages with limited training data represents a significant technical strategy. These methods leverage knowledge from well-resourced languages to improve performance on underrepresented ones, helping to address the data scarcity problem. The development of evaluation metrics that consider both technical performance and cultural appropriateness supports more comprehensive assessments of language technologies. The establishment of funding mechanisms that prioritize underrepresented languages helps direct resources toward addressing existing disparities. These strategies combine to create a more equitable landscape for language technology development.

9.5.5 Cultural Sensitivity in AI Development

The incorporation of cultural sensitivity into AI development processes represents a crucial component of language justice. Language technologies must accommodate not only linguistic structures but also the cultural contexts in which they are used. This requirement demands the involvement of native speakers and cultural experts throughout the development lifecycle, from initial design through implementation and evaluation. The consideration of cultural protocols and traditional knowledge systems helps ensure that technologies respect and preserve the unique heritage embodied in each language.

The practical implementation of cultural sensitivity involves several key considerations. The adaptation of user interfaces to accommodate local communication styles and interaction patterns makes technologies more accessible and relevant. The incorporation of cultural knowledge into training datasets helps models understand the nuances of language use in specific contexts.

The establishment of review processes that include cultural experts helps identify potential issues before deployment. The development of documentation that explains cultural considerations in technology use supports more appropriate adoption. These approaches create AI systems that better serve diverse linguistic communities while respecting their cultural heritage.

9.5.6 Policy and Governance for Language Justice

The establishment of policy frameworks and governance structures represents an essential component of promoting language justice in AI development. These mechanisms help ensure that technological progress serves all linguistic communities equitably while protecting cultural heritage.

The creation of standards for language technology development that prioritize underrepresented languages helps guide more equitable practices. The implementation of funding programs that support research on diverse languages directs resources toward addressing existing disparities. The development of certification processes that assess both technical performance and cultural appropriateness creates incentives for more responsible development.

The practical realization of these policy frameworks involves several important considerations. The inclusion of language community representatives in governance structures ensures that policies reflect actual needs and values. The establishment of transparent evaluation processes helps maintain accountability in technological development. The creation of mechanisms for reporting and addressing concerns about language technologies supports more responsive governance. The development of educational programs that raise awareness about language justice issues fosters broader understanding and support. These policy approaches combine to create an environment where language technologies can develop in ways that serve diverse linguistic communities while respecting their cultural heritage.

CHAPTER 10

Evaluation and Benchmarking

10.1 BENCHMARK SUITES (XTREME, XGLUE, MASSIVE)

The rapid development of multilingual artificial intelligence has demanded rigorous evaluation frameworks to measure the performance of models across languages and tasks. Benchmark suites serve as standardized platforms where models can be tested for their ability to understand, translate, and process language in diverse contexts. Unlike single-task benchmarks, multilingual suites are designed to assess cross-lingual generalization, ensuring that models are not overly reliant on dominant languages such as English. Instead, they provide a holistic view of how models perform in languages with varying data availability, typologies, and cultural contexts. Among the most influential benchmarks are XTREME, XGLUE, and MASSIVE, each of which offers distinct datasets, tasks, and evaluation methodologies. Together, these suites have shaped the trajectory of multilingual natural language processing and continue to be central in advancing the inclusivity and fairness of language models.

Benchmark suites such as XTREME, XGLUE, and MASSIVE are central to the progress of multilingual AI. They provide structured, standardized frameworks for evaluating how models handle diverse languages and tasks, from general natural language understanding to applied dialogue systems. XTREME pioneered large-scale evaluation of zero-shot cross-lingual transfer, XGLUE expanded evaluation into practical and reasoning-based tasks, and MASSIVE addressed the critical need for reliable multilingual conversational AI.

Together, these benchmarks have transformed the field by setting high standards for performance, inclusivity, and applicability. They not only highlight the strengths of multilingual models but also expose their limitations, guiding the development of more robust, equitable, and globally relevant AI systems. As AI continues to integrate into everyday life across cultures and languages, benchmarks will remain indispensable in ensuring that these technologies serve all of humanity, not just a select few.

As AI systems become increasingly global, future benchmark development will likely expand in several directions. Greater inclusion of low-resource and endangered languages is essential to ensure linguistic equity. Current benchmarks, while diverse, still underrepresent many languages spoken by millions of people. Expanding beyond written text to incorporate speech, multimodal communication, and dialectal variations will also be key.

Moreover, benchmarks may evolve to measure not only accuracy but also fairness, robustness, and cultural sensitivity. Evaluating how models handle idioms, metaphors, or culturally specific references will be crucial for building systems that truly understand language in human terms. The next generation of benchmarks may integrate explainability, offering insights not only into how well a model performs but also into why it produces specific outputs.

10.1.1 Need for Multilingual Benchmarks

Language models are often trained on massive corpora that disproportionately represent high-resource languages. While this training allows impressive performance in English and a handful of other languages, it does not guarantee comparable outcomes for languages with limited digital presence. Without benchmarks, it is difficult to determine whether models can generalize beyond the training distribution or whether they fail to provide meaningful outputs in underrepresented languages. Benchmarks address this gap by offering structured tasks across a wide variety of languages, making it possible to systematically measure strengths and weaknesses.

Multilingual benchmarks also provide a foundation for progress tracking. Researchers can compare new models against established baselines to determine whether innovations in architecture, pretraining, or fine-tuning translate into real improvements across diverse linguistic settings. This standardization fosters healthy competition and collaboration in the field, driving continual improvement.

10.1.2 XTREME Benchmark

The Cross-lingual TRansfer Evaluation of Multilingual Encoders, better known as XTREME, is one of the most comprehensive benchmarks designed to evaluate cross-lingual natural language understanding. It consists of nine tasks spanning forty different languages. These tasks are drawn from diverse domains such as sentence classification, part-of-speech tagging, question answering, and sentence retrieval, thereby covering multiple aspects of language comprehension.

One of the distinguishing features of XTREME is its focus on zero-shot cross-lingual transfer. Models are fine-tuned on English data and then evaluated directly on non-English test sets without additional training. This design tests a model's ability to generalize knowledge learned in one language to many others, which is critical for real-world multilingual applications. For example, a model fine-tuned on English sentiment analysis is tested on Hindi or Swahili sentiment analysis datasets without further adaptation. By including both high-resource and low-resource languages, XTREME highlights the disparities in performance across the linguistic spectrum. Models that excel in European languages may falter when confronted with morphologically complex or low-resource languages, thus revealing weaknesses that would remain hidden in English-only benchmarks.

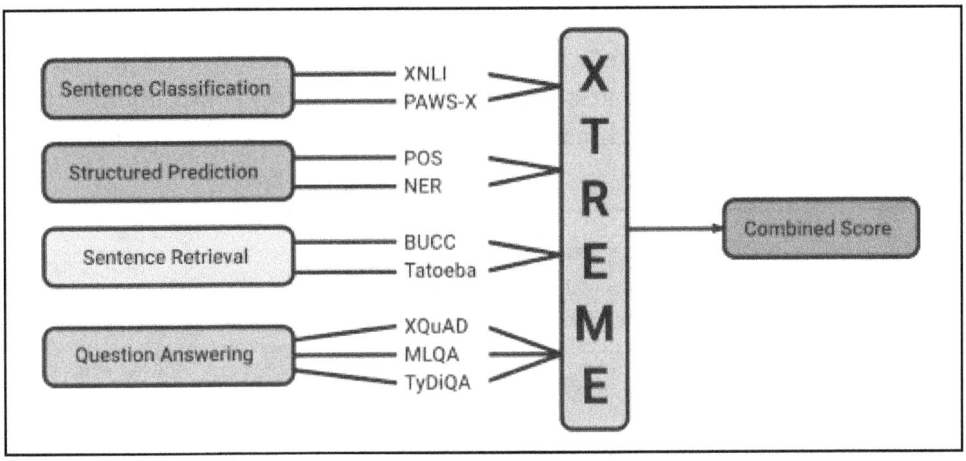

Fig: XTREME

XTREME has had a profound influence on multilingual AI research. It introduced a clear framework for evaluating cross-lingual generalization, emphasizing the importance of zero-shot transfer. Before XTREME, many models were only tested on multilingual translation or limited classification tasks. With XTREME, the community could assess models across a broader set of tasks, promoting more balanced development.

Another major contribution is the way XTREME elevated the discussion around inclusivity in language technologies. By including languages from multiple families and geographic regions, it drew attention to linguistic diversity and the necessity of building systems that do not exclude entire populations. Furthermore, XTREME inspired subsequent benchmarks and has been frequently cited in research introducing new multilingual models, such as XLM-R and mT5, providing a standardized yardstick for evaluation.

10.1.3 XGLUE Benchmark

The Cross-lingual General Language Understanding Evaluation benchmark, or XGLUE, complements XTREME by expanding the range of tasks and focusing on multilingual understanding in more applied contexts. It covers eleven natural language understanding tasks across nineteen languages, including both classification and ranking challenges. Unlike XTREME, which emphasizes zero-shot transfer, XGLUE places greater weight on cross-lingual learning across diverse tasks such as natural language inference, news classification, question answering, and paraphrase identification. These tasks mirror real-world applications such as information retrieval, customer support automation, and knowledge extraction, making XGLUE highly relevant for industrial as well as academic use.

A unique feature of XGLUE is its inclusion of machine reading comprehension tasks, where models must not only recognize sentence-level patterns but also understand longer passages of text. This pushes models to develop deeper semantic understanding rather than relying on surface-level token matching. The balance between classification, ranking, and reading comprehension tasks makes XGLUE a holistic benchmark for testing cross-lingual natural language processing systems.

Task Name	Model Task	Languages
News Classification (NC)	Identifies an article's news category (i.e., sports, entertainment, or world news)	English, French, German, Spanish, and Russian
Query-Ad Matching (QADSM)	Determines if an ad recommendation is "good" or "bad"	English, French, and German
Web Page Ranking (WPR)	Ranks the relevance of results on a scale of 0 (bad) to 4 (perfect)	English, French, German, Spanish, Italian, Portuguese, and Chinese
QA Matching (QAM)	Determines if a passage is relevant to a query	English, French, and German
Question Generation (QG)	Provides a query when given a passage	English, French, German, Spanish, Italian, and Portuguese
News Title Generation (NTG)	Creates news article based on a headline	English, French, German, Spanish, and Russian

Fig: XGLUE

XGLUE's significance lies in its ability to simulate real-world challenges faced by multilingual applications. Its task diversity forces models to go beyond simple transfer and tackle problems requiring reasoning, contextual understanding, and semantic representation across languages. This breadth has been instrumental in testing the limits of pretraining approaches such as multilingual BERT and evaluating how well new architectures handle cross-lingual challenges.

XGLUE also emphasized the practical relevance of multilingual AI. Many organizations rely on automated systems for customer support, news aggregation, or online moderation across multiple languages. By introducing benchmarks tied to such practical scenarios, XGLUE bridged the gap between academic research and industry application. As a result, it accelerated adoption of multilingual benchmarks as a standard in both research publications and product development.

10.1.4 MASSIVE Benchmark

Multilingual Amazon SLU for Slot-filling, Intent classification, and Virtual-assistant Evaluation, or MASSIVE, is a benchmark designed with conversational AI in mind. Unlike XTREME and XGLUE, which focus primarily on general natural language understanding tasks, MASSIVE targets natural language understanding in spoken dialogue systems. It includes fifty-one languages and supports the evaluation of intent classification and slot-filling, two key tasks in conversational AI.

The MASSIVE dataset consists of parallel utterances across all included languages, making it especially valuable for training and evaluating virtual assistants that must handle global user bases. For example, a query such as "Book me a flight to Paris" is available in dozens of languages, allowing models to learn intent classification and slot extraction consistently across linguistic contexts.

This benchmark is particularly relevant in an era where conversational interfaces are becoming ubiquitous. From customer service chatbots to personal assistants, the demand for reliable multilingual dialogue systems is growing rapidly. MASSIVE provides the evaluation framework necessary to ensure these systems function accurately across diverse linguistic populations.

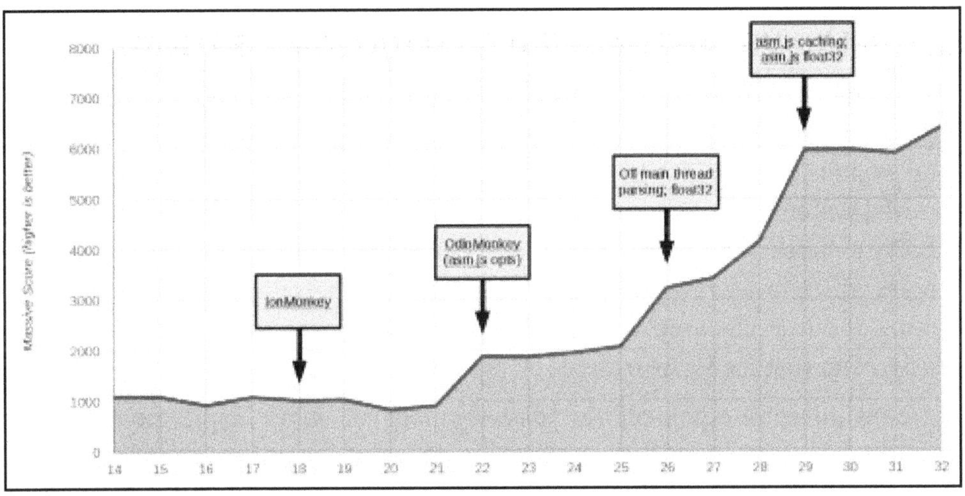

Fig: MASSIVE

The MASSIVE benchmark plays a vital role in moving multilingual AI from research to deployment. Conversational systems are often the most direct point of interaction between users and technology, and failures in intent recognition or slot-filling can lead to frustration and exclusion. By covering a wide spectrum of languages, MASSIVE helps ensure that conversational AI works reliably not just in English or other dominant languages but also in languages with fewer resources.

Additionally, MASSIVE emphasizes parallelism across languages, which allows developers to identify systematic gaps in model performance. This design makes it easier to pinpoint whether poor results stem from model limitations or from deeper linguistic challenges such as complex morphology or free word order. As a result, MASSIVE has quickly become a key benchmark for evaluating dialogue systems and multilingual virtual assistants.

10.1.5 Comparing XTREME, XGLUE, and MASSIVE

Although XTREME, XGLUE, and MASSIVE share the common goal of advancing multilingual AI, they differ in scope, focus, and application. XTREME is primarily designed for evaluating zero-shot cross-lingual transfer across a broad range of natural language understanding tasks. XGLUE emphasizes applied tasks with a balance of classification, ranking, and comprehension challenges, reflecting real-world multilingual applications. MASSIVE, in contrast, focuses on conversational AI, making it highly specialized for dialogue systems and virtual assistants.

Together, these benchmarks complement one another by covering different dimensions of multilingual performance. XTREME stresses transferability, XGLUE emphasizes practical versatility, and MASSIVE addresses deployment in dialogue-based systems. Researchers and developers can use them in combination to gain a comprehensive view of a model's multilingual capabilities.

10.2 HUMAN VS. AUTOMATED EVALUATION METHODS

The debate between human and automated evaluation methods is not about choosing one over the other but rather about finding the right balance between them. Human evaluation provides the depth, nuance, and contextual understanding that automated systems lack, while automated methods offer the speed, consistency, and scalability necessary for large-scale AI development. The most effective evaluation strategies will leverage both approaches, using automated metrics for preliminary screening and iterative improvements while relying on human judgment for final validation and nuanced assessment.

As AI continues to advance, the development of more sophisticated, hybrid evaluation frameworks will be crucial in ensuring that these systems are not only technically proficient but also aligned with human values and expectations. By combining the strengths of human insight and automated efficiency, the AI community can build evaluation methods that are as intelligent and adaptable as the systems they aim to measure. Ultimately, the goal is to create AI that is not just powerful but also trustworthy, fair, and truly beneficial to society—a goal that can only be achieved through rigorous, multifaceted evaluation.

The future of AI evaluation lies in developing more nuanced, context-aware methods that combine the depth of human judgment with the scalability of automated systems. One key area of focus is the creation of evaluation frameworks that account for ethical considerations, such as bias detection and fairness. As AI systems are deployed in high-stakes domains like healthcare and criminal justice, ensuring that evaluations measure not just accuracy but also equity and transparency becomes imperative. Researchers are also exploring real-time evaluation techniques, where AI systems are continuously monitored and adjusted based on user feedback, creating a more dynamic and responsive assessment process.

Another critical direction is the standardization of evaluation protocols across the AI community. Currently, disparate methodologies make it difficult to compare results across studies, hindering progress. Initiatives like the General Language Understanding Evaluation (GLUE) benchmark and its successors aim to establish unified standards, but more work is needed to extend these frameworks to diverse languages and applications. Furthermore, as AI systems become more interactive and multimodal, evaluation methods must evolve to assess not just text but also speech, images, and their integration, requiring innovative cross-modal evaluation techniques.

10.2.1 Role of Human Evaluation in AI Assessment

Human evaluation has long been considered the gold standard for assessing AI-generated outputs, particularly in tasks where meaning, fluency, and cultural appropriateness are paramount. Unlike automated metrics, human evaluators can assess nuanced aspects of language that machines may overlook, such as coherence, stylistic appropriateness, and emotional resonance. In machine translation, for example, human judges can determine whether a translated passage not only conveys the correct meaning but also maintains the tone and intent of the original text. Similarly, in creative text generation, human evaluators are better equipped to judge narrative flow, originality, and engagement—qualities that automated systems struggle to quantify.

Another significant advantage of human evaluation is its adaptability to context. Human judges can account for cultural, situational, and domain-specific factors that influence how language is interpreted. For instance, a legal document and a casual conversation require vastly different linguistic standards, and human evaluators can adjust their assessments accordingly. This flexibility makes human evaluation indispensable for applications where precision and appropriateness are critical, such as medical diagnosis systems, legal document analysis, and customer service chatbots. However, despite its strengths, human evaluation is not without drawbacks, including subjectivity, scalability issues, and high costs, which have led to the widespread adoption of automated alternatives.

10.2.2 Automated Evaluation Methods: Efficiency at Scale

Automated evaluation methods have gained prominence due to their ability to provide quick, consistent, and scalable assessments of AI systems. These methods rely on predefined algorithms and statistical measures to evaluate performance without human intervention. In machine translation, metrics like BLEU (Bilingual Evaluation Understudy) and METEOR compare AI-generated translations against human reference texts, measuring overlap in n-grams and semantic similarity. For text summarization, ROUGE (Recall-Oriented Understudy for Gisting Evaluation) assesses the overlap between generated summaries and reference content. These automated approaches are particularly valuable during the iterative development phase, where rapid feedback is necessary to refine models.

One of the primary benefits of automated evaluation is its objectivity. Unlike human evaluators, who may be influenced by personal biases or fatigue, automated systems apply the same criteria uniformly across all assessments. This consistency is crucial for benchmarking AI models across different research teams and ensuring reproducibility in experiments. Additionally, automated methods can process vast amounts of data in a fraction of the time required for human evaluation, making them indispensable for large-scale deployments. However, these methods also face criticism for their inability to capture linguistic subtleties, over-reliance on surface-level features, and occasional misalignment with human judgments, raising questions about their validity as standalone evaluation tools.

10.2.3 Comparative Strengths and Limitations

When comparing human and automated evaluation methods, it becomes clear that each approach excels in different areas while falling short in others. Human evaluation shines in tasks requiring deep semantic understanding, creativity, and contextual awareness. For example, in dialogue systems, human judges can detect whether a chatbot's responses are socially appropriate, empathetic, and logically coherent—qualities that automated metrics often miss. Conversely, automated methods provide unmatched speed and scalability, enabling researchers to evaluate models across thousands of samples in minutes, a feat impractical for human assessors. However, the limitations of each method highlight the need for a hybrid approach. Automated metrics, while efficient, frequently fail to align with human judgments, particularly in open-ended tasks like story generation or poetry. Studies have shown that high BLEU or ROUGE scores do not always correlate with human-perceived quality, as these metrics prioritize lexical overlap over meaning preservation. On the other hand, human evaluation is resource-intensive and prone to inconsistencies due to varying annotator expertise and subjective interpretations. These challenges underscore the importance of combining both methods to leverage their respective strengths while mitigating weaknesses.

10.2.4 Emerging Trends and Hybrid Approaches

Recent advancements in AI evaluation have focused on bridging the gap between human and automated methods through hybrid approaches. One promising direction is the use of AI-assisted human evaluation, where automated tools pre-screen outputs to identify potential issues before human reviewers conduct deeper analysis. This method reduces the workload on human evaluators while maintaining high-quality assessments. Another innovation is the development of more sophisticated automated metrics, such as BERTScore and BLEURT, which leverage neural embeddings to better capture semantic similarity and fluency, bringing automated evaluations closer to human judgment.

Crowdsourcing platforms have also emerged as a middle ground, enabling large-scale human evaluation at reduced costs. By distributing assessment tasks across diverse annotators, researchers can gather more representative judgments while minimizing individual biases. Additionally, techniques like dynamic evaluation, where models are assessed based on their ability to adapt to new, unseen data, are gaining traction as a way to measure real-world applicability beyond static benchmarks. These evolving methodologies reflect a growing recognition that neither human nor automated evaluation alone can fully capture the complexities of AI performance, necessitating integrated solutions.

10.3 ROBUSTNESS ACROSS LANGUAGES AND DIALECTS

The development of artificial intelligence systems capable of processing multiple languages and dialects has made remarkable progress in recent years, transforming global communication and information access. However, as these technologies become increasingly sophisticated, significant challenges emerge in ensuring consistent performance across the diverse spectrum of human languages. The concept of robustness in multilingual AI systems refers to the ability to maintain accurate and reliable performance despite variations in linguistic structures, cultural contexts, and dialectal differences. Achieving this robustness represents one of the most significant challenges in contemporary natural language processing, demanding innovative approaches that can accommodate the rich diversity of human communication while maintaining technical efficiency. The development of robust multilingual AI systems capable of maintaining consistent performance across languages and dialects represents one of the most significant challenges in contemporary natural language processing. The complexities of linguistic diversity, combined with cultural and contextual variations, create a challenging environment for building resilient systems. However, innovative approaches that combine computational methods with linguistic and cultural knowledge offer promising pathways for addressing these challenges.

As research in this area continues to advance, the creation of more sophisticated architectures, comprehensive evaluation frameworks, and culturally aware systems will support the development of AI technologies that can serve diverse global communities. The future of multilingual AI is marked by opportunities for innovation that will enhance our ability to build systems accommodating the rich spectrum of human communication. Through continued efforts in this domain, we can work toward creating technologies that better understand and process the world's linguistic diversity, supporting more inclusive and effective global communication.

The future of robust multilingual AI systems is marked by exciting opportunities for advancement and innovation. The continued development of model architectures that can better accommodate linguistic diversity will enhance the ability to maintain consistent performance across languages. The integration of cultural knowledge into computational frameworks promises to create more culturally aware systems that can handle diverse communication contexts. The expansion of training datasets to include more representative samples from underrepresented languages and dialects will support more comprehensive linguistic capabilities.

The development of more sophisticated evaluation frameworks that consider both technical performance and cultural appropriateness will support better assessment of multilingual systems. The creation of adaptive architectures that can adjust to different linguistic structures without sacrificing performance will enhance the systems' ability to handle diverse inputs. The establishment of international collaborations that share knowledge and resources across linguistic communities will foster more comprehensive solutions. As these efforts continue to evolve, they promise to create AI systems that can maintain robust performance despite the rich diversity of human languages and dialects, supporting more inclusive and effective global communication technologies.

10.3.1 Complexity of Linguistic Diversity

The landscape of human language presents a remarkably complex array of structures, patterns, and variations that challenge the development of robust AI systems. Languages differ fundamentally in their phonological, morphological, syntactic, and semantic characteristics, creating substantial obstacles for models that must process diverse linguistic inputs. These variations extend beyond formal language structures to include dialectal differences, regional variations, and sociolectal distinctions that reflect cultural and social dimensions of communication. The dynamic nature of language, with its constant evolution and adaptation, adds another layer of complexity to the challenge of building resilient multilingual systems.

The development of robust AI systems must account for several key dimensions of linguistic diversity. Phonological variations across languages and dialects affect how speech is processed and recognized. Morphological differences influence how words are formed and inflected, creating challenges for systems that must handle diverse word structures. Syntactic variations determine how sentences are constructed and understood, demanding flexible parsing capabilities. Semantic distinctions affect how meaning is conveyed and interpreted, requiring sophisticated understanding of contextual nuances. These linguistic complexities combine to create a challenging environment for developing AI systems that can perform consistently across diverse languages and dialects.

10.3.2 Challenges in Cross-Lingual Consistency

The achievement of consistent performance across multiple languages presents one of the most significant challenges in multilingual AI development. Current systems often demonstrate substantial variations in accuracy and reliability when processing different languages, with performance typically degrading for those with limited training data or complex linguistic structures. This inconsistency stems from several fundamental factors that affect how models handle diverse linguistic inputs. The availability of training data varies dramatically across languages, creating disparities in model performance that reflect these resource imbalances. The structural characteristics of languages influence how well existing architectures can process their unique patterns and features.

The development of robust multilingual systems faces several key technical challenges that must be addressed to achieve cross-lingual consistency. The adaptation of model architectures to accommodate diverse linguistic structures without sacrificing performance on well-resourced languages represents a fundamental challenge. The creation of balanced training datasets that adequately represent all languages in a system helps mitigate performance disparities.

The optimization of computational resources to handle multiple languages efficiently while maintaining accuracy creates practical limitations. The evaluation of model performance across diverse linguistic contexts demands sophisticated metrics that can assess both technical capabilities and cultural appropriateness. These challenges necessitate innovative solutions that can achieve consistent performance despite the inherent complexities of human language.

10.3.3 Dialectal Variation and Regional Differences

The accommodation of dialectal variation and regional differences presents particular difficulties for developing robust AI systems. Dialects often exhibit substantial differences from standard language forms in their phonological, lexical, and grammatical characteristics, creating challenges for models trained primarily on formal language data. These variations reflect not only linguistic differences but also cultural and social distinctions that affect how language is used in different contexts. The dynamic nature of dialectal evolution, with its continuous adaptation to local conditions, adds another layer of complexity to the challenge of building systems that can handle these linguistic variations. The development of dialect-aware AI systems requires several key considerations to achieve robust performance across regional variations. The collection of representative training data that captures the diversity of dialectal forms helps models learn to recognize and process these linguistic patterns. The adaptation of model architectures to accommodate dialectal structures without compromising performance on standard language forms creates technical challenges. The incorporation of sociolinguistic knowledge about how dialects are used in different social contexts enhances the systems' ability to understand and process these variations. The evaluation of dialectal performance demands specialized metrics that can assess accuracy across diverse regional forms. These considerations combine to create a complex landscape for developing AI systems that can maintain consistent performance despite dialectal variations.

10.3.4 Strategies for Building Robust Multilingual Systems

The construction of robust multilingual AI systems demands innovative strategies that can accommodate linguistic diversity while maintaining technical efficiency. Transfer learning approaches that leverage knowledge from well-resourced languages to improve performance on low-resource ones have shown particular promise in addressing cross-lingual consistency challenges. These methods enable models to adapt to new languages with limited training data, helping to mitigate performance disparities. The development of language-agnostic architectures that can process diverse linguistic inputs within a unified framework creates more flexible systems that can handle variations across languages.

The implementation of robust multilingual systems involves several key strategies that address the fundamental challenges of linguistic diversity. The creation of balanced training corpora that include representative samples from all target languages helps models develop more comprehensive linguistic capabilities. The adaptation of tokenization methods to handle diverse morphological structures without losing linguistic information enhances the systems' ability to process different languages.

The incorporation of linguistic typology knowledge into model architectures enables better handling of structural variations across languages. The development of evaluation frameworks that consider both technical performance and cultural appropriateness supports more comprehensive assessments of system robustness. These strategies combine to create more resilient AI systems that can maintain consistent performance across the spectrum of human languages.

10.3.5 Cultural and Contextual Understanding

The achievement of robust performance in multilingual AI systems demands not only linguistic capabilities but also cultural and contextual understanding. The variations in how different cultures express ideas and communicate affect how language should be processed and interpreted. The development of culturally aware systems requires the incorporation of sociolinguistic knowledge into computational frameworks, enabling models to recognize and accommodate cultural nuances in language use. This cultural understanding enhances the systems' ability to maintain consistent performance across diverse linguistic and social contexts.

The implementation of cultural understanding in AI systems involves several key considerations that affect their robustness across languages. The annotation of training data with cultural context information helps models learn to recognize and process language in culturally appropriate ways. The adaptation of model architectures to accommodate cultural variations in communication patterns without sacrificing linguistic accuracy creates technical challenges. The development of evaluation metrics that assess cultural appropriateness alongside technical performance supports more comprehensive assessments of system capabilities. The involvement of cultural experts in the development process helps ensure that systems understand and respect cultural nuances in language use. These considerations combine to create AI systems that can maintain robust performance despite cultural and contextual variations.

10.3.6 Evaluation Metrics for Multilingual Robustness

The assessment of robustness in multilingual AI systems requires sophisticated evaluation metrics that can accurately measure performance across diverse languages and dialects. Traditional metrics that focus solely on technical accuracy often fail to capture the complexities of cross-lingual consistency and cultural appropriateness. The development of comprehensive evaluation frameworks involves several key components that address the fundamental challenges of linguistic diversity. The creation of language-specific benchmarks that assess performance on representative tasks helps identify areas where models struggle with particular linguistic structures. The incorporation of dialectal variations into evaluation datasets tests the systems' ability to handle regional differences in language use.

The implementation of robust evaluation metrics involves several important considerations that affect their effectiveness in assessing multilingual systems. The development of cross-lingual consistency measures that compare performance across languages helps identify disparities that need to be addressed. The creation of cultural appropriateness metrics that evaluate how well systems accommodate cultural nuances in language use provides additional dimensions for assessment. The establishment of dialectal robustness tests that examine performance across regional variations helps ensure that systems can handle diverse forms of language use. The involvement of native speakers in the evaluation process helps provide cultural and linguistic insights that enhance the assessment's validity. These evaluation approaches combine to create more comprehensive frameworks for assessing the robustness of multilingual AI systems.

10.4 ADVERSARIAL TESTING IN MULTILINGUAL SETTINGS

Adversarial testing in multilingual settings is an indispensable aspect of ensuring the robustness, fairness, and reliability of AI systems. The challenges are amplified in multilingual contexts due to the diversity of linguistic features, cultural nuances, and the vulnerability of low-resource languages. While progress has been made in developing adversarial defenses, significant work remains to build models that can withstand manipulation across languages and contexts. Ultimately, adversarial testing is not only about exposing weaknesses but also about building stronger, more inclusive, and ethically responsible multilingual AI systems. By embracing the complexities of adversarial testing, the field moves closer to developing AI that can serve a truly global and linguistically diverse population.

Adversarial testing in multilingual AI also raises important ethical questions. While the goal is to improve robustness, adversarial methods can themselves be misused to deliberately deceive systems or spread misinformation. For example, adversarially generated content in multilingual social media could be employed for political manipulation or disinformation campaigns. Thus, while adversarial testing is vital for strengthening systems, safeguards must be implemented to ensure that these methods are not weaponized. Transparency in the development and sharing of adversarial testing frameworks is necessary, as is collaboration between researchers, policymakers, and communities to ensure that multilingual adversarial testing promotes fairness and safety rather than exploitation.

The future of adversarial testing in multilingual settings will likely focus on building more realistic adversarial scenarios. As AI systems are increasingly deployed in high-stakes applications such as healthcare, education, and governance, the need for resilience under adversarial conditions becomes critical. Advances in generative adversarial networks and large-scale language modeling may allow for the creation of sophisticated adversarial examples that mirror real-world linguistic diversity. Furthermore, interdisciplinary collaboration between linguists, computer scientists, and sociologists will be essential to capture the full spectrum of multilingual adversarial challenges. By integrating cultural, linguistic, and technical expertise, researchers can develop testing frameworks that truly reflect the complexities of human language.

- **Complexity of Multilingual Adversarial Inputs:** Multilingual adversarial testing is more complex than its monolingual counterpart due to the sheer diversity of linguistic systems. For example, adversarial attacks can exploit morphological richness in languages like Finnish, the tonal systems of Mandarin, or the complex gendered forms in languages like Spanish. Models trained predominantly on English often fail to generalize effectively when confronted with these linguistic features. Furthermore, adversarial inputs can include code-switching, where multiple languages are mixed within a single sentence, creating confusion for the model. Spelling variations, regional dialects, and borrowed words further complicate the process. These linguistic intricacies make multilingual adversarial testing a unique challenge requiring specialized design strategies.

- **Categories of Adversarial Attacks in Multilingual Settings:** Adversarial testing can be categorized into several types depending on the nature of the attack. One common form is lexical substitution, where words are replaced with synonyms, homophones, or words from related dialects to mislead the model. Another method involves syntactic perturbations, in which the word order is altered in a way that is grammatically correct but confusing for the system. Semantic adversarial attacks go a step further, maintaining grammatical correctness but altering meaning in subtle ways. In multilingual contexts, phonetic similarities across languages can be exploited, as can false cognates that appear similar but differ in meaning. Such adversarial strategies highlight how multilingual adversarial testing must account for both within-language and cross-language vulnerabilities.
- **Cultural and Contextual Challenges:** Language is deeply intertwined with culture, and adversarial testing in multilingual settings must consider cultural nuances. A phrase that is neutral in one culture might be offensive in another, creating opportunities for adversarial exploitation. For example, idiomatic expressions often lack direct translations, and adversaries can introduce misleading idioms to confuse the system. Similarly, politeness markers, honorifics, and culturally sensitive terms can be manipulated in adversarial inputs. These cultural dimensions make it essential to design adversarial tests that go beyond purely linguistic manipulations and include sociolinguistic and pragmatic considerations. The challenge lies not only in testing how well the model handles words but also how it interprets intent, tone, and context across languages.
- **Benchmarking Adversarial Robustness in Multilingual Models:** Benchmark suites like XTREME, XGLUE, and MASSIVE have provided standardized ways to evaluate multilingual AI performance. However, adversarial testing requires an additional layer of benchmarking specifically designed to measure robustness under attack. Adversarial

multilingual benchmarks can include synthetic datasets where noise, misspellings, and code-switching are systematically introduced. They may also involve real-world datasets curated from social media or user-generated content, which naturally contain adversarial-like patterns. By systematically benchmarking models under adversarial conditions, researchers can compare their resilience across languages and identify which languages or linguistic features pose the greatest challenges. This process is vital for ensuring that AI systems are not only accurate but also resistant to manipulation.

- **Low-Resource Languages and Adversarial Vulnerabilities:** Low-resource and endangered languages are particularly vulnerable in adversarial testing scenarios. Because models are often trained on limited data for these languages, they are more easily misled by small perturbations. For instance, a model trained on only a few thousand examples of a low-resource language might struggle to handle adversarial variations in spelling or syntax. Moreover, the scarcity of annotated data makes it difficult to design robust adversarial training pipelines for such languages. This creates a digital inequality where high-resource languages benefit from stronger adversarial defenses, while low-resource languages remain highly susceptible to errors. Addressing these disparities requires deliberate efforts to expand multilingual datasets and adapt adversarial strategies to languages with fewer resources.
- **Strategies for Adversarial Defense in Multilingual AI:** To counter adversarial vulnerabilities, researchers have developed several defensive strategies. Adversarial training is one such method, where models are intentionally exposed to adversarial examples during the training process so that they learn to resist them. In multilingual settings, this involves generating adversarial examples across a wide range of languages and linguistic phenomena. Data augmentation techniques, such as paraphrasing, transliteration, or simulated noise, can also enhance robustness. Another approach is ensemble modeling, where predictions are aggregated from multiple models trained with different linguistic perspectives, reducing the likelihood of consistent errors under adversarial attack. Furthermore, researchers are exploring explainability tools to help detect when a model is being misled, allowing for real-time defense against adversarial inputs.

10.4.1 Case Studies of Multilingual Adversarial Testing

Several recent studies have illustrated the importance of adversarial testing in multilingual contexts. For instance, models evaluated on cross-lingual natural language inference tasks have been shown to fail when adversarial examples include false cognates or code-switched sentences. In another case, adversarial testing revealed that sentiment analysis models trained on English and applied to Spanish performed poorly when idiomatic expressions were introduced. These case studies highlight that adversarial vulnerabilities are not merely theoretical but manifest in real-world applications such as machine translation, sentiment analysis, and content moderation. They demonstrate that without robust adversarial evaluation, multilingual AI systems risk misinterpretation and potential harm.

10.5 ERROR ANALYSIS AND PERFORMANCE DISPARITIES

Error analysis and the study of performance disparities represent essential disciplines in the responsible development of artificial intelligence systems. As AI applications proliferate across increasingly consequential domains, the thorough investigation of system failures transitions from an academic exercise to an ethical imperative.

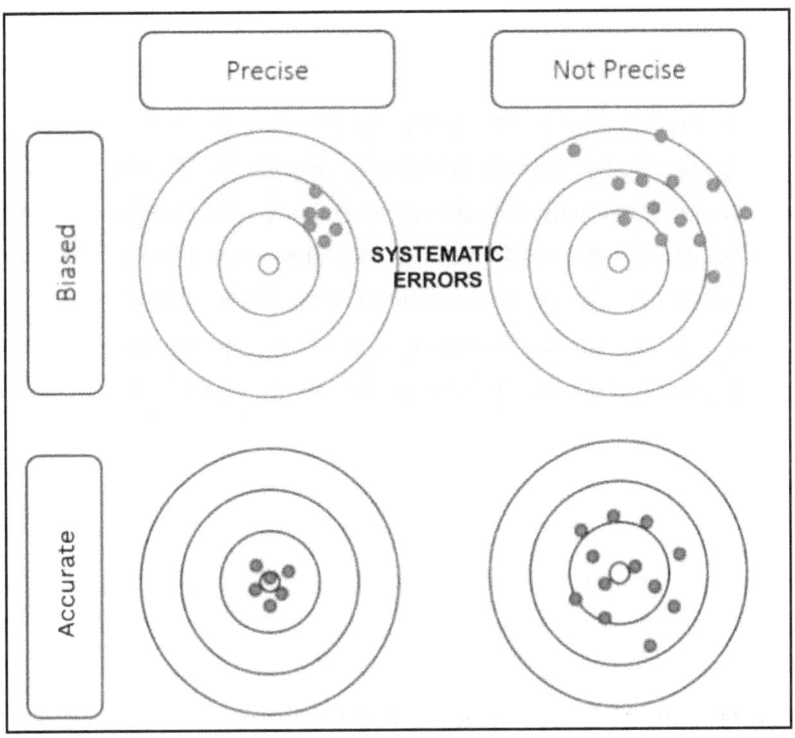

Fig: Error Analysis

The patterns revealed through rigorous error analysis frequently illuminate deeper issues in data collection practices, model architectures, and evaluation paradigms that might otherwise remain hidden beneath aggregate performance metrics. Performance disparities across demographic groups, languages, and use cases demand particular attention, as they risk exacerbating existing societal inequalities if left unaddressed.

Moving forward, the AI community must institutionalize comprehensive error analysis as a fundamental component of system development rather than an afterthought. This requires not only technical innovations in analysis methodologies but also cultural shifts toward greater transparency and accountability. By embracing the study of failures as enthusiastically as the pursuit of benchmarks, researchers and practitioners can build AI systems that are not just powerful but also reliable, equitable, and worthy of the public trust they increasingly demand. The path to truly robust artificial intelligence necessarily runs through the careful, honest examination of where and why our current systems fall short.

The frontier of error analysis research is moving toward more sophisticated, proactive approaches that anticipate rather than just react to system failures. Causal analysis techniques that distinguish between correlation and causation in error patterns promise deeper insights into the mechanisms underlying performance disparities.

The development of "self-diagnosing" models that can not only detect when they are likely to be wrong but also characterize the nature of their uncertainty represents an exciting direction for building more reliable systems. Researchers are also exploring human-AI collaboration frameworks where automated error detection works in concert with human expertise to identify and address subtle failure modes that might elude purely algorithmic approaches.

Another promising area involves the creation of comprehensive error taxonomies and benchmarking suites that systematically cover known failure modes across different AI domains. These resources would enable more standardized and comparable error analysis across research teams and industry applications.

Simultaneously, advances in interpretability techniques are providing new tools for understanding the internal decision processes that lead to errors, moving beyond surface-level pattern recognition to uncover the computational origins of failures. As these methodologies mature, they will enable more targeted interventions that address the root causes rather than just the symptoms of performance disparities.

10.5.1 Importance of Systematic Error Analysis

Error analysis in machine learning serves multiple critical functions that extend far beyond basic performance measurement. When conducted thoroughly, it provides diagnostic insights that help researchers understand the root causes of model failures rather than just observing their surface manifestations. This analytical process typically involves categorizing errors by type, frequency, and impact, then tracing these failures back to specific components of the model's architecture or training regimen. For natural language processing systems, common error categories might include semantic misunderstandings, syntactic errors, factual inaccuracies, or contextual misinterpretations, each requiring different remediation strategies.

The value of systematic error analysis becomes particularly evident when examining complex AI applications such as medical diagnosis systems or autonomous vehicles, where errors can have life-altering consequences. In these high-stakes domains, understanding whether failures stem from data limitations, algorithmic biases, or edge-case scenarios informs targeted improvements that enhance both performance and safety. Furthermore, comprehensive error analysis helps prioritize development efforts by distinguishing between rare but catastrophic failures and frequent but low-impact mistakes, enabling teams to allocate resources where they will yield the most significant improvements in real-world reliability.

10.5.2 Performance Disparities across Demographics and Languages

One of the most pressing challenges in contemporary AI development involves addressing performance disparities that emerge across different demographic groups, languages, and cultural contexts. Numerous studies have documented how facial recognition systems exhibit higher error rates for women and people with darker skin tones, how speech recognition struggles with certain accents and dialects, and how language models produce lower-quality outputs for non-dominant languages. These disparities often originate from imbalanced training datasets that overrepresent majority populations while underrepresenting marginalized groups, creating systems that perform unevenly across the spectrum of human diversity.

The consequences of these performance gaps extend beyond technical limitations into the realm of social equity. When AI systems used in hiring, lending, or law enforcement demonstrate biased performance patterns, they risk amplifying existing societal inequalities rather than mitigating them. In multilingual contexts, performance disparities between high-resource languages like English and low-resource languages can exacerbate digital divides, limiting access to technology for entire linguistic communities. Addressing these issues requires concerted efforts to audit system performance across diverse populations, identify the sources of disparity, and implement corrective measures that may include dataset rebalancing, algorithmic adjustments, or the development of specialized evaluation benchmarks.

10.5.3 Methodologies for Conducting Error Analysis

Effective error analysis employs a variety of methodological approaches tailored to the specific characteristics of the AI system and its application domain. One foundational technique involves confusion matrix analysis, which systematically tracks what types of mistakes a classifier makes and how frequently they occur. This approach proves particularly valuable for understanding whether errors are randomly distributed or concentrated in specific categories that might indicate underlying biases or knowledge gaps in the model. For generative AI systems, error analysis often takes the form of output quality assessment across different input categories, examining how factors like input complexity, domain specificity, or linguistic features correlate with output quality.

More sophisticated error analysis frameworks incorporate adversarial testing methodologies designed to probe system weaknesses deliberately. These approaches might involve stress-testing models with carefully constructed edge cases, ambiguous inputs, or counterfactual scenarios that reveal brittle decision boundaries.

In natural language processing, this could involve testing whether language models maintain consistent factual accuracy when presented with negated statements or whether translation systems preserve meaning when handling culturally specific references. Such rigorous testing not only identifies failure modes but also provides valuable data for improving model robustness through techniques like adversarial training or architecture modifications.

10.5.4 Root Causes of Performance Disparities

Delving deeper into the origins of performance disparities reveals multiple interconnected factors that contribute to uneven AI system behavior. Dataset composition stands as one of the primary determinants, with models trained on unrepresentative or biased data invariably reproducing those biases in their outputs.

The phenomenon of "representation bias" occurs when certain groups or language varieties appear insufficiently in training data, while "labeling bias" stems from subjective or problematic annotations that reflect human prejudices. Even when datasets appear balanced at a surface level, subtle correlations between protected attributes and other features can lead to disparate impacts that only emerge through careful analysis.

Algorithmic factors also play a significant role in performance disparities. Model architectures optimized for dominant languages or majority populations may inherently struggle with linguistic structures or visual patterns common in other contexts. The choice of loss functions, optimization strategies, and evaluation metrics can inadvertently prioritize performance on majority groups at the expense of minorities. Additionally, the transfer learning paradigm common in contemporary AI, where models pre-trained on large generic datasets are fine-tuned for specific tasks, can propagate and amplify biases present in the foundational models. These technical factors combine with societal and structural issues to create complex patterns of disparity that require multifaceted solutions.

10.5.5 Mitigation Strategies for Reducing Disparities

Addressing performance disparities in AI systems demands a comprehensive approach that intervenes at multiple stages of the development lifecycle. At the data level, techniques such as strategic oversampling of underrepresented groups, synthetic data generation for rare cases, and rigorous dataset auditing help create more balanced training environments.

Algorithmic interventions might include the development of fairness-aware loss functions that explicitly optimize for equitable performance across subgroups or the implementation of post-processing techniques that adjust model outputs to reduce disparate impact. Architectural innovations like modular networks that handle different linguistic or demographic groups through specialized components have shown promise in reducing performance gaps while maintaining overall system efficiency.

Evaluation protocols themselves require rethinking to properly assess and mitigate disparities. Traditional metrics that report aggregate performance often mask significant variations across subgroups, necessitating the development of disaggregated evaluation frameworks that measure and track performance separately for different populations.

The creation of specialized challenge sets that deliberately test known weak points, combined with ongoing monitoring of real-world performance, helps maintain awareness of potential disparities as systems evolve. Perhaps most importantly, establishing feedback mechanisms that allow affected communities to report and help analyze system failures ensures that mitigation efforts remain grounded in real-world impacts rather than abstract statistical measures.

10.5.6 Role of Transparency and Accountability

Building truly equitable AI systems requires institutionalizing transparency and accountability throughout the development and deployment process. Comprehensive documentation of model limitations, known error patterns, and performance disparities should become standard practice, enabling downstream users to make informed decisions about system applicability. Version control systems that track not just model parameters but also the evolution of training data and evaluation methodologies create audit trails that facilitate retrospective analysis of performance changes. Responsible organizations are increasingly adopting impact assessment frameworks that systematically evaluate potential harms before deployment and establish protocols for addressing disparities that emerge in production environments. The movement toward algorithmic accountability also benefits from external oversight mechanisms. Independent audits, standardized benchmarking initiatives, and regulatory requirements for disparity reporting all contribute to an ecosystem where performance gaps cannot be easily ignored or concealed.

Academic conferences and journals are increasingly emphasizing the importance of thorough error analysis by requiring submissions to include detailed discussions of failure modes and limitations. This cultural shift toward transparency represents a maturation of the field, recognizing that understanding and addressing system weaknesses is as important as touting performance benchmarks.

CHAPTER

Infrastructure and Deployment 11

11.1 APIS AND CLOUD-BASED LANGUAGE SERVICES

APIs and cloud-based language services have become central to the modern digital ecosystem, reshaping how humans and machines communicate. By providing scalable, accessible, and multilingual tools, these technologies have empowered businesses, institutions, and individuals to engage across languages and cultures. While challenges such as privacy, bias, and inclusivity remain, ongoing innovations and responsible practices offer pathways to overcome them.

The integration of APIs into everyday life underscores their transformative power, and their continued evolution promises to further democratize access to advanced language technologies. In this way, APIs and cloud-based services are not just technical solutions but enablers of global connectivity, inclusivity, and understanding.

The growing influence of APIs and cloud-based language services carries significant ethical and social implications. These technologies can either promote inclusivity or deepen inequalities depending on how they are developed and deployed. For example, expanding language coverage to include low-resource languages supports cultural preservation and broadens access to digital resources. Conversely, neglecting such languages risks reinforcing linguistic hierarchies. There is also the question of how AI-driven language services might impact jobs, particularly in areas such as translation and customer service. Balancing efficiency with human oversight is necessary to avoid displacing human expertise entirely. Ethical guidelines and transparent governance are needed to ensure that the benefits of these technologies are equitably distributed across societies.

The future of APIs and cloud-based language services promises to be both transformative and inclusive if guided thoughtfully. As language models grow more sophisticated, APIs will likely provide even more nuanced and context-sensitive interactions, bridging cultural and linguistic divides. Cloud infrastructure will continue to expand, enabling faster, more reliable, and more secure delivery of services. Collaboration between cloud providers, researchers, and policymakers will play a critical role in addressing challenges related to bias, inclusivity, and data governance. Furthermore, advancements in multimodal AI may lead to APIs that seamlessly integrate text, voice, image, and video inputs, creating richer and more human-like interactions. Ultimately, the trajectory of APIs and cloud-based language services points toward a future where communication is not constrained by linguistic or technological barriers but is instead facilitated by intelligent, accessible, and ethically designed systems.

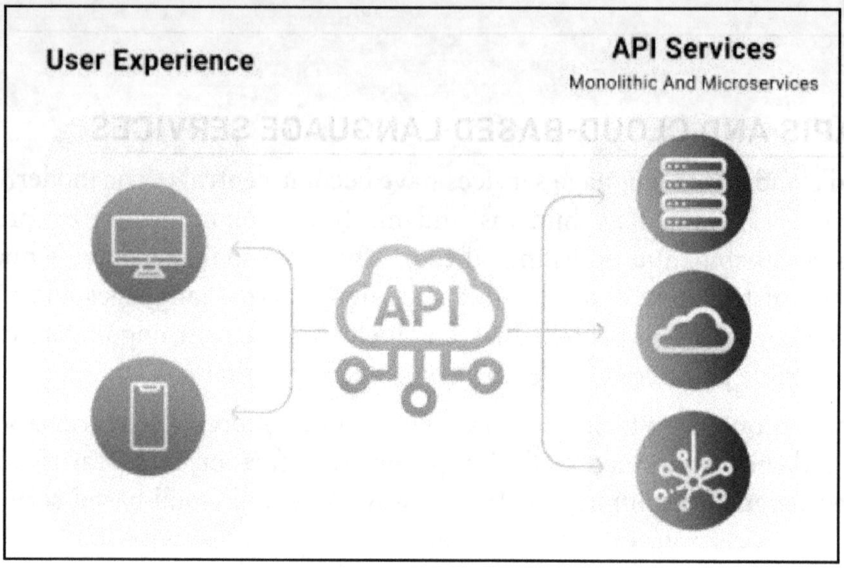

Fig: APIs in Cloud Computing

11.1.1 Role of APIs in Language Technology

APIs serve as the backbone of modern language services. They act as gateways that enable software applications to request and receive specific language capabilities, such as detecting the sentiment of a review, translating a text into multiple languages, or generating summaries of long documents. Instead of building complex language models from scratch, developers can integrate APIs provided by major cloud service providers into their applications. This reduces development costs, accelerates deployment, and ensures access to continuously improving language capabilities. For example, companies can add real-time translation to their websites or customer service platforms by calling translation APIs, or they can embed chatbots with natural language understanding features by leveraging conversational AI APIs. In essence, APIs allow the modularization of language technology, ensuring flexibility and adaptability across multiple use cases.

11.1.2 Cloud-Based Infrastructure and Its Advantages

The cloud plays a central role in hosting and delivering language services through APIs. Traditionally, advanced language processing required powerful computing resources that were costly and limited to research institutions or large corporations.

With cloud-based infrastructure, these capabilities are now available on a pay-as-you-go basis, eliminating the need for expensive on-premises hardware. This accessibility benefits small and medium-sized enterprises that want to leverage language technologies without making large upfront investments. Cloud-based solutions also offer scalability, meaning that services can handle fluctuating demands such as spikes in translation requests or sudden increases in chatbot usage. Moreover, cloud providers ensure regular updates, security, and maintenance, which further reduces the technical burden on users. The combination of APIs and cloud computing thus fosters a more inclusive ecosystem where advanced language services are available globally.

11.1.3 Key Language Services Delivered via APIs

Cloud-based APIs deliver a wide array of language services that cover nearly every aspect of natural language processing. Machine translation is one of the most common, enabling communication across linguistic boundaries in real time. Speech recognition and speech-to-text APIs allow spoken language to be converted into written text for applications such as transcription services, virtual assistants, and accessibility tools. Sentiment analysis APIs are used to interpret customer feedback, monitor brand reputation, and analyze public opinion on social media. Other popular services include named entity recognition, text classification, summarization, and question answering. With the growth of generative AI, APIs are increasingly being used to provide conversational agents, content creation tools, and personalized learning systems. These services collectively support industries such as healthcare, education, e-commerce, customer service, and entertainment.

11.1.4 Multilingual Capabilities and Global Communication

One of the most impactful aspects of APIs and cloud-based language services is their ability to facilitate multilingual communication. Globalization has heightened the demand for systems that can interact seamlessly across languages. Translation APIs make it possible for businesses to engage customers in their native languages, increasing inclusivity and market reach. Similarly, multilingual sentiment analysis allows companies to monitor opinions and trends across different regions. Cloud-based services often support dozens or even hundreds of languages, which is particularly beneficial for global enterprises, government organizations, and international NGOs. These capabilities are not only breaking down linguistic barriers but also ensuring that cultural nuances are respected in interactions, thereby fostering more authentic communication across diverse audiences.

11.1.5 Integration into Business and Everyday Applications

The integration of APIs into business operations has revolutionized how organizations interact with customers and manage internal processes. In customer service, chatbots powered by natural language understanding APIs provide instant responses to common inquiries, reducing the workload on human agents. In healthcare, speech recognition APIs assist doctors in creating electronic health records more efficiently. In education, translation and transcription APIs enable the creation of multilingual resources and real-time captions for lectures, enhancing accessibility for students.

On a daily basis, individuals use cloud-based language services when they ask a digital assistant for weather updates, use real-time translation apps while traveling, or rely on predictive text suggestions when writing messages. The widespread adoption of these services highlights how deeply APIs and cloud-based language technologies are integrated into modern life.

11.1.6 Challenges in APIs and Cloud-Based Language Services

Despite their advantages, APIs and cloud-based language services also face several challenges. Data privacy and security are among the most pressing concerns, as sensitive information is often processed by external cloud providers. Users must trust that providers comply with regulations such as GDPR and employ robust security measures. Another challenge is the issue of bias in language models, as AI systems trained on large-scale data can inadvertently reproduce societal stereotypes or exhibit performance disparities across languages.

Additionally, while many APIs support a wide range of languages, low-resource and endangered languages are often underrepresented, limiting inclusivity. There are also concerns about dependency on a few dominant cloud providers, which can create monopolistic tendencies and restrict innovation. Addressing these challenges is essential to ensure that APIs and cloud-based language services remain fair, secure, and accessible to all.

11.1.7 Innovations and Trends in Language APIs

The field of APIs and cloud-based language services is evolving rapidly. One significant trend is the integration of generative AI models into APIs, enabling more advanced conversational agents, content generation, and contextual understanding. Another innovation is the development of domain-specific APIs tailored to industries such as legal, medical, or financial sectors, which require specialized vocabularies and knowledge bases. Cloud providers are also exploring federated learning and edge computing to process data closer to users, thereby enhancing privacy and reducing latency. Additionally, APIs are being designed with greater adaptability, allowing them to handle code-switching, dialectal variations, and multimodal inputs that combine text, speech, and images. These innovations signal a future where language services become more intelligent, context-aware, and tailored to user needs.

11.2 ON-DEVICE VS. CLOUD-BASED PROCESSING

11.2.1 Fundamental Differences in Architecture and Operation

On-device and cloud-based processing systems differ fundamentally in their architectural design and operational characteristics. On-device solutions leverage the computational power embedded within end-user hardware, executing algorithms directly on smartphones, sensors, or specialized edge computing devices. This approach eliminates the need for constant data transmission to external servers, keeping information flows localized and contained within physical device boundaries.

Modern smartphones exemplify this capability, with their increasingly powerful system-on-chip designs incorporating dedicated neural processing units capable of handling complex machine learning tasks without external assistance. The self-contained nature of on-device processing creates a closed-loop system where input data never leaves the ownership perimeter of the device user.

Cloud-based processing operates on an entirely different paradigm, centralizing computational workloads in remote data centers that aggregate requests from multiple users and devices. These hyperscale facilities house thousands of interconnected servers equipped with high-performance processors and accelerators, providing nearly unlimited scaling potential for demanding computational tasks. The cloud model transforms local devices into relatively thin clients that primarily serve as input and output interfaces, while the heavy computational lifting occurs in geographically distributed server farms.

This architecture enables access to cutting-edge processing capabilities that would be impractical to embed in every end-user device, particularly for resource-intensive applications like large language models or complex scientific simulations. The centralized nature of cloud computing allows for continuous updates and improvements that immediately propagate to all connected users.

11.2.2 Performance Considerations and Latency Implications

Performance characteristics diverge significantly between on-device and cloud-based approaches, with each excelling in different operational scenarios. On-device processing provides deterministic latency since computations occur immediately on local hardware without dependency on network conditions. This proves critical for applications requiring real-time responsiveness, such as augmented reality filters, industrial control systems, or autonomous vehicle decision-making. The absence of network round-trip delays ensures consistent performance unaffected by internet congestion or server load fluctuations. Modern mobile processors have become sufficiently powerful to handle many AI workloads with acceptable speed, though they remain constrained by thermal limits and energy budgets that don't affect cloud infrastructure. Cloud-based processing offers superior raw computational throughput for tasks that can tolerate some latency, enabling the execution of models that would be impossible to run on constrained edge devices. The elastic nature of cloud resources allows for dynamic scaling to meet sudden demand spikes, a capability particularly valuable for services with unpredictable usage patterns.

However, the inherent latency introduced by data transmission to and from remote servers creates challenges for time-sensitive applications. Even with high-speed internet connections, the physical limitations of data traveling through network infrastructure impose unavoidable delays that may disrupt user experience in interactive applications. Advanced content delivery networks and edge computing hybrids attempt to mitigate these issues by bringing computation closer to end users without fully committing to on-device processing.

11.2.3 Privacy and Data Security Implications

The privacy and security implications of processing location represent one of the most significant differentiators between these architectures. On-device processing provides inherent privacy advantages by ensuring sensitive data never leaves the user's control. This proves particularly valuable for applications handling personal health information, financial data, or private communications where users rightfully demand maximum confidentiality. Local processing eliminates the risks associated with data breaches at cloud providers or interception during transmission, reducing the attack surface available to malicious actors. Many modern smartphones now incorporate secure enclave processors that provide hardware-level isolation for sensitive operations, further enhancing the security proposition of on-device computation.

Cloud-based processing introduces unavoidable privacy trade-offs by necessitating data transmission to third-party infrastructure. While cloud providers invest heavily in security measures including encryption and access controls, the fundamental requirement to send information outside organizational or personal boundaries creates potential vulnerabilities. Regulatory frameworks like GDPR and HIPAA impose strict requirements on data handling that become more complex to implement in cloud environments. That said, cloud providers can offer robust security postures that surpass what many organizations could achieve independently, with dedicated security teams and advanced threat detection systems that would be cost-prohibitive for individual users or small businesses to implement on their own devices.

11.2.4 Energy Efficiency and Environmental Impact

The energy consumption profiles of these processing models reveal important environmental considerations that grow increasingly relevant in our climate-conscious era. On-device processing generally demonstrates superior energy efficiency for individual tasks by eliminating the power requirements of constant data transmission. Wireless communication modules represent some of the most energy-intensive components in mobile devices, and minimizing their use through local processing can significantly extend battery life. This efficiency comes at the cost of computational capability limits that may require more frequent device upgrades as software demands outpace hardware capabilities, contributing to electronic waste concerns.

Cloud data centers achieve remarkable energy efficiency at scale through advanced cooling systems, workload optimization, and renewable energy investments, but their aggregate power consumption remains enormous. The environmental impact depends heavily on the energy sources powering these facilities and the efficiency of workload distribution algorithms. Some analyses suggest that consolidating computation in highly optimized cloud facilities may prove more energy-efficient than distributing it across millions of less efficient end-user devices, particularly for intensive workloads. However, this equation changes when considering the energy costs of constant data transmission and the embodied energy in frequently replaced user devices that can't handle evolving computational demands locally.

11.2.5 Economic and Business Model Considerations

The economic implications of processing location create divergent business models and cost structures that influence organizational decisions. On-device processing typically requires higher upfront hardware costs to equip devices with sufficient computational resources, but eliminates recurring cloud service fees. This model favors one-time purchase products where manufacturers can amortize development costs across device sales. The economics become challenging for applications requiring frequent model updates or enhancements, as these may necessitate hardware refreshes to maintain compatibility. Apple's neural engine development exemplifies the investment required to make on-device processing viable at scale, with custom silicon designs optimized for local AI workloads.

Cloud-based processing shifts capital expenditures to operational expenses, allowing organizations to access cutting-edge capabilities without massive upfront hardware investments. The subscription-based revenue models enabled by cloud services provide predictable income streams for providers and flexible scaling for customers. This proves particularly advantageous for startups and small businesses that couldn't otherwise afford the infrastructure required for advanced computational tasks. However, long-term costs may exceed on-device alternatives for high-volume applications, and vendor lock-in risks create strategic vulnerabilities for businesses dependent on specific cloud providers. The emergence of hybrid models attempts to blend these economic approaches, combining local processing for common tasks with cloud offloading for demanding operations.

11.2.6 Use Case Suitability and Application-Specific Demands

The optimal choice between on-device and cloud-based processing ultimately depends on specific application requirements and operational contexts. On-device solutions excel in scenarios demanding real-time responsiveness, offline functionality, or strict privacy guarantees. Examples include smartphone camera processing, voice assistant wake-word detection, and industrial equipment monitoring where network connectivity cannot be assumed. The automotive industry increasingly adopts on-device processing for advanced driver assistance systems, where split-second decision-making cannot tolerate network latency or dropout risks. These applications prioritize predictable performance over maximum computational capability.

Cloud processing dominates when applications require massive computational resources, centralized data aggregation, or continuous model updates. Large language model inference, video streaming recommendation algorithms, and enterprise data analytics typically rely on cloud infrastructure to handle their intensive processing needs. Applications benefiting from collective learning across user bases also favor cloud architectures, as they can aggregate insights from diverse data sources to improve models. The medical imaging field demonstrates hybrid approaches, where initial processing occurs on scanning devices but complex analysis leverages cloud-based supercomputing resources. Emerging technologies like federated learning attempt to bridge these paradigms by enabling collaborative model improvement without centralized data collection.

11.2.7 Future Trends and Converging Architectures

The future of computing processing models points toward increasingly sophisticated hybrid architectures rather than pure on-device or cloud approaches. Edge computing represents an intermediate paradigm that brings computational resources closer to end users without fully committing to on-device implementation. 5G networks enable new possibilities for distributed processing by providing high-bandwidth, low-latency connections that blur the traditional boundaries between local and remote computation. Advances in model compression techniques like quantization and pruning allow more sophisticated algorithms to run on resource-constrained devices, while hardware improvements continue to enhance local processing capabilities.

The growing emphasis on privacy-preserving technologies may accelerate adoption of on-device processing for sensitive applications, even as cloud providers develop more sophisticated confidential computing solutions. Differential privacy and homomorphic encryption techniques attempt to reconcile the benefits of cloud-scale computation with privacy requirements, though they currently impose substantial performance overheads. Semiconductor innovations like neuromorphic chips and photonic processors could radically reshape the balance between local and remote processing capabilities in coming years. Ultimately, the optimal processing strategy will continue to evolve alongside technological capabilities and shifting user expectations around performance, privacy, and sustainability.

11.3 EDGE AI AND MULTILINGUAL VOICE INTERFACES

The convergence of edge AI and multilingual voice interfaces represents a significant advancement in global communication technologies. By bringing sophisticated language processing capabilities to local devices, these systems enable more natural, culturally appropriate interactions with technology across diverse linguistic landscapes. The challenges of accommodating linguistic diversity while operating within computational constraints demand innovative solutions that combine technical sophistication with cultural understanding.

As research and development in this area continue to advance, the creation of more efficient architectures, culturally adaptive interfaces, and privacy-preserving systems will support the development of technologies that serve diverse global communities. The future of edge AI and multilingual voice interfaces is marked by opportunities for innovation that will enhance our ability to create more inclusive and effective communication technologies. Through continued efforts in this domain, we can work toward developing systems that better understand and accommodate the world's rich linguistic and cultural diversity, supporting more natural and accessible global communication.

The future of edge AI and multilingual voice interfaces is marked by exciting opportunities for innovation and advancement. The continued development of more efficient model architectures that can process diverse linguistic inputs while operating within computational constraints will enhance the capabilities of these systems. The integration of multimodal processing that combines voice with visual or contextual information presents new possibilities for more natural and intuitive interfaces. Advances in on-device learning techniques that enable continuous adaptation to user interactions will support more personalized and responsive voice interfaces. The realization of these future directions involves several important considerations that will shape their development. The creation of more comprehensive evaluation frameworks that assess both technical performance and cultural appropriateness will support better system development. The establishment of international collaborations that share knowledge and resources across linguistic communities will foster more inclusive technology development. The development of standards for privacy-preserving voice processing will enhance the security of these systems. As these technologies continue to evolve, they promise to create more accessible and culturally appropriate interfaces that can serve diverse global populations effectively.

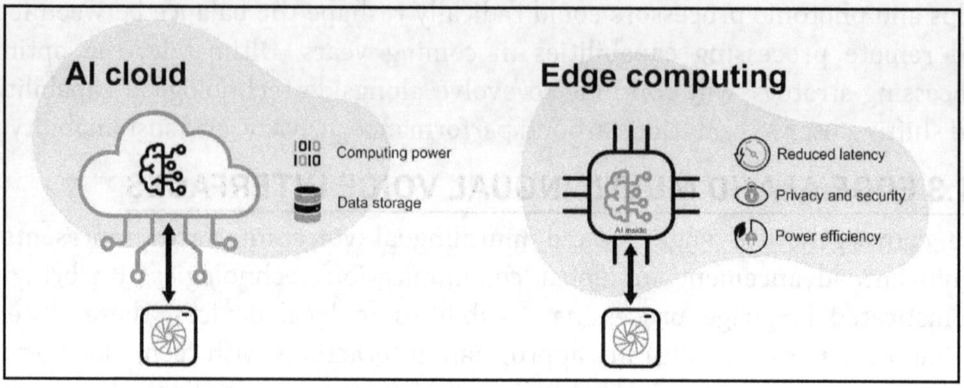

Fig: Edge AI and Vision for Data Automation and Privacy

11.3.1 Evolution of Edge Computing in AI

Edge computing has emerged as a paradigm shift in artificial intelligence deployment, moving computational processes closer to where data is generated rather than relying on distant cloud servers. This architectural transformation addresses several critical challenges in modern computing, including latency issues, bandwidth limitations, and privacy concerns associated with centralized processing. By bringing AI capabilities to local devices, edge computing enables real-time processing of voice inputs and other data streams while maintaining user privacy and reducing reliance on continuous internet connectivity.

The development of edge AI has been particularly transformative for voice interfaces, where low latency and real-time processing are essential for natural interaction. This evolution has enabled voice assistants and other spoken language systems to operate more efficiently in diverse environments, including those with limited connectivity. The ability to process voice inputs locally also enhances privacy by reducing the need to transmit sensitive audio data to remote servers. These advantages have made edge AI particularly valuable for developing multilingual voice interfaces that can serve users across different linguistic and cultural contexts.

11.3.2 Multilingual Voice Interfaces: Bridging Language Barriers

Multilingual voice interfaces represent a significant advancement in making technology more accessible to diverse linguistic communities. These systems enable users to interact with devices and applications using their native languages, breaking down barriers that have traditionally limited access to digital technologies. The development of effective multilingual voice interfaces requires sophisticated natural language processing capabilities that can understand and respond appropriately across different languages and dialects.

The challenges in creating these interfaces are substantial, as they must accommodate not only the linguistic structures of various languages but also their cultural contexts and use patterns. Successful multilingual voice interfaces incorporate several key components that address these challenges. Advanced speech recognition systems that can process diverse phonological patterns form the foundation of these interfaces. Natural language understanding models that capture semantic relationships across languages enable more accurate interpretation of user inputs. Culturally aware response generation ensures that system outputs are appropriate for different linguistic and social contexts. These components combine to create voice interfaces that can serve users from diverse backgrounds more effectively.

11.3.3 Technical Foundations of Edge AI for Voice Processing

The implementation of edge AI for multilingual voice interfaces builds upon several technical foundations that enable efficient local processing of voice inputs. Neural network architectures optimized for edge devices form the core of these systems, allowing sophisticated language processing to occur on resource-constrained hardware. Model compression techniques that reduce the size of language models while maintaining their accuracy enable deployment on devices with limited computational capacity. On-device training methods that allow models to adapt to specific users or environments without requiring cloud connectivity enhance the personalization and responsiveness of voice interfaces.

The development of these technical foundations involves several key considerations that affect their effectiveness. The optimization of model architectures to balance performance with computational efficiency creates systems that can operate effectively on edge devices. The adaptation of training methods to accommodate the constraints of local processing ensures that models can learn from user interactions while maintaining privacy. The implementation of efficient inference algorithms that minimize latency enables real-time processing of voice inputs. These technical approaches combine to create edge AI systems that can support sophisticated multilingual voice interfaces while operating within the constraints of local devices.

11.3.4 Challenges in Multilingual Voice Interface Development

The development of effective multilingual voice interfaces presents several significant challenges that reflect the complexities of human language and communication. The linguistic diversity of the world's languages creates substantial obstacles for systems that must understand and respond appropriately across different linguistic structures. The cultural context of language use adds another layer of complexity, as the same words or phrases may carry different meanings or implications in various social settings. The resource constraints of edge devices present practical limitations for implementing sophisticated language processing capabilities locally.

Addressing these challenges requires innovative approaches that can accommodate linguistic diversity while operating within computational limitations. The development of language-agnostic architectures that can process diverse linguistic inputs within unified frameworks helps create more flexible systems. The implementation of efficient attention mechanisms that focus computational resources on the most relevant parts of voice inputs enhances processing efficiency. The adaptation of model architectures to handle the specific characteristics of different languages while maintaining cross-lingual capabilities creates more robust systems. These approaches combine to enable the development of multilingual voice interfaces that can operate effectively on edge devices.

11.3.5 Cultural Adaptation in Voice Interfaces

The cultural adaptation of voice interfaces represents a crucial component in creating effective multilingual systems that serve diverse user populations. This adaptation involves several key considerations that affect how well voice interfaces accommodate different cultural contexts. The incorporation of culturally specific vocabulary and expressions enables systems to understand and respond appropriately to language use patterns in different communities. The adaptation of interaction styles to match cultural norms for communication creates more natural and comfortable user experiences. The implementation of culturally aware response generation ensures that system outputs respect local values and social protocols. The practical realization of cultural adaptation involves several important strategies that enhance the effectiveness of multilingual voice interfaces.

The collection of culturally representative training data that captures diverse language use patterns helps models learn appropriate responses for different contexts. The involvement of native speakers and cultural experts in the development process ensures that systems accommodate actual communication norms. The creation of evaluation frameworks that assess cultural appropriateness alongside technical performance supports more comprehensive system development. These strategies combine to create voice interfaces that can serve users from diverse cultural backgrounds more effectively.

11.3.6 Privacy and Security Considerations

The implementation of edge AI for multilingual voice interfaces raises important privacy and security considerations that must be carefully addressed. The local processing of voice inputs on edge devices enhances privacy by reducing the transmission of sensitive audio data to remote servers. However, this architectural shift also introduces new security challenges that require careful management. The protection of user data stored on local devices demands robust security measures to prevent unauthorized access. The implementation of secure communication protocols for any necessary data transmission helps maintain privacy while enabling essential connectivity.

Addressing these considerations involves several key strategies that support responsible development and deployment of edge AI systems. The implementation of differential privacy techniques that protect individual user data while enabling system learning enhances privacy protection. The development of secure enclaves that isolate sensitive processing on devices helps prevent unauthorized access to personal information. The creation of transparent data handling policies that inform users about how their information is processed and protected supports more ethical system implementation. These approaches combine to create edge AI systems that can process voice inputs securely while respecting user privacy.

11.4 COST AND COMPUTE CONSIDERATIONS IN MULTILINGUAL TRAINING

Cost and compute considerations represent some of the most significant challenges in multilingual training. The scale of data, infrastructure requirements, and training cycles make these models expensive and resource-intensive, often limiting access to large corporations and well-funded institutions. However, growing awareness of environmental impacts, financial constraints, and data imbalances is driving the development of more efficient methods and collaborative frameworks. By innovating in both algorithms and infrastructure, the field is moving toward a future where multilingual models can be trained sustainably and inclusively. Balancing performance, efficiency, and accessibility will be key to ensuring that language technologies serve diverse global communities without imposing prohibitive financial or computational barriers.

The future of multilingual training lies in developing more efficient, cost-effective, and sustainable approaches. Advances in hardware design, such as more energy-efficient GPUs and TPUs, will reduce compute demands. On the software side, innovations in model compression, efficient training algorithms, and low-rank adaptation techniques will continue to lower costs. Additionally, expanding collaborative frameworks and creating multilingual benchmarks will help distribute the financial burden and ensure balanced representation of languages. Ethical considerations, such as minimizing environmental impacts and ensuring equitable access, will also shape the trajectory of multilingual training.

Ultimately, the goal is to achieve high-quality multilingual models that are both computationally feasible and financially sustainable.

- **Scale of Multilingual Models:** Multilingual models such as multilingual BERT, XLM-R, and GPT-based systems are built to accommodate hundreds of languages with varying linguistic properties. Supporting this diversity requires architectures that are both expansive and flexible. To handle different scripts, syntactic structures, and vocabularies, these models often contain billions of parameters and require massive datasets. The computational scale for pretraining such models is immense, often involving high-performance clusters with thousands of GPUs or TPUs running for weeks or even months. The sheer size of these models results in high financial costs, making them feasible mainly for large corporations, research consortia, or government-supported institutions. For smaller organizations and academic groups, replicating these efforts often becomes prohibitive.
- **Data Collection and Processing Costs:** A significant portion of multilingual training costs arises before the training process even begins. Collecting, curating, and preprocessing multilingual datasets is resource-intensive. For high-resource languages like English, vast amounts of text data are readily available, but for low-resource languages, researchers may need to engage in costly data acquisition efforts such as web scraping, digitizing print materials, or collaborating with local communities. Once collected, the data must be cleaned, normalized, and tokenized across multiple scripts, which requires significant compute power. For example, handling languages with complex morphology, non-Latin scripts, or right-to-left writing directions demands additional preprocessing steps that increase computational costs. Thus, data considerations significantly affect the financial and computational investment required for multilingual models.
- **Computational Infrastructure Requirements:** Training multilingual models demands advanced infrastructure capable of handling large-scale computations. High-performance GPUs and TPUs are essential for managing massive datasets and large parameter counts. These hardware systems not only need to be powerful but also require extensive memory, storage, and bandwidth to efficiently process data. Furthermore, training multilingual models often involves distributed computing, which adds complexity in coordinating parallel processing across multiple nodes. The infrastructure costs extend beyond hardware to include electricity consumption, cooling systems, and long-term maintenance. As a result, compute requirements make multilingual

training one of the most resource-intensive endeavors in the field of artificial intelligence.

- **Energy Consumption and Environmental Costs:** An often-overlooked aspect of multilingual training is its environmental footprint. Training massive models requires significant energy consumption, which in turn leads to increased carbon emissions. Studies have shown that the carbon footprint of training a single large-scale model can be equivalent to that of several cars over their lifetimes. With multilingual models being even larger and more complex, their environmental cost is even more substantial. Organizations are increasingly being called upon to adopt greener practices, such as using renewable energy for data centers, improving model efficiency, or developing methods like distillation and pruning to reduce computational demands. Balancing the need for multilingual inclusivity with environmental sustainability is therefore a crucial consideration in future research.
- **Financial Constraints for Academic and Low-Resource Institutions:** The high cost of compute and infrastructure places academic institutions and organizations in low-resource regions at a disadvantage. While large corporations like Google, Microsoft, and Meta can afford to train massive multilingual models, smaller players often lack the budget and hardware capacity. This creates inequalities in access to cutting-edge language technologies and risks marginalizing low-resource languages that rely heavily on academic and community-driven efforts. The cost barriers also limit innovation, as independent researchers may be unable to experiment with large-scale models or propose alternative architectures. Addressing these disparities requires collaborative frameworks, open-source initiatives, and shared infrastructure that reduce financial barriers and democratize access to multilingual training.
- **Trade-Offs between Model Size and Efficiency:** In multilingual training, a key consideration is the trade-off between model size and efficiency. Larger models generally provide better performance across diverse languages but come with significantly higher computational and financial costs. Smaller models, while more affordable, may struggle with coverage and accuracy, particularly in low-resource languages. Researchers are therefore exploring approaches such as parameter sharing, modular architectures, and transfer learning to balance performance with efficiency. Knowledge distillation, where a smaller model is trained to replicate the outputs of a larger one, has

also emerged as a way to reduce compute demands while maintaining reasonable performance. These strategies highlight the importance of optimizing architectures to minimize cost without sacrificing inclusivity and accuracy.

- **Challenges of Multilingual Data Imbalance:** Another factor that influences cost and compute considerations is the imbalance of data across languages. High-resource languages dominate datasets, leading to skewed training that favors them over low-resource languages. Addressing this imbalance often requires oversampling underrepresented languages or creating synthetic data, both of which increase computational costs. Additionally, training strategies such as adaptive sampling or curriculum learning may be employed to better balance performance across languages, but these methods further extend training cycles and resource requirements. Thus, data imbalance compounds the financial and computational challenges of multilingual training.
- **Advances in Reducing Compute Costs:** Despite the challenges, researchers are developing innovative methods to reduce the cost of multilingual training. Techniques such as sparse modeling, mixture-of-experts architectures, and efficient fine-tuning approaches aim to reduce the number of active parameters during training, thereby lowering compute demands. Transfer learning, where knowledge from high-resource languages is applied to low-resource ones, also reduces the need for extensive data and training cycles. Cloud-based services and federated learning approaches further allow distributed, collaborative training, which can share costs across institutions. These advancements signal a shift toward more efficient training methods that balance inclusivity with affordability.
- **Role of Cloud Providers in Cost Management:** Cloud computing providers play a significant role in managing costs for multilingual training. Platforms like Google Cloud, Amazon Web Services, and Microsoft Azure offer access to high-performance computing resources on a pay-as-you-go basis, enabling smaller organizations to access advanced infrastructure without massive upfront investment. However, long-term reliance on cloud providers can also become costly, particularly for extended training cycles. Optimizing resource allocation, using spot instances, and employing cost-monitoring tools are strategies that organizations can adopt to manage expenses. The competitive landscape among cloud providers is also pushing prices downward, which may improve accessibility over time.

- **Collaboration and Shared Resources:** To mitigate the high costs of multilingual training, collaboration has emerged as a vital strategy. Research consortia, government initiatives, and open-source communities are pooling resources to create multilingual models and datasets. Projects such as Hugging Face's BigScience initiative exemplify how shared resources and collective efforts can reduce individual costs while advancing the field as a whole. By distributing the financial and computational burden across institutions, collaborative efforts make it possible to build inclusive multilingual systems that no single organization could achieve alone. This cooperative model also encourages transparency, reproducibility, and equitable access to language technologies.

11.5 SECURITY AND PRIVACY IN LANGUAGE AI DEPLOYMENT

The security and privacy challenges posed by language AI deployment represent one of the most complex technical and ethical puzzles of our digital age. Balancing the transformative potential of these systems with fundamental rights to privacy and data protection requires ongoing collaboration between researchers, developers, policymakers, and civil society. The solutions will necessarily be multifaceted—combining technical innovations in model architecture, cryptographic techniques, and system design with robust governance frameworks and ethical guidelines. Organizations that prioritize security and privacy throughout the AI lifecycle will not only mitigate legal and reputational risks but also build sustainable competitive advantage in an era of increasing scrutiny over data practices. As language AI capabilities continue their rapid advancement, the parallel development of strong security and privacy protections will determine whether these technologies ultimately empower or endanger the societies they aim to serve.

The security landscape for language AI will continue evolving as both attack techniques and defensive measures grow more sophisticated. Adaptive defense mechanisms that leverage AI itself to detect and respond to emerging threats in real-time represent a promising research direction. The development of standardized security benchmarks for language models will enable more systematic evaluation of vulnerabilities across different architectures and deployment scenarios. Explainability advances that provide meaningful insights into model decision processes may enhance the ability to identify and mitigate security flaws before exploitation.

Long-term solutions may require fundamental rethinking of language model architectures to incorporate security and privacy as first-class design constraints rather than afterthoughts. Techniques like modular networks that isolate sensitive functions, dynamic architecture adaptation based on threat detection, and biologically-inspired self-healing mechanisms could lead to more robust systems. The emergence of certified AI security professionals and standardized auditing frameworks will help institutionalize best practices across industries. As language AI becomes increasingly embedded in critical infrastructure, the development of fail-safe mechanisms and damage containment protocols will grow in importance to prevent localized vulnerabilities from cascading into systemic failures.

11.5.1 Data Privacy Challenges in Language Model Training

The training process for contemporary language models presents fundamental privacy dilemmas that challenge conventional data protection frameworks. Modern language AI systems typically ingest vast corpora of text data scraped from public and proprietary sources, potentially containing sensitive personal information, confidential business material, or protected intellectual property. Unlike structured databases where sensitive fields can be easily redacted, unstructured language data makes comprehensive identification and removal of private information extraordinarily difficult. Research has demonstrated that large language models can memorize and later reproduce fragments of their training data, including personally identifiable information, medical records, and confidential documents, even when such content appeared only briefly in the training corpus.

The scale of data collection required for training state-of-the-art models exacerbates these privacy risks. Training datasets often comprise trillions of tokens sourced from diverse origins, making thorough privacy auditing practically impossible with current tools and methodologies. Even when organizations implement data filtering and anonymization techniques, the complex statistical patterns learned by neural networks can enable reconstruction of sensitive attributes through careful analysis of model outputs. Differential privacy methods, which add controlled noise to training processes, offer partial solutions but frequently degrade model performance when applied at scales sufficient to provide meaningful protection. These tensions between model capability and privacy preservation represent one of the most pressing challenges in responsible language AI development.

11.5.2 Security Vulnerabilities Specific to Language AI Systems

Language AI systems introduce novel attack vectors that differ significantly from traditional software vulnerabilities, requiring specialized defensive strategies. Adversarial prompt engineering has emerged as a particularly insidious threat, where malicious actors craft inputs designed to bypass content filters, extract training data, or manipulate model behavior. These attacks range from simple prompt injections that override system instructions to sophisticated multi-step attacks that exploit emergent properties in large language models. The black-box nature of neural networks makes comprehensive vulnerability assessment exceptionally challenging, as harmful behaviors may surface only under rare combinations of inputs that evade standard testing protocols. Model inversion attacks represent another critical security concern, where adversaries use carefully designed queries to reconstruct sensitive information from a model's training data. Recent studies have demonstrated successful extraction of complete email addresses, phone numbers, and other personal identifiers from production language models through systematic probing. The deployment of language AI as APIs or cloud services amplifies these risks by providing attackers with unlimited query access to probe for vulnerabilities. Even when direct training data extraction proves impossible, attackers can often infer sensitive statistical properties about the training corpus through careful analysis of model outputs, potentially revealing demographic biases, commercial secrets, or security vulnerabilities in source systems.

11.5.3 Enterprise Security Considerations for AI Integration

The integration of language AI into enterprise environments introduces complex security considerations that extend beyond the models themselves to encompass entire business processes. Organizations deploying conversational AI for customer service must safeguard against accidental disclosure of proprietary information through chatbot responses, while simultaneously preventing malicious actors from extracting business intelligence through carefully crafted dialogues. The internal use of language models for document processing and analysis creates risks of sensitive data being incorporated into model weights or temporary processing artifacts that may persist in unexpected locations.

Access control mechanisms designed for traditional software systems often prove inadequate for language AI deployments, as the fluid nature of natural language interactions enables privilege escalation through social engineering-like techniques. Employees interacting with AI assistants may inadvertently disclose credentials or sensitive operational details unless rigorous guardrails are implemented. The growing practice of fine-tuning foundation models on corporate data creates additional attack surfaces, as the training pipelines themselves become targets for data exfiltration. Security teams must develop new monitoring frameworks capable of detecting anomalous usage patterns in language AI systems that may indicate attempted breaches or internal misuse.

11.5.4 Privacy-Preserving Deployment Architectures

Emerging architectural approaches aim to reconcile the utility of language AI with stringent privacy requirements through innovative system designs. Federated learning frameworks enable model improvement across distributed datasets without centralizing raw data, keeping sensitive information localized to originating devices or organizations. This approach proves particularly valuable in regulated industries like healthcare and finance, where data residency requirements constrain traditional cloud-based AI deployment. Secure multi-party computation techniques allow collaborative model training and inference across organizational boundaries while mathematically preventing participants from accessing each other's raw data.

On-device processing represents another promising direction for privacy-preserving language AI, where sensitive queries are processed locally without ever being transmitted to external servers. Modern smartphones and edge devices increasingly incorporate specialized hardware capable of running sophisticated language models while maintaining end-to-end encryption. Hybrid architectures that partition processing between local and cloud components based on sensitivity levels offer a practical compromise, allowing resource-intensive tasks to leverage cloud scalability while keeping personal data confined to user-controlled devices. These technical solutions must be complemented by rigorous data governance policies that clearly define retention periods, usage limitations, and access controls throughout the AI system lifecycle.

11.5.5 Regulatory Compliance and Ethical Considerations

The regulatory landscape for language AI privacy and security remains in flux as policymakers worldwide grapple with the unique challenges posed by these technologies. The European Union's General Data Protection Regulation (GDPR) establishes strict requirements for data minimization, purpose limitation, and user consent that directly conflict with standard practices in language model development. Right to be forgotten requests present particular difficulties, as completely removing an individual's data from a trained neural network without retraining from scratch remains an unsolved technical challenge. Emerging regulations like the EU AI Act introduce additional requirements for transparency and risk assessment that will fundamentally shape how language AI systems are developed and deployed. Ethical considerations extend beyond legal compliance to encompass broader societal impacts of language AI deployment. The potential for these systems to erode privacy norms through pervasive monitoring and analysis of human communication raises profound questions about the future of interpersonal interaction. Organizations deploying language AI must balance innovation with respect for individual autonomy, ensuring users maintain meaningful control over how their linguistic data is collected, analyzed, and utilized. The development of auditable AI systems that can demonstrate their handling of sensitive information without revealing proprietary model details represents an important direction for maintaining accountability while protecting intellectual property.

CHAPTER 12

Real-World Applications and Case Studies

12.1 MULTILINGUAL AI IN HEALTHCARE, EDUCATION, AND DISASTER RESPONSE

Multilingual AI stands at the forefront of efforts to make essential services more accessible across linguistic divides in healthcare, education, and disaster response. When thoughtfully implemented, these technologies can save lives through improved medical communication, transform educational opportunities for language minority students, and ensure equitable access to critical information during emergencies. Realizing this potential requires ongoing collaboration between AI researchers, domain experts, and local communities to address technical limitations, ethical concerns, and implementation challenges. As multilingual AI systems become more sophisticated and widespread, their responsible development and deployment will play a crucial role in building more inclusive global systems that serve all people, regardless of language. The measure of success will be not just technological advancement, but tangible improvements in health outcomes, educational achievement, and disaster resilience for linguistically diverse populations worldwide.

The deployment of multilingual AI in sensitive domains demands rigorous ethical scrutiny to prevent unintended harm and ensure equitable benefits. In healthcare, strict confidentiality protocols must govern how patient data in various languages is processed and stored by AI systems, with particular attention to compliance with regional data protection laws.

Algorithmic bias presents another critical concern, as models trained predominantly on data from certain language groups may provide inferior service to speakers of marginalized languages, potentially exacerbating existing healthcare disparities. Similar risks exist in education, where overreliance on AI translation could inadvertently privilege certain linguistic groups or academic traditions. Disaster response scenarios introduce acute ethical dilemmas regarding resource allocation based on AI-processed multilingual information. Systems must be designed to avoid giving preferential treatment to populations speaking more widely documented languages, and human oversight should verify critical decisions involving life-saving resources. All three sectors must address the risk of technological dependency, ensuring that multilingual AI supplements rather than replaces essential human services in healthcare delivery, education, and emergency management. Transparent documentation of system limitations in various languages helps manage user expectations and prevents overreliance on imperfect technologies.

The frontier of multilingual AI applications in these vital sectors points toward increasingly sophisticated and integrated solutions. In healthcare, next-generation systems may combine real-time translation with diagnostic support, analyzing patient speech patterns across languages to detect neurological conditions or mental health indicators. Educational applications are moving toward immersive language environments where AI facilitates multilingual collaborative learning among geographically dispersed students. Disaster response systems are incorporating predictive multilingual capabilities, analyzing social media chatter in various languages to anticipate emerging crises before they fully develop.

Advancements in speech technology will enable more natural interactions with multilingual AI systems, particularly important in high-stress medical and disaster scenarios where users may struggle with complex interfaces. The integration of visual communication with language technologies—such as AI that can interpret and describe medical images or disaster damage in multiple languages—promises to further enhance cross-linguistic understanding. Perhaps most importantly, the growing emphasis on community involvement in AI development for these sectors ensures that systems are designed with direct input from the diverse populations they aim to serve, leading to more culturally appropriate and effective solutions.

12.2 GLOBAL CUSTOMER SUPPORT AUTOMATION

Global customer support automation is redefining the way businesses interact with their customers. By combining artificial intelligence, multilingual capabilities, and data-driven insights, automation enables companies to meet the demands of an interconnected world. It reduces costs, enhances efficiency, and delivers consistent customer experiences across borders and cultures. While challenges such as complexity, trust, and ethical concerns remain, the continuous evolution of technology promises more advanced and effective solutions.

Ultimately, automation is not about replacing humans but empowering them to focus on high-value interactions while ensuring that customers everywhere receive timely and personalized support. Despite its advantages, global customer support automation faces several challenges. AI-driven systems still struggle with highly complex queries that require nuanced judgment, empathy, or negotiation. Misinterpretations of intent, especially in languages with limited training data, can frustrate customers rather than assist them. Additionally, customers sometimes prefer human interactions, particularly when dealing with sensitive or urgent matters. Over-reliance on automation risks alienating users if not balanced with human support. Ethical concerns such as data privacy, transparency, and algorithmic bias also need to be addressed to build trust in automated systems. These limitations highlight the importance of hybrid models that combine automation with human oversight.

Global businesses face unique challenges in customer support, including language diversity, cultural differences, and round-the-clock availability. Traditional human-driven support systems often fail to keep up with the volume of queries and the expectation of instant responses. Customers today demand immediacy, accuracy, and personalization, regardless of their location. Automation addresses these demands by enabling scalable systems that operate continuously, providing quick resolutions to common problems while freeing human agents to handle complex cases. As customer loyalty increasingly depends on service quality, automation becomes a vital tool for maintaining competitiveness in international markets.

Artificial intelligence lies at the core of global customer support automation. AI-driven chatbots, virtual assistants, and automated helpdesks are capable of understanding natural language, detecting intent, and providing contextually relevant responses. These systems are continuously trained on large datasets, which allows them to improve accuracy and efficiency over time. Machine learning models can analyze past customer interactions to predict common issues and proactively suggest solutions. In multilingual contexts, natural language processing technologies enable chatbots to communicate across different languages, thereby breaking down barriers that previously hindered global support systems. AI ensures that automation is not just about speed but also about quality and personalization.

One of the most significant challenges in global customer support is language diversity. Customers expect to communicate in their native languages, and failure to meet this expectation often results in dissatisfaction and brand mistrust. Automation tools equipped with multilingual capabilities allow companies to deliver seamless support in dozens of languages without needing to hire extensive teams of translators or multilingual agents. Natural language translation models and sentiment analysis tools also help organizations adapt responses to different cultural contexts. This reduces misunderstandings and ensures that communication feels natural and respectful, enhancing the overall customer experience.

Global customer support automation dramatically reduces the costs associated with staffing large call centers and training human agents. Automated systems can handle repetitive tasks such as answering frequently asked questions, resetting passwords, or providing order status updates. This minimizes the workload for human representatives, allowing them to focus on complex or sensitive issues where human empathy and critical thinking are required. Additionally, automation enables organizations to scale quickly without incurring proportional increases in labor costs. For businesses expanding into new markets, automation provides an efficient way to offer support without building costly regional support centers.

Contrary to the perception that automation makes customer service impersonal, advanced systems are increasingly capable of providing tailored interactions. By leveraging customer data such as purchase history, browsing behavior, and prior interactions, automated tools can deliver personalized recommendations and responses. For example, a chatbot can greet a returning customer by name, recall their past issues, and suggest relevant solutions. This creates a sense of continuity and care, which strengthens customer trust and satisfaction. The combination of personalization with automation ensures that global businesses can provide both efficiency and empathy in their support systems.

Modern customers interact with businesses through multiple channels, including email, social media, live chat, mobile apps, and voice assistants. Global customer support automation is most effective when integrated seamlessly across these channels. Omnichannel automation ensures that a customer's history and context follow them across platforms, preventing repetitive explanations and fragmented experiences. For instance, a query initiated on social media can be continued via live chat with full continuity. This holistic approach creates a unified customer experience while reducing friction and enhancing satisfaction on a global scale.

Automation not only handles customer interactions but also generates valuable data. Each automated exchange provides insights into customer behavior, common pain points, and emerging issues. By analyzing this data, businesses can identify trends, refine their support strategies, and improve product offerings. Global support systems particularly benefit from data-driven insights, as they reveal regional differences in customer needs and expectations. This allows companies to tailor services to specific markets and continuously optimize their support strategies. Automation thus plays a dual role: it improves immediate efficiency while driving long-term organizational growth.

The future of global customer support automation lies in greater sophistication, adaptability, and collaboration between humans and machines. Advances in natural language processing and conversational AI will continue to make automated systems more accurate and human-like. Emerging technologies such as generative AI are expected to enhance the creativity and flexibility of automated responses. Additionally, as businesses adopt more advanced predictive analytics, support systems will shift from reactive to proactive, anticipating customer issues before they arise. The integration of automation with the Internet of Things and smart devices will also expand customer support into new domains. The long-term trajectory points to fully intelligent support ecosystems that deliver seamless, personalized, and globally inclusive experiences.

12.3 MEDIA AND CONTENT LOCALIZATION

Traditional localization practices focused primarily on linguistic accuracy, employing direct translation techniques that often failed to capture cultural context or regional nuances. Contemporary approaches recognize localization as a multidimensional process involving linguistic, visual, and contextual adaptation tailored to specific markets. Subtitling and dubbing have advanced through AI-assisted speech recognition and text-to-speech technologies that maintain vocal characteristics while adapting dialogue pacing to different languages. Visual localization now routinely alters on-screen text, graphics, and even scene compositions to accommodate reading direction variations and cultural symbolism preferences across regions.

The emergence of transcreation as a specialized discipline reflects this evolution, where marketing messages and branded content undergo creative reinterpretation rather than literal translation. This approach preserves emotional impact and persuasive power across cultural contexts, addressing the reality that humor, metaphors, and social references rarely translate directly. Simultaneously, automated quality assurance systems scan localized content for potential cultural insensitivities, religious conflicts, or political implications that might resonate differently in target markets than in the original production context.

Artificial intelligence has transformed media localization workflows, enabling unprecedented scalability without sacrificing quality. Neural machine translation engines trained on domain-specific media corpora produce first-draft translations with contextual awareness of genre conventions, whether adapting legal dramas, romantic comedies, or documentary narration. Computer vision algorithms automatically identify and track on-screen text for replacement, significantly reducing manual effort in graphic localization for news broadcasts or streaming platform interfaces.

Voice cloning technologies now support multilingual voiceovers that preserve the original performer's vocal timbre and emotional range, while speech synthesis systems adjust lip movements in dubbed content to better match translated dialogue timing. For live broadcasts, real-time translation and captioning systems combine automatic speech recognition with AI-mediated language conversion, enabling near-instantaneous accessibility for global events. These technological solutions integrate with asset management platforms that maintain version control across hundreds of localized variants, ensuring consistency when updating source content or addressing regional compliance requirements.The most sophisticated localization strategies confront persistent challenges in navigating cultural differences that extend beyond language. Visual storytelling conventions vary significantly between markets, influencing decisions about scene selection, editing pace, and even color grading for different regional preferences. Social norms surrounding depictions of gender, religion, and authority figures require careful consideration, as content that resonates positively in one culture may provoke unintended reactions elsewhere.

Historical contexts present particular difficulties, where references familiar to source audiences may carry completely different connotations abroad. Localization teams must decide whether to adapt such elements, add explanatory context, or in some cases, recommend content modifications for specific markets. Even seemingly universal concepts like family relationships or humor styles contain cultural specificity that demands thoughtful localization strategies. The most effective solutions combine algorithmic analysis of successful regional content patterns with human cultural consultants who provide nuanced guidance on sensitive adaptations.

Media localization must navigate an increasingly complex web of regional content regulations that govern everything from advertising claims to historical representation. Age rating systems vary significantly between countries, requiring localized versions to meet different standards for language, violence, or sexual content. Product placement regulations differ across markets, sometimes necessitating visual edits or disclosure text adaptations in localized versions.

Accessibility mandates represent another critical consideration, with countries enforcing distinct requirements for closed captioning, audio descriptions, and sign language interpretation. Automated compliance checking systems now scan localized content against regional regulatory databases, flagging potential issues before distribution. For news organizations operating internationally, localization extends to verifying the accuracy of translated facts and figures against regional source materials, ensuring journalistic integrity across language versions.

The economics of content localization have shifted dramatically with changing consumption patterns and technological capabilities. Streaming platforms employ predictive analytics to determine localization priorities, analyzing subscriber demographics and viewing patterns to allocate resources among languages and content types. Dynamic cost-benefit models help rights holders decide between full dubbing, subtitling, or partial localization based on market size, audience preferences, and platform requirements.

Crowdsourced localization platforms now complement professional services, particularly for user-generated content and niche media, though quality control remains challenging. Hybrid models leverage community input for cultural authenticity while maintaining professional oversight for technical execution.

For major studios and publishers, centralized localization management systems coordinate workflows across dozens of languages, tracking progress and budgets while ensuring brand consistency across territories.

Emerging technologies promise to further revolutionize how content crosses linguistic and cultural boundaries. Real-time adaptive localization may soon allow viewers to select personalized localization preferences that blend translated dialogue with culturally appropriate visual elements. Advances in contextual AI could enable dynamic content adjustment based on viewer location, age, or cultural background while maintaining narrative coherence.

Generative AI applications may produce localized versions that adapt not just language but cultural references and storytelling conventions to match regional preferences. Blockchain-based rights management could streamline the complex licensing required for international distribution while ensuring proper attribution and compensation for localization contributors. As these technologies mature, they will enable more granular and responsive localization strategies that keep pace with the accelerating global demand for culturally resonant digital content.

12.4 GOVERNMENT AND NGO USE CASES

Governments and non-governmental organizations (NGOs) play a crucial role in addressing societal challenges, delivering public services, and supporting vulnerable populations across the globe. As the complexity of governance and humanitarian work increases, both sectors are turning to digital technologies, artificial intelligence, and data-driven systems to enhance their efficiency and effectiveness. Use cases for governments and NGOs highlight how technology is not only transforming operations but also redefining the way these entities engage with citizens, communities, and stakeholders.

- One of the most significant areas where governments are using technology is in public service delivery. E-governance platforms allow citizens to access services such as tax filing, identification documents, and welfare applications online. By digitizing these services, governments reduce bureaucracy, improve transparency, and cut costs. In countries like India, digital identity systems such as Aadhaar have allowed millions of citizens to gain access to essential services without intermediaries. Similarly, NGOs working in rural areas use mobile-based platforms to connect communities with healthcare, education, and financial services, bridging gaps that traditional systems cannot address effectively.
- Governments and NGOs frequently collaborate in healthcare and humanitarian relief efforts, particularly during crises. During the

COVID-19 pandemic, technology-enabled systems were used to track infections, schedule vaccinations, and disseminate accurate information to the public. NGOs played a vital role in extending these services to vulnerable groups, ensuring no community was left behind. Artificial intelligence has also been used in predicting disease outbreaks, analyzing medical records, and optimizing the distribution of medical supplies. For NGOs engaged in humanitarian aid, satellite imagery, drones, and data analytics help in mapping disaster-affected areas, coordinating relief supplies, and ensuring timely assistance to people in need.

- Education is another domain where governments and NGOs have developed significant use cases. Many countries have adopted e-learning platforms to ensure access to quality education for students in remote or underserved regions. Governments integrate online resources into formal school systems, while NGOs often focus on marginalized groups such as refugees, children in conflict zones, or those without internet access. By using low-cost digital devices, community learning centers, and offline educational applications, NGOs bring learning opportunities to communities that would otherwise remain excluded. These efforts not only address educational disparities but also promote digital literacy, preparing individuals for the demands of the modern economy.

- Governments are increasingly using digital systems to manage welfare programs, ensuring benefits reach the intended populations directly. Cash transfer programs enabled through digital banking and mobile money have become popular methods of providing financial support to low-income families. NGOs complement these efforts by focusing on grassroots poverty alleviation projects, offering microfinance programs, vocational training, and women's empowerment initiatives. Technology plays a key role in monitoring these programs, assessing their effectiveness, and reducing the corruption or leakage often associated with manual distribution of resources. Together, governments and NGOs are building more inclusive welfare ecosystems that support long-term development.

- Disaster preparedness and response represent critical use cases for governments and NGOs. Governments rely on data-driven early warning systems for floods, earthquakes, and hurricanes to protect citizens and coordinate evacuations. NGOs, on the other hand, work closely with communities during crises, often serving as the first responders in remote or hard-to-reach areas. Mobile communication networks, geospatial data, and real-time analytics have improved the ability to deliver timely assistance. For example, during natural disasters, governments and NGOs use digital platforms to coordinate relief operations, allocate resources, and connect volunteers with communities in need. The integration of advanced technologies ensures faster and more efficient crisis management, saving lives and reducing long-term damage.

- Governments and NGOs use digital tools for advocacy and engagement with citizens. Governments employ online portals, feedback systems, and social media to interact with citizens, gather feedback on policies, and maintain transparency in decision-making. NGOs often use similar platforms to advocate for human rights, environmental protection, or social justice. Campaigns powered by digital media allow NGOs to amplify their voices, reach global audiences, and mobilize support for pressing issues. Technology enables grassroots campaigns to influence policy at national and international levels, creating stronger collaboration between governments, NGOs, and civil society.
- Corruption and inefficiency are persistent challenges in governance and development work. Governments and NGOs increasingly rely on digital systems to improve accountability and build public trust. Open data initiatives allow citizens to track government spending, monitor development projects, and verify whether resources are being used effectively. NGOs adopt similar tools to share project outcomes with donors and stakeholders, ensuring transparency in their operations. Blockchain technology is also emerging as a way to ensure secure and tamper-proof transactions in aid distribution and procurement. These measures strengthen accountability, reduce misuse of funds, and increase public confidence in institutions.
- Global challenges such as climate change, pandemics, and refugee crises require collaboration across borders. Governments and NGOs use digital platforms to share information, coordinate projects, and pool resources for international initiatives. For example, governments collaborate on cross-border health monitoring, while NGOs engage in international partnerships to tackle environmental issues or provide humanitarian relief. Cloud-based platforms and real-time communication systems enable global teams to work together seamlessly, regardless of geography. Such collaborative use cases demonstrate how technology fosters unity in addressing problems that transcend national boundaries.
- Despite the promise of digital transformation, governments and NGOs face challenges in implementing these use cases. Limited infrastructure,

particularly in developing countries, restricts access to digital systems for many communities. Data privacy and cybersecurity are growing concerns, especially when sensitive information such as health records or welfare data is involved. Additionally, the digital divide continues to exclude marginalized populations from accessing essential services. NGOs often struggle with limited funding, making it difficult to sustain long-term technological projects. These challenges highlight the need for balanced approaches that combine innovation with inclusivity and ethical considerations.

- The future of government and NGO use cases lies in greater integration of artificial intelligence, machine learning, and advanced analytics. Predictive models will allow governments to forecast social and economic challenges more accurately, enabling proactive policy-making. NGOs will benefit from using AI-driven tools to track the impact of their projects, optimize resource allocation, and expand their outreach. The adoption of blockchain and decentralized technologies is expected to strengthen transparency and accountability. Furthermore, as digital ecosystems expand, partnerships between governments, NGOs, and private technology companies will play a vital role in creating scalable, sustainable solutions for global challenges.

12.5 CROSS-BORDER BUSINESS AND E-COMMERCE ENABLEMENT

Cross-border business and e-commerce enablement represent a fundamental shift in the way trade operates in the twenty-first century. By leveraging technology, businesses of all sizes can reach international markets, providing consumers with access to a wider range of products and services. Although challenges in logistics, regulation, and cultural adaptation remain, the opportunities far outweigh the obstacles. With continued innovation in payment systems, artificial intelligence, and supply chain management, cross-border commerce will not only become more efficient but also more inclusive and sustainable. Governments, businesses, and consumers alike stand to benefit from this interconnected marketplace, which promises to shape the future of global trade.

Cross-border business has always existed in the form of international trade, but its scale and accessibility have grown dramatically with the advent of the internet and digital marketplaces. In earlier decades, only large corporations had the resources to manage international trade complexities. Today, however, small and medium-sized enterprises can leverage e-commerce platforms to connect with customers across continents. This democratization of trade has been fueled by online marketplaces such as Amazon, Alibaba, and eBay, which provide global storefronts and facilitate the distribution of goods and services worldwide. Technology is the cornerstone of cross-border e-commerce enablement. Cloud-based platforms allow businesses to host websites and manage transactions without the need for expensive infrastructure. Artificial intelligence is increasingly applied in areas such as recommendation engines, fraud detection, and personalized customer experiences. Language translation tools and multilingual chatbots bridge communication gaps, making it possible for businesses to provide customer support and marketing materials in multiple languages. Secure payment gateways and blockchain solutions also enhance the trustworthiness of international transactions, ensuring customers feel confident purchasing from foreign merchants.

One of the biggest challenges in cross-border commerce is logistics. Efficient movement of goods across borders requires coordination between customs authorities, shipping providers, and last-mile delivery networks. Advances in supply chain management systems and real-time tracking technologies have enabled businesses to provide customers with transparent updates on shipping status. Additionally, partnerships with global courier companies allow small businesses to offer competitive delivery times even across vast distances. The integration of digital customs clearance systems also speeds up the process of getting goods through regulatory checkpoints, reducing delays and operational costs.

Payment systems are critical in enabling cross-border transactions. Customers expect secure, convenient, and locally relevant payment methods. E-commerce platforms now integrate global solutions such as PayPal, Stripe, and Alipay, while also offering region-specific methods like UPI in India or M-Pesa in Africa. Currency conversion tools and digital wallets make it easier for businesses to accept payments in multiple currencies, lowering the barriers for international customers. For many developing countries, this digital financial inclusion also creates opportunities for small entrepreneurs to participate in global markets without traditional banking infrastructure.

Cross-border e-commerce faces challenges in navigating different regulatory systems across countries. Governments impose laws around taxation, data protection, consumer rights, and import restrictions that businesses must comply with. For example, the European Union's General Data Protection Regulation sets strict rules on data privacy, impacting how businesses handle customer information globally.

To support businesses, international trade agreements and regional collaborations are being designed to harmonize standards and reduce trade friction. Understanding these frameworks and ensuring compliance is a crucial component of successful cross-border business. Cross-border e-commerce enables businesses to expand into new markets without setting up physical stores or offices. By analyzing consumer demand across regions, companies can strategically target new demographics and diversify their revenue streams. For consumers, the benefit lies in greater choice, access to niche products, and competitive pricing. Businesses can also capitalize on global shopping events such as Black Friday, Singles' Day, and Cyber Monday, which attract massive international sales. The expansion of digital marketplaces ensures that even small artisans and startups can reach customers in countries far from their own.

Despite its advantages, cross-border e-commerce comes with significant challenges. Language barriers, cultural differences, and varying consumer expectations can affect customer satisfaction. Businesses must adapt marketing strategies and product descriptions to suit local preferences, which requires investment in localization. Cybersecurity threats, fraud risks, and data breaches also remain concerns in international digital commerce. Additionally, logistical complexities, customs delays, and fluctuating exchange rates add uncertainty to operations. These challenges highlight the importance of careful planning and the adoption of reliable digital solutions.

Artificial intelligence and automation are becoming increasingly vital in supporting cross-border e-commerce. AI-powered analytics help businesses forecast demand, identify market trends, and optimize pricing strategies. Automated translation tools allow product descriptions and customer support to be provided in multiple languages. Intelligent chatbots provide 24/7 assistance to customers across different time zones, improving satisfaction and trust. In logistics, AI-driven route optimization enhances delivery efficiency, while automation in customs clearance speeds up international shipments. These technologies are making cross-border commerce faster, more reliable, and more personalized.

As e-commerce continues to grow, sustainability has become a pressing concern. Governments, businesses, and NGOs are increasingly focusing on reducing the environmental impact of cross-border logistics. Eco-friendly packaging, carbon-neutral shipping, and optimized delivery networks are being adopted to minimize emissions. Consumers are also becoming more conscious of sustainability, preferring brands that demonstrate responsible practices. Businesses engaging in cross-border commerce must balance growth with environmental responsibility, as sustainable practices are not only ethical but also contribute to long-term customer loyalty.

CHAPTER 13

Future of Multilingual AI

13.1 UNIVERSAL LANGUAGE MODELS

The rise of universal language models has transformed the field of artificial intelligence and natural language processing. Unlike earlier systems that were designed for specific languages or limited tasks, universal language models aim to understand, generate, and translate text across multiple languages using a single unified framework. These models bring together advances in machine learning, multilingual corpora, and large-scale training techniques to create powerful tools capable of bridging linguistic divides. Their potential lies not only in enabling seamless communication across borders but also in supporting low-resource languages, enhancing accessibility, and democratizing knowledge globally.

Universality in language models refers to the ability of a single model to handle multiple languages and tasks without being restricted to one linguistic system. Traditional models were often monolingual, trained to perform well in a single language environment, which limited their applicability in multilingual contexts. Universal models, however, are designed to share representations across languages. This means that the same underlying framework can process English, Hindi, Arabic, or Swahili, while leveraging similarities and patterns across languages to improve performance. By building shared embeddings and representations, universal models reduce duplication of effort and provide a more scalable approach to multilingual AI.

The development of universal language models is closely tied to innovations in multilingual pretraining. Large-scale corpora containing texts from multiple languages are used to train these models in a way that allows them to learn general linguistic structures. Models such as mBERT, XLM-R, and GPT-based multilingual frameworks have demonstrated how pretraining across diverse data enables generalization. This pretraining allows the model to identify shared patterns such as syntax, grammar, and semantics that transcend linguistic boundaries. As a result, the model can adapt more easily to low-resource languages by leveraging knowledge learned from high-resource counterparts. One of the most significant advantages of universal language models is their efficiency. Instead of training and maintaining separate models for different languages, organizations can deploy a single universal system. This not only reduces computational costs but also ensures consistency in performance across languages. Universal models also enable zero-shot and few-shot learning, where a model can perform tasks in a language it was never explicitly trained on by relying on its generalized understanding. Additionally, universal models enhance inclusivity by supporting a wide range of languages, giving speakers of underrepresented languages access to AI-driven tools.

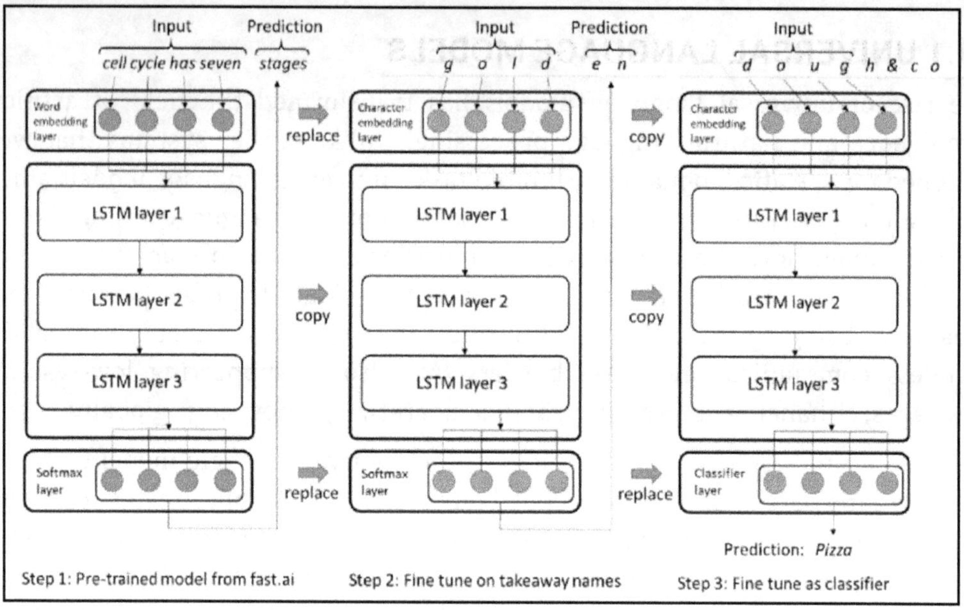

Fig: Universal Language Models

Universal language models have proven to be particularly powerful in machine translation. By capturing relationships between multiple languages within the same model, they achieve higher translation accuracy and fluency compared to traditional bilingual systems. This enables real-time communication across linguistic barriers, powering applications like multilingual chatbots, cross-border customer support, and global collaboration platforms. Beyond translation, universal models are used in summarization, sentiment analysis, and content moderation across different languages, ensuring that global digital platforms can function seamlessly in diverse linguistic environments.

While universal language models offer immense promise, their development is not without challenges. Training these models requires vast amounts of computational resources and diverse datasets that cover many languages. However, linguistic representation is highly uneven, with some languages having abundant digital data while others remain underrepresented. This imbalance can result in biased performance, where high-resource languages dominate while low-resource ones are not adequately supported. Furthermore, differences in grammar, writing systems, and cultural contexts make it difficult to build truly universal systems that perform equally well across all languages. Universal language models raise important questions about fairness, representation, and linguistic equity. If most of the training data comes from languages like English, Chinese, or Spanish, the resulting model may unintentionally marginalize smaller or endangered languages.

This creates a risk of reinforcing existing power imbalances in global communication. Ensuring that universal models fairly represent diverse linguistic communities requires intentional inclusion of low-resource languages and collaboration with local communities to create representative datasets. Ethical practices also extend to respecting cultural nuances, avoiding harmful biases, and ensuring that marginalized voices are amplified rather than erased.

One of the most transformative aspects of universal language models is their potential to support low-resource and endangered languages. By transferring knowledge from high-resource languages, universal models can provide translation, transcription, and information access in languages that otherwise lack digital resources.

This can play a crucial role in preserving linguistic diversity and promoting cultural heritage. Educational tools powered by universal models can make knowledge accessible in native languages, empowering communities to participate in the digital economy without having to adopt dominant languages. Cross-lingual transfer is a central mechanism enabling universal language models to function effectively. By learning representations that are shared across languages, these models can apply knowledge from one language to another.

For instance, a sentiment analysis model trained on English text may also perform well on French or German without retraining. This transferability greatly reduces the need for task-specific datasets in every language, lowering barriers to entry for multilingual applications. However, achieving effective cross-lingual transfer depends on the quality and diversity of the training data as well as the architecture of the model.

The future of universal language models is likely to be shaped by innovations that address current challenges while expanding capabilities. Advances in efficiency will be crucial, with research focused on reducing the computational costs of training and deploying these massive models.

Efforts to improve inclusivity by incorporating more low-resource languages into training datasets will also be central. Moreover, multimodal universal models, which integrate text with speech, images, and video, represent the next frontier, enabling richer and more contextualized communication across languages. Governance, regulation, and open collaboration between governments, researchers, and industry will play an essential role in ensuring that these models are developed responsibly.

13.2 BEYOND TEXT: MULTILINGUAL MULTIMODAL AI

Multilingual multimodal AI represents more than just the convergence of separate technological strands - it embodies a fundamental shift toward artificial intelligence systems that perceive and communicate about the world with human-like sensory integration across language boundaries. As these technologies mature, they will enable more natural cross-cultural interactions, more inclusive accessibility solutions, and more sophisticated analysis of our increasingly multimodal digital landscape. The ultimate promise lies in creating AI systems that don't just process different languages and modalities separately, but genuinely understand the unified human experience they represent - where words, images, sounds and context intertwine to create meaning that transcends any single mode of expression. Realizing this potential will require ongoing advances in neural architectures, training methodologies, and evaluation frameworks that can capture the rich complexity of truly multimodal multilingual intelligence.

Modern multilingual multimodal AI systems build upon sophisticated neural architectures that create shared embedding spaces for different data modalities. Transformer-based models with cross-attention mechanisms learn to align visual concepts with their linguistic representations across dozens of languages simultaneously. A single forward pass through such systems might process Spanish speech waveforms, Japanese text captions, and visual scene graphs while maintaining coherent contextual understanding across all inputs. The technical challenge lies not merely in handling each modality separately but in developing deep correlations between them that remain consistent across linguistic variations.

Training these systems requires carefully curated multilingual multimodal datasets where images, videos, or sensor data are annotated with parallel descriptions in multiple languages. Techniques like contrastive learning help align representations so that the vector embedding for an "apple" in English text closely matches its French and Mandarin equivalents in the visual domain. Recent breakthroughs in parameter-efficient modular designs allow knowledge transfer from high-resource language-vision pairs to boost performance in low-resource language combinations, addressing the data scarcity problem that affects many multimodal applications.

Multilingual multimodal AI is dramatically improving accessibility services for diverse linguistic communities. Real-time sign language translation systems now combine computer vision for gesture recognition with multilingual natural language generation, enabling seamless communication between sign language users and non-signers across language barriers. These systems can interpret American Sign Language and output spoken Japanese, or process Indian Sign Language while displaying Spanish text, with visual context helping disambiguate signs that may have multiple meanings. For visually impaired users worldwide, advanced multimodal assistants describe environments using culturally appropriate references in the listener's native language while processing visual inputs. A system might identify currency notes for a blind traveler, not just stating "banknote" but specifying "a 5000 Korean won bill with King Sejong's portrait" when interacting with an English speaker or "un billete de 10 euros con la imagen de Europa" for a Spanish user. The multilingual capability ensures these critical services remain effective regardless of the user's primary language or geographical location.

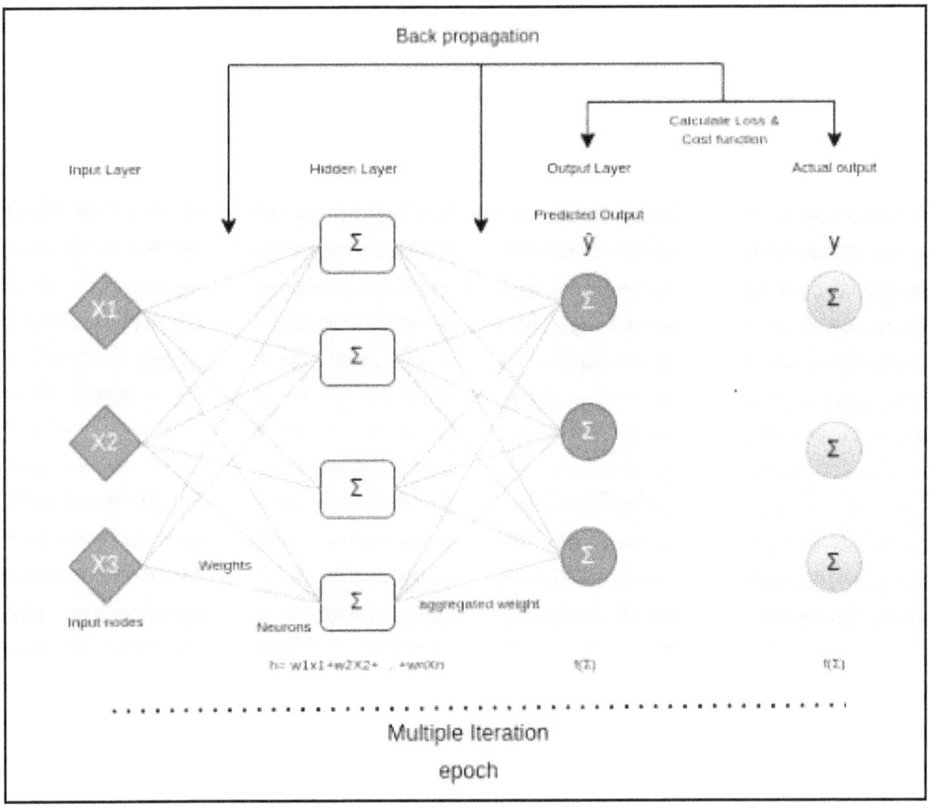

Fig: Multimodal AI Agents and Applications

Content moderation at global scale benefits immensely from multilingual multimodal analysis that examines text, images, audio, and video in tandem across hundreds of languages. Where traditional systems might separately analyze German text and an accompanying image, advanced models detect subtle correlations like culturally specific hate symbols paired with coded vernacular across languages. This proves particularly valuable for identifying emerging threats that combine visual elements with language-specific slang or regional dialects. Media monitoring systems now track news narratives as they evolve across languages and formats, recognizing when a political cartoon in one language version of a publication relates to an editorial column in another. For global brands, this capability provides comprehensive sentiment analysis that understands how visual marketing campaigns resonate differently when localized across markets. The technology also aids cultural preservation efforts by helping scholars analyze connections between indigenous art forms and oral traditions that exist in fragile multilingual ecosystems.

The development of robust multilingual multimodal systems faces several persistent technical challenges. Temporal synchronization proves difficult when aligning speech, text, and visual elements across languages with different information densities - a concept that might require ten words in German but only three in Mandarin must still match the same visual timeline. Cultural variations in visual interpretation present another hurdle, where images considered neutral in one context may carry strong connotations in others, requiring models to understand these nuances across all supported languages. The "modality gap" between how different languages describe the same visual content creates training complications. While English might emphasize actors and actions in describing an image, other languages may focus more on relationships or states of being, requiring models to learn these divergent descriptive patterns without losing factual accuracy. Evaluation methodologies also struggle to assess true multimodal multilingual understanding, as most benchmarks test modalities and languages in isolation rather than their complex interactions.

The next generation of multilingual multimodal AI points toward unified interfaces that fluidly combine speech, text, touch, and visual interaction across language barriers. Experimental systems already demonstrate real-time multilingual visual question answering where users can ask about an image in Hindi and receive answers in Portuguese, with the visual context maintaining semantic consistency throughout the translation. Retail applications allow customers to photograph products and receive specifications in their preferred language while the system processes shelf signage in another language. Educational technology stands to benefit tremendously from these advancements, with prototypes enabling immersive language learning where students interact with multilingual visual environments. A learner might point at objects in a virtual marketplace scene to hear their names in Swedish while seeing descriptive text in Arabic, with the system correcting pronunciation based on visual lip movement analysis. Such applications promise to make language acquisition more intuitive by embedding it in rich multimodal contexts that mirror naturalistic learning environments.

13.3 AI FOR LANGUAGE REVITALIZATION

AI is transforming the field of language revitalization by providing innovative tools for documentation, education, and preservation. While challenges remain, the integration of AI technologies offers hope for the survival of endangered languages. By leveraging AI responsibly and collaboratively, communities can work toward a future where linguistic diversity is celebrated and preserved. The continued development of AI-driven solutions will be essential in ensuring that no language is left behind in the digital age.

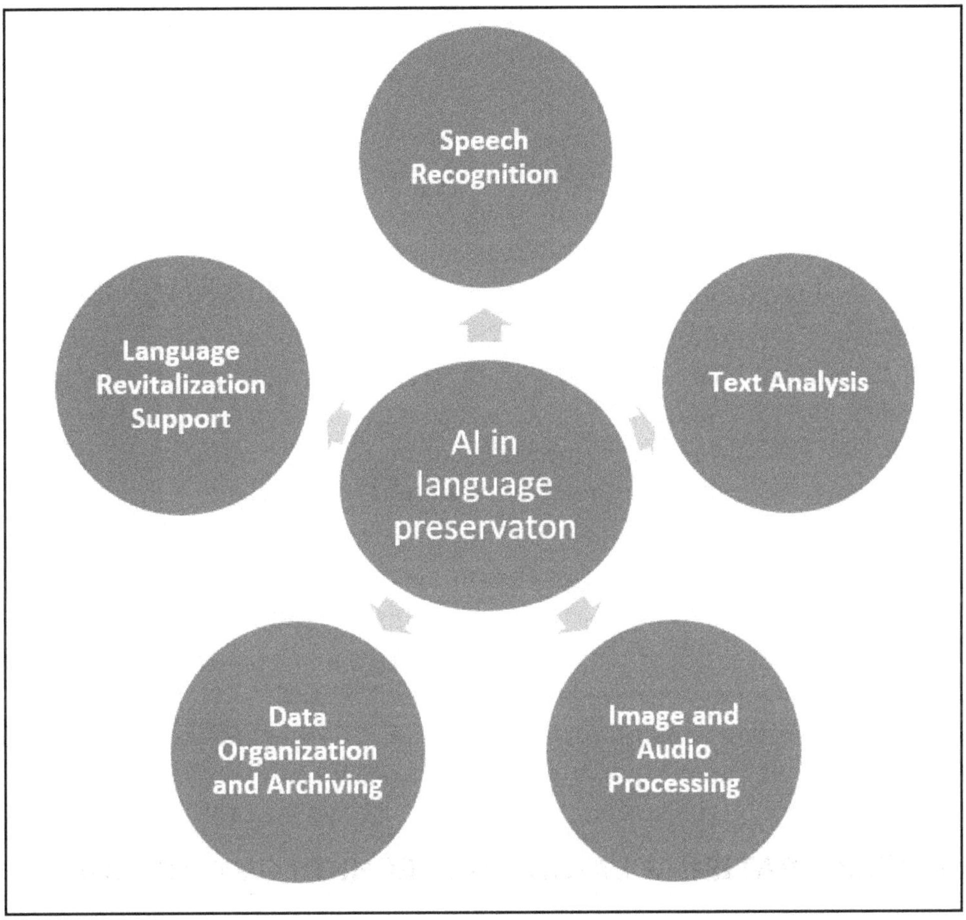

Fig: Reviving Indigenous Languages using Machine Learning

One of the primary challenges in language revitalization is the lack of comprehensive documentation. Many endangered languages exist only in oral form, making them vulnerable to being lost forever. AI technologies, such as automatic speech recognition (ASR) and natural language processing (NLP), can assist in transcribing spoken language into written form. Machine learning models trained on limited datasets can help linguists and researchers analyze grammatical structures, phonetics, and vocabulary, creating digital archives that preserve linguistic knowledge for future generations. AI has significantly enhanced language learning by making it more accessible and interactive. For endangered languages with few speakers, traditional learning resources are often scarce. AI-driven applications, such as language learning apps and chatbots, can simulate conversations, provide pronunciation guidance, and offer personalized learning experiences. These tools can be particularly useful for younger generations who may not have regular exposure to their heritage language. By integrating AI into educational platforms, communities can foster language acquisition in engaging and effective ways.

Another critical application of AI in language revitalization is speech synthesis. Many endangered languages lack digital voice representations, making it difficult for learners to hear proper pronunciation. AI-powered text-to-speech (TTS) systems can generate synthetic speech in these languages, allowing users to listen to words and phrases even when native speakers are unavailable. This technology can be integrated into educational materials, mobile apps, and online dictionaries, providing learners with essential auditory support.

While AI offers promising solutions for language revitalization, several challenges and ethical concerns must be addressed. One major issue is the lack of sufficient data for training AI models, as many endangered languages have limited written or recorded material. Additionally, there is a risk of misrepresentation or cultural insensitivity if AI tools are developed without input from native speakers. Ethical considerations also include data privacy, consent from indigenous communities, and ensuring that AI applications respect cultural values and traditions.

The future of AI in language revitalization looks promising, with advancements in machine learning and computational linguistics continually improving the accuracy and effectiveness of language preservation tools. Collaborations between AI researchers, linguists, and indigenous communities will be crucial in developing culturally appropriate and sustainable solutions. As AI technology evolves, it has the potential to play an even greater role in safeguarding linguistic diversity and ensuring that endangered languages continue to thrive for generations to come.

13.4 DEMOCRATISING LANGUAGE TECHNOLOGY ACCESS

Democratising language technology access is not just a technical goal but a social imperative. It ensures that technological progress benefits everyone, regardless of the language they speak. By addressing barriers, supporting multilingual AI, embracing open-source initiatives, and empowering communities, it is possible to build a more inclusive digital ecosystem.

The integration of policy, ethics, and cultural preservation into this process ensures that democratisation is holistic and sustainable. Ultimately, making language technologies accessible to all is a step toward greater equity, cultural resilience, and human empowerment in the digital age. Language technologies are integral to everyday life. From using digital assistants to navigate tasks, to relying on translation tools for cross-border business, and depending on automated captions for accessibility, these technologies are deeply embedded in human interaction. For communities whose languages are underrepresented in AI systems, the lack of access translates into limited opportunities for education, employment, and participation in the digital economy. Democratising access therefore ensures that the benefits of technological innovation are not restricted to a select group of linguistic communities but are shared broadly and fairly.

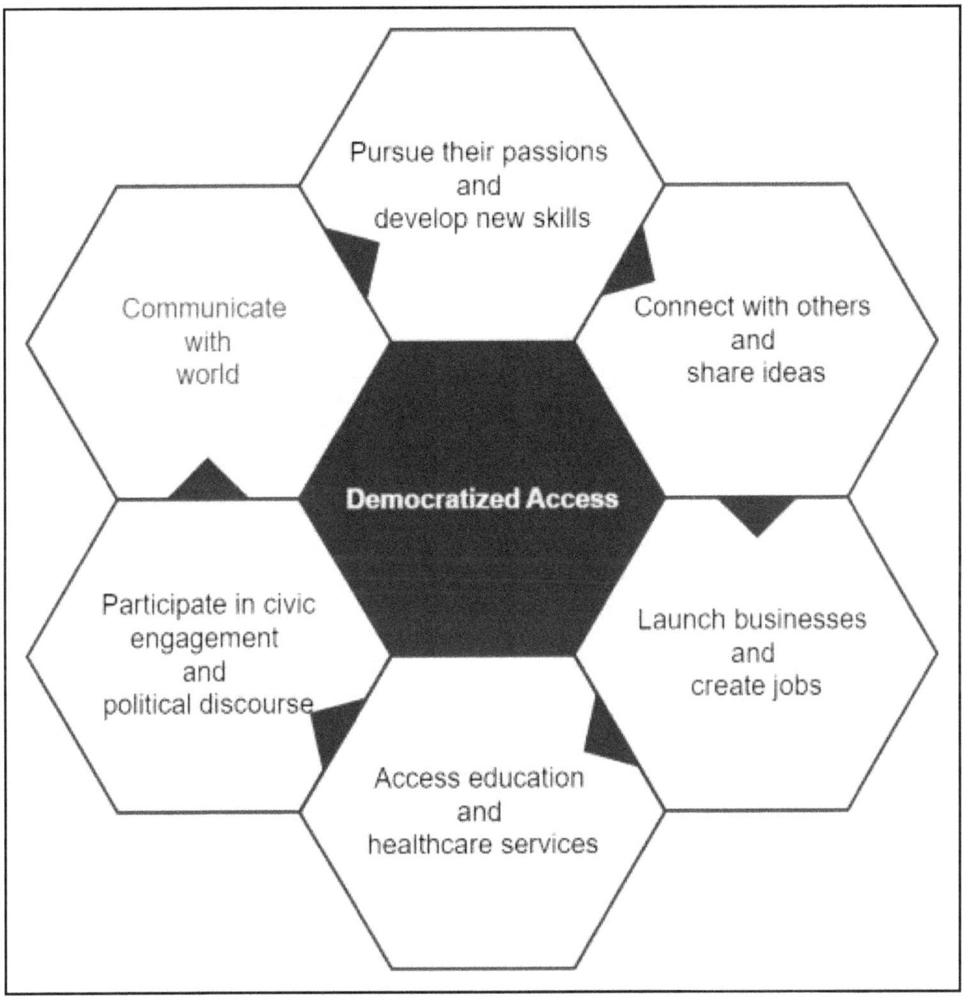

Fig: Democratized Access

Despite the promise of language technology, significant barriers prevent equitable access. One major challenge is the imbalance of digital resources. Languages with vast amounts of digital data are easier to model and integrate into AI systems, while low-resource languages lack sufficient text and speech corpora to train effective models. Another barrier is the concentration of AI development in a few global tech companies, which often focus on commercially profitable languages. This prioritisation excludes smaller languages, reinforcing inequalities. Moreover, socio-economic factors, such as limited infrastructure or lack of funding for linguistic research, also restrict the ability of some communities to benefit from language technologies.

Multilingual AI has become a promising solution to the challenge of inclusion. By training models on multiple languages simultaneously, researchers can leverage similarities across languages to improve performance in low-resource contexts. Transfer learning and universal language models allow knowledge from high-resource languages to benefit others, reducing the gap between dominant and underrepresented languages. Democratising language technology access thus requires continued investment in multilingual AI frameworks that are not restricted to a handful of languages but are designed to cover as many linguistic groups as possible.

Open-source projects are at the heart of democratising language technology. Platforms such as Hugging Face, Mozilla Common Voice, and Masakhane have shown how collaborative and community-driven initiatives can expand access. By allowing researchers, developers, and communities to contribute data, models, and tools, open-source initiatives lower barriers to entry and empower grassroots efforts to build language technologies. They also create opportunities for local innovation, as communities themselves can adapt and develop technologies in ways that align with their cultural and social needs. The open-source approach challenges the monopoly of large corporations and makes technological progress more transparent and accessible.

Governments and policy makers play a critical role in ensuring equitable language technology access. Public investment in data collection, linguistic research, and AI infrastructure can significantly accelerate progress for underrepresented languages. Policies that support digital inclusion and promote linguistic diversity can encourage technology companies to prioritize equitable language representation. Governments also have the responsibility to safeguard cultural heritage, and ensuring that local languages are integrated into digital platforms is an essential aspect of this. Democratising language technology requires a collective effort that brings together governments, academia, industry, and civil society.

One of the most profound areas where democratised access can make a difference is education. Students who speak low-resource languages often face challenges in accessing digital learning tools, which are typically available only in global languages. Language technologies such as machine translation, speech-to-text systems, and digital learning platforms can bridge this gap, enabling students to learn in their native language while accessing global knowledge. This not only improves educational outcomes but also fosters pride and confidence in one's linguistic identity. Democratising access ensures that knowledge is not limited by language barriers, creating more equal opportunities for learners worldwide. Languages are more than communication tools; they carry history, traditions, and cultural identity. Many endangered languages face the risk of extinction as they are excluded from digital technologies. Democratising access to language technology helps preserve these languages by making them usable in digital contexts, from social media to digital assistants. This visibility strengthens cultural identity and empowers communities to engage with modern technology without abandoning their linguistic heritage. By enabling underrepresented languages to thrive digitally, technology can contribute to the broader effort of cultural preservation.

The process of democratising language technology also raises ethical questions that must be carefully addressed. It is essential to ensure that the voices of local communities are central to decision-making about how their languages are represented and used. Exploitative practices, where data is extracted from communities without their consent or benefit, must be avoided. Ethical frameworks should guide the creation of inclusive technologies that respect linguistic rights and cultural ownership. Democratisation should not merely be about technological access but also about ensuring that access is just, fair, and empowering.

The future of language technology lies in inclusivity, and democratisation is the pathway to achieving it. Emerging techniques such as low-resource language modeling, unsupervised learning, and multimodal AI offer new opportunities to expand access. Collaboration between global technology companies and local communities will be vital in ensuring that development is equitable. As more resources become available and ethical practices are emphasized, it is possible to envision a digital world where every language has a place. Democratising language technology access has the potential to transform societies by breaking down barriers, expanding opportunities, and preserving linguistic diversity.

13.5 TOWARD TRULY INCLUSIVE GLOBAL COMMUNICATION

The path toward truly inclusive global communication represents one of the most complex and consequential challenges of our digitally connected age. It demands simultaneous advances in technology, design, policy, and infrastructure - all oriented toward the fundamental principle that every person deserves equal opportunity to communicate in ways that honor their linguistic and cultural identity. Realizing this vision will require moving beyond the paradigm of "internationalization" that simply extends dominant communication models to new markets, and instead embracing genuine "pluralization" that values diverse communication modes equally. The rewards for succeeding at this challenge extend far beyond commercial opportunity - they touch on fundamental human rights and dignity. In a world where so much conflict stems from failures of communication and understanding, building systems that foster connection across differences may prove essential to addressing larger global challenges. The technologies now emerging - from language-aware AI to adaptive interfaces - provide powerful tools for this work, but the ultimate determinant of success will be our collective commitment to designing communication ecosystems that leave no voice unheard.

Traditional digital communication systems have privileged a handful of dominant languages, forcing billions of users to adapt to linguistic frameworks that don't reflect their native modes of expression. Truly inclusive systems must move beyond this paradigm by developing interfaces that dynamically adjust to users' preferred languages, dialects, and communication styles. This involves creating writing systems that accommodate non-Latin scripts with equal fluency, voice interfaces that recognize regional accents without bias, and visual communication tools that transcend linguistic barriers entirely. The technical hurdles are substantial, requiring advances in rendering complex scripts, processing low-resource languages, and developing culturally aware design paradigms.

The representation challenge extends to signed languages, which have been particularly marginalized in digital communication platforms. Next-generation interfaces must incorporate sign language recognition and generation as first-class communication methods rather than accessibility afterthoughts. This demands multimodal AI systems that can interpret and produce the rich spatial grammar of sign languages while maintaining synchronization with text and speech outputs. Similarly, tonal languages and those with unique phonetic inventories require specialized treatment in voice interfaces to prevent the systematic exclusion of speakers whose speech patterns deviate from "standard" models.

Language forms just one dimension of inclusive communication - cultural context fundamentally shapes how messages are composed, interpreted, and valued. Communication systems must account for variations in conversational norms, from appropriate levels of formality to expectations around turn-taking and silence. In some cultures, indirect communication carries important social meaning that direct translation might erase, while others value explicit precision that might seem abrupt elsewhere. These cultural frameworks influence everything from emoji interpretation to expectations about response times in digital conversations.

Inclusive design must also consider varying cultural relationships with technology itself. Some communities may prefer voice-based interfaces over text, while others might prioritize privacy-preserving communication methods that don't rely on cloud processing. The timing and pacing of digital interactions often carry cultural significance that platforms frequently overlook - whether instant messaging is expected to be truly instantaneous or whether delayed responses are culturally appropriate. Truly inclusive systems will need to surface and adapt to these preferences rather than imposing a single culturally specific communication model on all users. Building infrastructure for inclusive global communication requires rethinking several fundamental technical architectures. Current natural language processing systems typically route all languages through English-centric intermediate representations, introducing subtle biases and inefficiencies. Emerging approaches develop language-agnostic neural architectures that process each language according to its unique structure rather than forcing conformity to dominant language patterns. This shift enables more accurate handling of languages with different word orders, morphological complexity, or contextual dependencies.

On the hardware front, inclusive communication demands devices and interfaces that accommodate diverse input methods - from tactile writing systems to gaze-based controls for users with limited mobility. Network infrastructure must evolve to support efficient transmission of multimodal communication (sign language video, complex scripts) even in bandwidth-constrained environments. Perhaps most challengingly, these systems must maintain interoperability across different platforms and protocols to prevent the creation of new communication silos along technological lines.

Inclusive global communication must serve users across the entire spectrum of literacy and technical proficiency. An estimated 773 million adults worldwide lack basic literacy skills, while billions more experience varying degrees of digital literacy challenges. Systems designed for truly universal access incorporate multiple parallel communication channels - combining voice, text, and visual elements to ensure comprehension regardless of reading ability. This multimodal approach proves particularly important for communicating essential information about health, safety, and civic participation.

Accessibility features cannot remain segregated as specialized options but must be integrated into core communication architectures. Text-to-speech and speech-to-text capabilities should function seamlessly across all supported languages, including those with limited digital representation. Visual communication tools need to incorporate automatic description generation for users with visual impairments, while voice interfaces must accommodate speech differences without degrading performance.

The goal is to create systems where accessibility is inherent rather than added, benefiting all users while specifically empowering those who have been historically excluded. Achieving genuinely inclusive communication requires moving beyond traditional top-down design approaches to embrace community-centered development models. This means involving speakers of marginalized languages not just as test subjects but as co-designers of communication tools. Participatory design processes can surface unique communication needs and preferences that might otherwise be overlooked, from the importance of oral storytelling traditions to culturally specific protocols for group discussions.

Several promising initiatives demonstrate this approach, such as crowdsourced development of language resources for AI systems and community review processes for translation outputs. These methods help prevent the cultural flattening that often occurs when communication systems are designed without input from the communities they intend to serve. They also foster local capacity building, ensuring that technological advances don't create new dependencies but rather empower communities to shape their own communication futures. The challenge lies in scaling these participatory models while maintaining their authenticity and effectiveness.

Inclusive global communication cannot be achieved through technology alone - it requires supportive policy frameworks and infrastructure investments. Governments and international bodies must recognize language diversity as critical digital infrastructure, funding the development of language technologies for marginalized languages just as they would physical transportation networks. Intellectual property regimes need adaptation to protect indigenous knowledge systems while enabling technological innovation. Spectrum allocation policies should prioritize connectivity for underserved linguistic communities rather than favoring commercially dominant regions.

Education systems play a crucial role in preparing populations to participate in inclusive digital communication, requiring investments in multilingual digital literacy programs. At the same time, technology companies must be incentivized - whether through regulation or market mechanisms - to prioritize inclusion over mere scale in their communication products. This might involve requirements for proportional language support based on user populations or standards for interoperable accessibility features. The ultimate goal is to create an ecosystem where inclusive communication is rewarded rather than treated as a cost center.

Current metrics for evaluating communication technologies focus overwhelmingly on scale and efficiency, neglecting crucial dimensions of inclusion. Developing comprehensive frameworks for assessing inclusive communication requires new qualitative and quantitative measures. These might track language coverage depth (not just the number of languages supported but how fully each is implemented), accessibility feature adoption rates across demographics, or user satisfaction disparities between language groups.

CHAPTER

Appendices 14

14.1 GLOSSARY OF TERMS

Alignment: The process of matching sentences, words, or phrases across different languages in a parallel corpus to train translation or multilingual models.

Annotation: The act of labeling linguistic data with tags such as part-of-speech, sentiment, or entity information, which is crucial for supervised learning in multilingual AI.

Bias: Systematic errors in AI models that may favor certain languages, dialects, or cultural norms, often due to imbalanced training data.

Bilingual Lexicon: A dictionary or list of word pairs in two languages, used in cross-lingual applications and low-resource language modeling.

Code-Switching: The practice of alternating between two or more languages in communication, a phenomenon that presents unique challenges for multilingual AI systems.

Comparable Corpus: A collection of texts in different languages that are not direct translations but cover similar domains or topics, used for training cross-lingual models.

Cross-Lingual Transfer: A technique in which knowledge learned in one language is applied to another, often benefiting low-resource languages.

Embedding: A numerical representation of words, sentences, or documents in vector space, enabling multilingual models to compare meanings across languages.

Endangered Languages: Languages at risk of falling out of use, which multilingual AI can help preserve by integrating them into digital applications.

Evaluation Metrics: Standards such as BLEU, F1 score, or accuracy used to measure the performance of multilingual AI models across languages.

Few-Shot Learning: A machine learning approach that enables models to generalize to new languages or tasks using only a small amount of training data.

Language Coverage: The extent to which a multilingual AI system supports different languages, including high-resource and low-resource ones.

Language Model (LM): A statistical or neural model that predicts the probability of word sequences, adapted in multilingual AI to work across multiple languages.

Low-Resource Languages: Languages with limited digital data, corpora, or computational resources, making them challenging for AI development.

Machine Translation (MT): An AI-driven process of automatically translating text or speech from one language to another, central to multilingual applications.

Massively Multilingual Models: Large-scale AI models trained on dozens or even hundreds of languages simultaneously, such as mBERT or XLM-R.

Monolingual Corpus: A dataset consisting of text in a single language, often used as a foundation for training models before applying cross-lingual techniques.

Morphological Complexity: The structural richness of a language in terms of word forms, inflections, and conjugations, which affects how AI models handle it.

Named Entity Recognition (NER): An NLP task in which entities such as names, places, and organizations are identified in text, complicated by multilingual variations.

Parallel Corpus: A collection of texts aligned across multiple languages, providing direct translations that serve as training material for multilingual AI.

Pretraining: The initial stage of training language models on large-scale datasets before fine-tuning for specific tasks, often used in multilingual AI.

Resource Scarcity: The lack of adequate data, tools, or computational resources for developing AI in specific languages.

Tokenization: The process of breaking text into smaller units (words, subwords, or characters), a crucial step in preparing data across different languages.

Transfer Learning: A method where knowledge gained in one task or language is applied to another, enabling efficient use of limited data in low-resource languages.

Universal Language Model: A model designed to process and understand multiple languages using a single shared architecture, supporting cross-lingual generalization.

Zero-Shot Learning: The ability of a model to perform tasks in a new language without having seen labeled training data for that language.

14.2 KEY MULTILINGUAL DATASETS AND TOOLS

The development of robust multilingual artificial intelligence systems relies heavily on the availability of high-quality datasets and specialized tools that enable training, evaluation, and deployment across diverse languages. As AI applications expand globally, the demand for comprehensive linguistic resources has grown exponentially, prompting both academic institutions and technology companies to create increasingly sophisticated multilingual datasets. These resources vary widely in scope, covering different language combinations, domains, and task-specific annotations. Parallel to dataset development, an ecosystem of tools has emerged to facilitate multilingual natural language processing, ranging from preprocessing utilities to model training frameworks. Together, these datasets and tools form the foundation upon which modern multilingual AI systems are built, addressing challenges from low-resource language support to cross-lingual transfer learning.

14.2.1 Major Multilingual Text Corpora

Several large-scale multilingual text corpora have become fundamental resources for training broad-coverage language models. The Common Crawl dataset stands as one of the most extensive web-derived multilingual collections, containing petabytes of text data from hundreds of languages, though with significant variation in coverage quality across languages. More curated alternatives like OSCAR apply rigorous deduplication and quality filtering to create standardized web text corpora for multiple languages. For parallel text essential to translation tasks, the OPUS collection aggregates aligned multilingual content from various sources including parliamentary proceedings, movie subtitles, and technical documentation. The United Nations Parallel Corpus provides high-quality professionally translated documents in six official languages, prized for its domain specificity and translation accuracy. For languages with limited digital representation, collections like the Leipzig Corpora Collection offer carefully sampled text across diverse genres, helping mitigate the bias toward web content that characterizes many larger datasets.

14.2.2 Specialized Multilingual Evaluation Benchmarks

Assessing multilingual model performance requires carefully designed benchmarks that control for language-specific factors. XTREME has emerged as a standard framework for evaluating cross-lingual generalization capabilities across dozens of languages and multiple NLP tasks. More recently, XTREME-R expanded this paradigm to include more languages and challenging retrieval tasks. For machine translation specifically, the WMT shared tasks provide annual benchmarks with carefully curated test sets across numerous language pairs, maintaining rigorous quality standards. GLUE and its multilingual successor XNLI focus on natural language understanding, offering parallel texts in multiple languages for tasks like textual entailment and sentiment analysis. Flores-101 provides high-quality evaluation data for low-resource neural machine translation across 101 languages, filling a critical gap in assessment capabilities for underserved languages. For question answering tasks, TyDi QA offers gold-standard annotations across typologically diverse languages, requiring models to handle language-specific structures rather than relying on English-centric patterns.

14.2.3 Multilingual Speech and Audio Datasets

Speech processing presents unique challenges for multilingual AI, requiring carefully collected and annotated audio resources. Common Voice by Mozilla represents the largest open multilingual speech dataset, with thousands of hours of crowd-sourced recordings across dozens of languages. More specialized collections like BABEL focus on conversational speech in low-resource languages critical for national security applications. VoxPopuli provides parliamentary speech data from European Union proceedings, offering aligned audio and text in multiple European languages. For speech translation tasks, CoVoST covers language pairs involving several low-resource languages with professionally verified translations. Multilingual LibriSpeech extends the popular English LibriSpeech corpus to include read audiobooks in multiple languages. Emerging datasets like MLS (Multilingual LibriSpeech) and CVSS (Common Voice Speech Synthesis) address the growing need for multilingual text-to-speech resources. These speech collections increasingly incorporate metadata about speaker demographics and recording conditions to facilitate research into bias mitigation and domain adaptation.

14.2.4 Essential Multilingual NLP Tools

The multilingual NLP ecosystem has developed specialized tools to handle the unique requirements of processing diverse languages. Stanza and UDPipe provide consistent morphological analysis and dependency parsing across numerous languages, crucial for understanding language-specific syntactic structures. FastText offers language identification and word embeddings trained on hundreds of languages, while LASER and LaBSE provide massively multilingual sentence embedding spaces. For practical deployment, the HuggingFace Transformers library has become indispensable, with pretrained multilingual models like mBERT, XLM-R, and mT5 readily available. OPUS-MT delivers open-source neural machine translation models for hundreds of language pairs, built on the MarianNMT framework. NLLB (No Language Left Behind) from Meta provides state-of-the-art translation models specifically targeting low-resource languages. For linguistic analysis, the UniMorph project offers standardized morphological paradigms across dozens of languages, enabling consistent cross-lingual comparison.

14.2.5 Low-Resource Language Support Tools

Addressing the data scarcity challenge for underserved languages has inspired specialized tool development. The ELRA and LDC catalogs provide access to professionally collected linguistic resources for many low-resource languages. Tools like BLOOM and NLLB-200 specifically target language inclusivity, with the latter supporting translations between 200 languages including many with limited digital presence. The Masakhane initiative fosters community-driven NLP for African languages, producing both datasets and tailored modeling approaches. SIL International's FieldWorks Language Explorer helps linguists document and analyze under-resourced languages, creating structured data usable for NLP applications. The Apertium platform provides rule-based machine translation systems for language pairs lacking sufficient parallel data for neural approaches. For phonetic analysis, the PHOIBLE database offers cross-linguistic phonological inventory data that can inform speech system development for undocumented languages. These tools collectively help bridge the digital divide in language technology access.

14.2.6 Challenges in Multilingual Data Curation

Creating high-quality multilingual datasets presents unique difficulties that single-language collections avoid. Alignment quality becomes exponentially harder to maintain as more languages are included, requiring sophisticated verification pipelines. The distribution of content across languages often reflects historical biases, with certain domains (like technical or legal text) being overrepresented for some languages and completely absent for others. Metadata standards must accommodate writing system variations, complex script rendering requirements, and differing annotation conventions across linguistic traditions. Legal and ethical concerns multiply in multilingual contexts, as consent protocols and data use restrictions may differ significantly between regions and cultures. Many languages lack standardized orthographies or have multiple competing writing systems, forcing dataset creators to make consequential decisions about representation. Dialectal variation presents another challenge, as treating mutually intelligible varieties as separate languages or unified under one code can significantly impact model performance and usability.

14.2.7 Future Directions in Multilingual Resources

The next generation of multilingual datasets and tools is likely to focus on three key areas: expanded language coverage, richer annotations, and improved interoperability. Efforts like the BigScience Workshop aim to create truly representative multilingual language models through inclusive data collection practices. There's growing emphasis on multimodal multilingual resources that align text with visual, auditory, and sensory data across languages. Improved standardization through initiatives like OLAC (Open Language Archives Community) promises better discovery and reuse of existing linguistic resources. Tool development is shifting toward more modular architectures that allow mixing and matching components for specific language needs. There's also increasing attention to continuous learning frameworks that can incorporate new languages without catastrophic forgetting of previously learned ones. Perhaps most importantly, the field is moving toward more equitable resource creation processes that involve speaker communities directly in dataset design and tool development, ensuring technologies serve rather than marginalize linguistic minorities. These advances collectively promise to make multilingual AI more robust, inclusive, and effective across the full spectrum of human languages.

14.3 OPEN-SOURCE LIBRARIES (FAIRSEQ, HUGGING FACE, OPENNMT)

The revitalization of endangered languages relies heavily on technological advancements, particularly in artificial intelligence and natural language processing. Open-source libraries play a crucial role in this effort by providing accessible, customizable, and cost-effective tools for researchers, linguists, and indigenous communities. Among the most influential open-source frameworks are Fairseq, Hugging Face, and OpenNMT, each offering unique capabilities for machine translation, speech recognition, and language modeling. These tools empower developers to build AI-driven solutions that can document, translate, and teach endangered languages, ensuring their survival in the digital age.

Open-source libraries such as Fairseq, Hugging Face, and OpenNMT are invaluable in the fight to preserve endangered languages. These tools provide the necessary infrastructure for machine translation, speech recognition, and language modeling, enabling researchers and communities to document and revitalize linguistic heritage. While challenges remain, the continued improvement of AI technologies and collaborative efforts will strengthen language preservation initiatives. By leveraging these open-source resources, the world can work toward a future where no language is lost to time, and cultural diversity is celebrated through technology.

- **Fairseq—Advancing Machine Translation and Speech Recognition:** Developed by Facebook AI Research, Fairseq is a sequence modeling toolkit designed for machine translation, speech recognition, and text generation. Its modular architecture allows researchers to train and fine-tune models for low-resource languages, making it particularly useful for endangered language preservation. Fairseq supports transformer-based models, which are highly effective in handling linguistic nuances and rare vocabulary. Additionally, its compatibility with self-supervised learning techniques enables the training of models even when labeled data is scarce. By leveraging Fairseq, linguists can develop translation systems that bridge communication gaps between endangered languages and widely spoken ones, facilitating cultural exchange and education.

- **Hugging Face—Democratizing NLP for Endangered Languages:** Hugging Face has become a cornerstone in the natural language processing (NLP) community, offering a vast repository of pre-trained models and an easy-to-use interface through its Transformers library. For language revitalization, Hugging Face provides tools for text generation, sentiment analysis, and multilingual translation, which can be fine-tuned for low-resource languages. The platform's model hub allows researchers to share and access language models, fostering collaboration in preserving endangered languages. Furthermore, Hugging Face's datasets library simplifies the process of collecting and preprocessing linguistic data, making it easier to train AI models on limited datasets. By utilizing these resources, developers can create applications that assist in language learning, documentation, and digital preservation.
- **OpenNMT—Specialized Tools for Neural Machine Translation:** OpenNMT (Open Neural Machine Translation) is an open-source framework specifically designed for neural machine translation (NMT). It supports multiple programming languages and provides pre-trained models that can be adapted for endangered languages. One of OpenNMT's key strengths is its ability to handle low-resource language pairs, making it ideal for translating between indigenous languages and dominant ones. The framework also includes tools for back-translation and data augmentation, which help improve translation quality when training data is limited. By using OpenNMT, linguists and developers can build translation systems that preserve linguistic structures and cultural context, ensuring that endangered languages remain accessible in digital communication.

14.4 LIST OF LANGUAGE CODES AND COVERAGE

14.4.1 High-Resource Languages

- **en / eng** – English – High-resource
- **zh / zho** – Chinese (Simplified & Traditional: zh-CN, zh-TW) – High-resource
- **es / spa** – Spanish – High-resource

- **fr / fra** – French – High-resource
- **de / deu** – German – High-resource
- **ru / rus** – Russian – High-resource
- **ar / ara** – Arabic (variants: ar-SA, ar-EG, ar-MA) – High-resource
- **pt / por** – Portuguese (pt-BR, pt-PT) – High-resource
- **ja / jpn** – Japanese – High-resource
- **ko / kor** – Korean – High-resource
- **it / ita** – Italian – High-resource
- **hi / hin** – Hindi – High-resource
- **bn / ben** – Bengali – High-resource

14.4.2 Medium-Resource Languages

- **tr / tur** – Turkish – Medium-resource
- **vi / vie** – Vietnamese – Medium-resource
- **th / tha** – Thai – Medium-resource
- **id / ind** – Indonesian – Medium-resource
- **pl / pol** – Polish – Medium-resource
- **nl / nld** – Dutch – Medium-resource
- **fa / fas** – Persian (Farsi, Dari, Tajik) – Medium-resource
- **uk / ukr** – Ukrainian – Medium-resource
- **he / heb** – Hebrew – Medium-resource
- **sv / swe** – Swedish – Medium-resource
- **fi / fin** – Finnish – Medium-resource
- **el / ell** – Greek – Medium-resource

14.4.3 Low-Resource Languages

- **am / amh** – Amharic – Low-resource
- **sw / swa** – Swahili – Low-resource
- **ta / tam** – Tamil – Low-resource
- **te / tel** – Telugu – Low-resource
- **kn / kan** – Kannada – Low-resource
- **ml / mal** – Malayalam – Low-resource
- **si / sin** – Sinhala – Low-resource

- **or / ori** – Odia – Low-resource
- **ne / nep** – Nepali – Low-resource
- **mr / mar** – Marathi – Low-resource
- **ur / urd** – Urdu – Low-resource
- **gu / guj** – Gujarati – Low-resource

14.4.4 Endangered or Very Low-Resource Languages

- **iu / iku** – Inuktitut – Endangered
- **gd / gla** – Scottish Gaelic – Endangered
- **cy / cym** – Welsh – Endangered
- **mi / mri** – Maori – Endangered
- **br / bre** – Breton – Endangered
- **ay / aym** – Aymara – Endangered
- **qu / que** – Quechua – Endangered
- **sm / smo** – Samoan – Endangered
- **lu / lub** – Luba-Katanga – Endangered
- **rw / kin** – Kinyarwanda – Endangered

14.5 MULTILINGUAL AI RESEARCH LABS AND INITIATIVES

Multilingual AI research labs and initiatives form the backbone of global communication in the digital age. From the industry leaders like Google, Meta, Microsoft, and Amazon, to community-driven projects such as Masakhane and AI4Bharat, the ecosystem is diverse and expanding. Open-source platforms like Hugging Face ensure democratization, while international collaborations secure long-term sustainability. Together, these initiatives not only push the boundaries of AI research but also ensure that technological progress respects and preserves the linguistic diversity of humanity.

- **Google AI and DeepMind:** Google AI has been one of the earliest pioneers in multilingual AI research. The development of models such as multilingual BERT (mBERT) and mT5 marked a turning point in cross-lingual understanding. Google's Translation Hub and Google Translate draw on decades of multilingual research and cover more than one hundred languages, including recent expansions into African and South Asian languages. DeepMind, Google's research arm, has contributed to ethical and low-resource language modeling. Their focus includes building efficient architectures that can scale across languages while maintaining fairness and inclusivity.

- **Meta AI and No Language Left Behind:** Meta AI has made a landmark contribution with the No Language Left Behind (NLLB) initiative. NLLB-200, one of the most comprehensive multilingual translation models, supports two hundred languages and was explicitly designed to give representation to marginalized and low-resource languages. Meta's research labs emphasize equitable access to AI tools and promote collaboration with regional linguists to ensure accuracy. In addition, projects such as LASER (Language-Agnostic Sentence Representations) provide embeddings for multiple languages, improving cross-lingual transfer learning.
- **Microsoft Research and Azure Cognitive Services:** Microsoft Research has invested heavily in building multilingual AI frameworks for both academic and commercial applications. The Microsoft Translator platform, available in Azure Cognitive Services, supports over a hundred languages with speech, text, and document translation. Beyond consumer tools, Microsoft researchers publish extensively on language representation, bias mitigation, and multilingual benchmarks. Their XGLUE benchmark was a groundbreaking contribution to evaluating multilingual language models across tasks such as sentiment analysis, natural language inference, and question answering.
- **Amazon AI and AWS Language Services:** Amazon AI focuses on integrating multilingual capabilities into its AWS ecosystem. Services like Amazon Translate, Amazon Comprehend, and Amazon Polly cover a broad range of languages, enabling businesses to localize content and automate multilingual customer support. While Amazon's research presence in multilingual AI is less visible than Google or Meta, its large-scale deployment demonstrates the practical applications of multilingual models in commerce, e-commerce, and enterprise cloud solutions.
- **Hugging Face and the Open-Source Community:** Hugging Face has become a hub for open-source multilingual AI research. Their Transformers library includes pre-trained models such as XLM-RoBERTa, mBERT, and mT5, making them accessible to researchers and developers worldwide. Through the BigScience Workshop and the BLOOM multilingual language model, Hugging Face has advanced transparency and inclusivity in multilingual AI. BLOOM supports forty-six languages and thirteen programming languages, offering open-access training data and documentation to democratize language technology.

- **Research Labs in Academia:** Several academic institutions have established dedicated multilingual AI labs. The Center for Speech and Language Processing at Johns Hopkins University, the Language Technologies Institute at Carnegie Mellon University, and the University of Edinburgh's School of Informatics are notable contributors. Their research focuses on machine translation, speech recognition, and cross-lingual embeddings. European initiatives like the European Language Grid (ELG) and CLARIN provide infrastructure for multilingual AI research and emphasize interoperability across national research communities. Regional and Non-Profit Initiatives: Multilingual AI research is not confined to global technology giants. Regional initiatives play a vital role in covering low-resource and indigenous languages. The Masakhane Project, led by African researchers, aims to build machine translation systems for African languages using community-driven collaboration. Similarly, the AI4Bharat initiative in India promotes AI solutions for Indian languages, bridging gaps in translation, speech, and digital accessibility. Non-profit organizations like the Mozilla Common Voice project crowdsource speech data to make multilingual speech technology more inclusive. United Nations and Global Organizations: International bodies have recognized the importance of multilingual AI for global communication. The United Nations uses multilingual NLP tools for translation and documentation in six official languages, while agencies like UNESCO highlight the importance of preserving linguistic diversity through AI. Partnerships between governments and AI labs are becoming increasingly common to ensure equitable access to AI technologies in developing nations.
- **Benchmarking and Shared Tasks:** Multilingual AI research labs also drive progress through shared benchmarking initiatives. Datasets such as XTREME, XGLUE, and MASSIVE were developed collaboratively by research labs and industry leaders to measure multilingual performance across multiple tasks. These benchmarks provide a common platform for comparing models, encouraging transparency, and accelerating innovation. They ensure that progress in multilingual AI does not favor only dominant languages but also includes diverse linguistic communities.

References

Computational Linguistics and Multilingual NLP by Pushpak Bhattacharyya (2020, Springer)

Cross-Lingual NLP by Xiaodong Shi (2019, CRC Press)

Cross-Lingual Word Embeddings by Anders Søgaard (2019, Morgan & Claypool)

Deep Learning for NLP and Speech Recognition by Uday Kamath (2019, Springer)

Low-Resource Neural Machine Translation by Raj Dabre (2022, Springer)

Machine Translation by Thierry Poibeau (2017, MIT Press)

Multilingual AI Ethics by Emily M. Bender (2022, MIT Press)

Multilingual Argument Mining by Elena Cabrio (2020, Springer)

Multilingual Author Profiling by Francisco Rangel (2018, Springer)

Multilingual Chatbots by Boris Galitsky (2020, Springer)

Multilingual Coreference Resolution by Vincent Ng (2021, Springer)

Multilingual Dependency Parsing by Ryan McDonald (2013, Morgan & Claypool)

Multilingual Dialogue Systems by Oliver Lemon (2018, Springer)

Multilingual Educational Technology by Scott Crossley (2020, Springer)

Multilingual Event Extraction by Leon Derczynski (2017, Springer)

Multilingual Fake News Detection by Paolo Rosso (2021, Springer)

Multilingual Financial Text Analysis by Mike Thelwall (2019, Springer)

Multilingual Hate Speech Detection by Thomas Davidson (2020, Springer)

Multilingual Information Extraction by Leon Derczynski (2019, Springer)

Multilingual Information Retrieval by Carol Peters (2012, Springer)

Multilingual Knowledge Graphs by Gerard de Melo (2021, Springer)

Multilingual Language Models by Sebastian Ruder (2021, MIT Press)

Multilingual Legal Text Processing by Adam Wyner (2018, Springer)

Multilingual Medical NLP by Dina Demner-Fushman (2017, Springer)

Multilingual Named Entity Recognition by Erik Tjong Kim Sang (2018, Springer)

Multilingual Natural Language Processing by Dipanjan Sarkar (2020, Packt Publishing)

Multilingual Ontology Learning by Paul Buitelaar (2010, Springer)
Multilingual Opinion Mining by Alexandra Balahur (2014, Springer)
Multilingual Plagiarism Detection by Martin Potthast (2011, Springer)
Multilingual Question Answering by Danilo Croce (2022, Springer)
Multilingual Semantic Similarity by Eneko Agirre (2017, Springer)
Multilingual Semantic Web by Paul Buitelaar (2013, Springer)
Multilingual Sentiment Analysis by Alexandra Balahur (2018, Springer)
Multilingual Social Media Analysis by Alexandra Balahur (2019, Springer)
Multilingual Speech Processing by Tanja Schultz (2012, Academic Press)
Multilingual Speech Recognition by William Hartmann (2020, Wiley)
Multilingual Speech Synthesis by Alan Black (2013, Springer)
Multilingual Stylometry by Efstathios Stamatatos (2017, Springer)
Multilingual Text Alignment by Michael Carl (2014, Springer)
Multilingual Text Analysis by Steven Bethard (2021, CRC Press)
Multilingual Text Classification by Paolo Rosso (2021, Springer)
Multilingual Text Generation by Ehud Reiter (2020, Springer)
Multilingual Text Mining by Michael Wiegand (2012, Springer)
Multilingual Text Normalization by Richard Sproat (2010, Springer)
Multilingual Text Reuse Detection by Benno Stein (2013, Springer)
Multilingual Text Summarization by Horacio Saggion (2017, Springer)
Multilingual Word Sense Disambiguation by Roberto Navigli (2009, Springer)
Neural Machine Translation by Philipp Koehn (2019, Cambridge University Press)
Neural Networks for Multilingual NLP by Yoav Goldberg (2022, MIT Press)

Index

www.ingramcontent.com/pod-product-compliance
Lightning Source LLC
LaVergne TN
LVHW081938200926
848484LV00009B/2460

* 9 7 8 1 7 8 7 1 5 6 1 9 7 *